Writings on Philosophy and Economy of Power

Peter Herrmann (Ed.)

New Princedoms

Critical Remarks on Claimed Alternatives by New Life Worlds

Writings on Philosophy and Economy of Power Vol. 1

EHV)

Herrmann, Peter (Ed.)

New Princedoms
Critical Remarks on Claimed Alternatives by New Life Worlds
Writings on Philosophy and Economy of Power Vol. 1

From the same author of "God, Rights, Law and a Good Society. Over-coming Religion and Moral as Social Policy Approach in a Godless and Amoral Society" (Vol. 2) and "Rights – Developing Ownership by Link-ing Control over Space and Time." (Vol. 3).

ISBN/EAN: 978-3-86741-812-6
First published in 2012 by Europaeischer Hochschulverlag GmbH & Co KG, Bremen, Germany.

EHV

The state is a palace one enters, but one without exit to the back. In this palace one can at most get upstairs. On e might enter the institutions, but then one remains therein. Many feel happy there. That is the fascination of the bourgeois power relations. However, it is a fascination from which, at the end, we all suffer.

(Agnoli, 2002: 21; translation P. H.)

Table of Contents

Preface by Hurriyet Babacan

New Princedoms – Critical Remarks on Claimed Alternatives by New Life Worlds:

A must reading for modern times

The way we view the world, envisage possibilities for social change and strive for improvement in the quality of life is highly complex, with significant challenges in rapidly changing landscapes of the 21st century.

This book, edited by Herrmann and with contributions from Earles and Kratzwald, revisits, with fresh insight, key sociological, philosophical, political and cultural theoretical frameworks of relevance to contemporary globalised world. The book is thought-provoking in its central thesis which posits that there is a tendency for the 're-feudalisation' of production and reproduction and where economics is enmeshed with all elements of social life. Herrmann takes us on a journey of revisiting the concept of citizenship, that all important, and yet unclear concept. We are confronted with how citizenship is redefined in the face of modern globalised capitalism where the state is an instrument of global economics. The author visits key questions of rights, inclusion-exclusion within bounded territoriality and spatial boundaries in the context of globalisation where borders are porous. The notion of citizenship calls into question its inextricable links to the nation-state. Herrmann challenges us to think through the complexity of this relationship including the technocratic nature of contemporary nation-states, what is the 'common good' and the relevance of collective rights. He also presents a critique of the nation state across the different historical stages of society (from slave society to global capitalist) and how the different stages of the nation state are characterised (i) on power, (ii) territoriality and (iii) on how it is related to economic structures and class division/division of labour.

These critiques focus us, through a historical journey, about the interpretation of citizenship as a political institution or a broader mechanism for society building and social cohesion. The analysis, Herrmann puts forward, is about how we make citizenship for society-building when the state is embedded in strong systems of economic relationships. Herrmann posits some key contradictions: power appropriation, dealing with societality and individuality and being part of engagement with systems theories or not. He excavates the nature of contemporary societies under advanced capitalism and examines the

1

process of reproduction – where the reintegration of societal functions is under the control of the economy. While the economy is assumed to have gained primacy, Herrmann, urges us to consider global shifts in modern capitalism and the implications, not just about the mode of production in the strict sense but about the wider societal mechanism of re-production, including a change of the understanding and meaning of citizenship.

Herrmann points to the notions of social hegemony and notes that this hegemony gains dominance to some extent as somewhat 'incontestable position' by which the contestation of the system itself easily shifts towards struggles engaged with lifestyle issues rather than with fundamental systemic issues. Two very important conclusions are drawn:

(i) that production moves beyond immediate consumption not only in terms of the productive/economic circles but in terms of the of the actual ultimate aim of the economic process that is – more than ever – solely based on producing the 'consumptive needs' that it aims to serve.

(ii) the redefinition of the social as part of an also socio-cultural system of thought that is guided by purely utilitarian hegemonic project.

The new form of socialization is the interpenetration of the social with utilitarian thinking, at the same time accompanied by the complete dissolution of the economy into a space that is suggested as being positioned outside of the social sphere. The result is subsuming of all elements of life under the economic – including self-alienation, governance, self-help, civic movement, participation, and empowerment. Envisaging any alternative social futures requires a rethinking of relationships between people and institutions and to ask questions about inclusion and who decides the boundaries of inclusion, beyond the nation state and beyond narrow territory boundaries.

This analysis paves the way for a consideration of contributions by the two other authors. The first is a consideration about broader conceptualization of space and looking at political spatial engagement. The focus is then on the third sector and the role of nongovernmental organisations – on the one hand as integrative factor, being themselves drawn into the maintenance of systemic processes, on the other hand as source of possible alternatives and agency for change. Earles, in her contribution, focuses our attention on the third sector within a market economy. The third sector, seen as separate from state and market, is interpreted in different ways. On the one hand, it is assumed to have a value base and an agency for change while on the other, it as an instrumental arm of the state. Earles provides a complex analysis of the not for profit sector and points to the boundaries (overlaps and separation) between the state, market and third and informal sectors. Providing an account of classic and market based paradigms of the third sector, she alerts us to think carefully about the role of the third sector as an actor for change and its precarious nature as created within the market realm.

Kratzwald, in another excellent contribution, examines the terrains of social struggles and compromises in organizing for social change. She argues that with crisis of capitalism, the agents of neoliberalism are confronted with increasing critique and resistance from social movements, and in search for regaining their legitimation often co-opt arguments of their critics to enhance their credibility. She identifies the precarity of the 'social' and degradation of living conditions, weakening of democratic structures and decline in social rights. Kratzwald points out that there is a change in the techniques of governing individuals, particularly, in Western Europe, to a focus on governing individuals from the distance. There is a fundamental shift from discourses of competition and human capital to a strong discourse of individual moral responsibility and hence the creation of 'the consumer-subject' who will achieve social change through individual action through the market mechanism as a consumer. The 'responsible consumer' emerges as the new mode of subjectivation and as way to resolve the major social, environmental and political crisis through consumer power, vesting responsibility to the individuals for significant social and systemic issues. Quite rightly, Kratzwald, concludes that such market based approaches will leave the status quo unchanged and not result in any significant change for social justice.

The final chapter of the book Herrmann leads us to think about 'empowerment'. Different perspectives of empowerment are covered and key themes unpacked for consideration, particularly perspectives on power, action, control, access, participation and the nature of social relations. Herrmann also takes us through the layers of empowerment from individuals, institutions, citizens and social actors. The chapter concludes with indicators of empowerment – for aims, structures and processes of empowerment and how these can be utilized by different social actors.

The ideas raised in the book lead us to an exploration of our basic knowledge base and urges us to interrogate and re-think our understanding relating to citizenship, the state, power relations and empowerment, historical meaning and sense-making, what constitutes the social and the economic, quality of life and, and the construction of a rights-based framework. It invites us to think about the greater human endeavour and possibilities for social transformation. Intellectually demanding and stimulating, this book enhances our thinking about possibilities for social transformation in an exciting way.

Professor Hurriyet Babacan, Director, The Cairns Institute, James Cook University, Australia.

8 August 2010

Acknowledgements and Dedication

From Peter Herrmann

Work as it is presented here is linked into very different contexts – and this is actually the fundamental idea behind it: not loosing the thread, rather: bringing issues together although there original context had been in some way dispersed. This intention had been also the editor's reason for inviting the contributions written by two colleagues – and if I may say so: friends – who kindly agreed to do. It had not been just about writing these contributions but the readiness of engaging in a debate for which I am especially grateful to Brigitte Kratzwald and Wendy Earles. I am especially thankful to Wendy who opened for me the opportunity of visiting the Cairns Institute at James Cook University, Cairns, Australia. After she made me aware of the fellowship I applied and had been accepted. So I am also grateful to the Institute: being an Institute in statu nascendi (or perhaps more appropriate to say: in the phase of a toddler) it had been nevertheless accepted that I follow for some time my own path of working on the finalisation of this book – I am grateful to the colleagues and especially to Hurriyet Babacan who gave me this opportunity and granted the stay, thus opening also a new world in many respects.

I got particular help from Fabrizio Vitali who supported me in the efforts of chasing up some literature – though the Internet puts just a mouse-click between us as scholars and some of the material needed there are remain other cases where we still need to overcome the hurdles of in this cases thousands of miles, between Australia and Ireland where he helped me with search for references in the Cork library en lieu. I want to thank him for his support.

In an entirely different way Yitzhak Berman had been a help – on many occasions we discussed issues that play in one or another way a role in the various instances. Though we never will come to a completely satisfying answer on the question about community and society and tough we have in several instances different viewpoints, it always had been an enriching exchange, in one or another way reflected in the work presented.

Also, working with a publisher as Rozenberg is not really work – more just a pleasure of bringing work and pleasure together. – I surely could go on, and fill many pages with words of Thanks.

Instead, I will stop here with only one further short remark – earlier I mentioned 'the readiness of engaging in a debate'. And in this respect I am grateful to the students of the Higher Diploma in Social Policy, School of Applied Social Studies at the University of Cork, academic year 2009/2010. The support I got from UCC had been really the support I received from the students, their readiness of engaging in a debate; and also their readiness to bear with me: while developing the ideas with them (though they had not necessarily being aware of it) and their readiness to accept frequently needed flexibility due to my travelling.

I want to dedicate the book to

Aine Maíre, Caroline, Catríona, Ciaran, Darelle Maeve, Fabrizio, Jack Anthony, Jenna, John (Shane), Marie Edel, Michelle Ann, Nora Mary, Oyindamola, Stephen Joseph

– and not least to

Joe Finnerty

who, as course director, gave me another time the huge privilege of having the freedom of 'doing my own thing' – in a supportive way, thus different to the way in which so many other people today allow freedom in princedoms of academia: letting people down by lack of support.

Cork, Kuopio, Munich, Cairns – 1ˢᵗ half of 2010

From Brigitte Kratzwald:

I want to thank those people who helped to develop the ideas presented in my contribution. I could draw on discussions with colleagues in University Seminars as well as people from the social movements. Andrea Bührmann introduced me in an inspiring way into Foucauldian thought and Leo Kühberger called my attention to the relation with Autonomist Marxism. Peter Herrmann finally not only helped to sharpen my arguments with his patient but persistent questions but also gave me the chance to contribute to this volume and supported me in manifold ways.

Graz, June 2010

6

From Wendy Earles:

I wish to acknowledge the opportunity provided by a one-year research fellow-in-residence position during 2009-2010 with the Cairns Institute at James Cook University, Australia. This enabled a greater focus on writing and international scholarly collaboration. I would like to thank Peter Herrmann for encouraging me to write beyond my immediate empirical work and local grounded theorising, and engage in wider debates on third sector developments.

Cairns, June 2010

Prolegomena
Encore Citizenship – Revisiting or Redefining?

Peter Herrmann

Abstract

In the following – meant to be an introduction of thought that lead my personal interest in and stance towards the different topics of the present book and two publications *(Herrmann, (b), (c))* – I want to carve out the foundation of an argument suggesting some tendency of 're-feudalisation' being characteristic of the current historical stage. However, this does not suggest that history repeats itself. Instead, the thesis is that we find a shift of both, (i) the state shifting more and more towards being an instrument of economics rather than being itself part of a wider form of economic organisation (precisely an intermediary for the management of distinct and to some extent independent subsystems) and (ii) the economy shifting towards an immediate societal actor. This is, however, seen as going beyond the array of a simple power shift and it is also pointing beyond a simple movement of the economic system. Seeing it as shift of the accumulation system may serve as point of departure. It is suggested that globalisation as such is not the core of current transformations. Instead, I assume a fundamental change of the mode of production that is equally ample as the emergence of modern capitalism. This formulation suggests that the change is not just about the mode of production in the strict sense but about the wider societal mechanism of (re-)production, including a change of the understanding and meaning of citizenship

Introduction

Citizenship is one of the core questions in multiple regards – for instance in debates on globalisation which is for many also a question of blurring the status of citizenship and the citizen's identity; or when it comes to rights, reference is frequently made to citizen's rights and also to the before mentioned blurring of citizenship and the danger of undermining criteria of deciding to whom these rights should be granted. Making reference to the world or global citizen or to human rights does not overcome the application of the principal standard of some kind of citizenship as point of reference. With some justification we then repeat the same question(s) as they had been brought up since the emergence of the ancient Greek and Roman empires. In such perspective we are dealing with the enhancement of spaces of rules and ruling and also the inclusion of groups under a regime but not with fundamental shifts in the meaning. This is at least true as long as we refer to space as (though possibly socially constructed, ands surely socially enclosed) territoriality. We may say as well, the discussion in such perspective is about quantitative shifts in range and scope of citizenship – and depending on this about the definition of citizens from one constituency to another; but it is not about the qualitative shifts as such.

The present author is however convinced of the necessity of emphasising what is implicitly as well assumed in the debates on quantitative shifts: that we are facing important qualitative, not reducible on quantitative leaps. I understand the contributions of this volume as part of a wider debate on this matter, aiming with this – and some publications that are already in the pipeline – on understanding societal change in a deeper time perspective, a view that links into Fernand Braudel's understanding of time and history respectively, in short characterised by saying that

> *[t]he stage on which humanity's endless dramas are played out partly determines their story-line and explains their nature. The cast will alter, but the set remains broadly the same.*

> *(Braudel, 1987:10)*

With this, Braudel outlines his concept of understanding time as social matter and he points out the distinction between long-distance history, recent history and history of events *(s. ibid.)*. He speaks of three 'planes' – using in French language the term *plan* which is much wider than the English 'plane' – saying

> *[t]hat the historian works on at least three planes.*

> *One ... is that of traditional history, habitual narrative, hurrying from one event to the next ...*

> *A second plane ... is that of episodes, each taken as a whole ...*

> *A third plane ... transcends these events: it considers only phenomena that can be measured over a century or more. At this level, the movement of history is slow and covers vast reaches of time ...*

In this final perspective ... civilizations can be seen as distinct from the accidents and vicissitudes that mark their development: they reveal their longevity, their permanent features, their structures – their almost abstract but yet essential diagrammatic form.

(ibid: 34 f.)

Charles Tilly puts this nicely in a metaphorical way, making clear that this has also a spatial perspective – and we may add already here the present understanding of space as social construct. He posits that

[t]he analysis of political development has had about the same relationship to historical experience as a dog on a long leash to the tree at the other end of the leash. The dog can roam in almost any direction. He can get even the illusion of rushing off on his own. But let him rush too far, too fast and his collar will jerk him back; it may even knock the wind out of him. Some political scientists want to break the leash or at least move the tree. ... . major political transformations which occurred in the past may not repeat themselves in the present and future, and are very unlikely to repeat themselves in the same way, but any theories which claim to encompass general processes of political transformation must be consistent with past experience, and ought to be checked carefully against that experience before gaining wide acceptance.

(Tilly, 1975: 3)

And of course this suggests the perspective of the third plane, frequently named as *longue durée* as the one of interest in the present consideration.

This is in line with suggestions from different perspectives of world systems theory – two points have to be emphasised.

History and Historical Analysis as Reflection on Complexities

First, it is the very general aspect of social science being concerned with the complexity of reality from which any departure has potentially fatal consequences. Immanuel Wallerstein contends that

[p]art of the problem is that we have studied thee phenomena in separate boxes to which we have given special names – politics, economics, the social structure, culture – without seeing that these boxes are constructs more of our imagination than of reality. The phenomena dealt with in these separate boxes are so closely intermeshed that each presumes the other, each affects the other, each is incomprehensible without taking into account the other boxes. And part of the problem is that we tend to leave out of our analysis of what

is and is not 'new' the tree important turning points of our modern world-system ...

(Wallerstein, 2004: X)

He points on the emergence of the capitalist world-economy during the 16th century, the centrist liberalism with the French Revolution and then the revolution of 1968, undermining the 'centrist liberal geoculture'. In the later course of the argument Wallerstein emphasises the 'divorce' between philosophy and science as being of special importance – a turning point that he characterises as claim to divorce truth and value *(see ibid.: 2; cf. e.g. Horkheimer, 1947)*.

In the present context this is of particular meaning as it can easily be traced that the citizenship analysis and debate is to some extent mislead by following a one-sided argument, namely that of political science as born from the enlightenment, resting on two of its main ideas.

The one is the Cartesian notion of science – in the limited understanding of 'science as investigation of nature' – being the foundational source of a – in tendency – complete subordination of – also social – development under the human will. This implies the orientation (i) on individual freedom as source and goal of any action and (ii) the understanding of 'well-being' as matter of enhancing individual (control over) resources.

The second is the orientation on the principle of separation of power being seen as fundamental, unquestionable issue, apparently set in place and valid independent of history – and thus: independent of society. Surely, all this happened with the best intentions. But this should not make us forget that we find in consequence a fundamental shortcoming of the perspective, namely the de-historisation even of the historical perspective. – Referring to Braudel's remarks, political history is then commonly limited on the perspective of events.

Historical Cut-off Point as Confirmation of Historical Meaning

The point in question is not simply the extension of the time perspective but the need to recognise that we enter with such long-term perspective an entirely different field. We can now say that widening the timeframe makes only sense if it is about deepening the qualitative orientation. This had been frequently discussed and practiced in world systems theory. *Cum grano salis* we can say the same for such a deepened historical perspective as what has been said with respect to the distinction between global and non-global *(see Babones, 2006)*.

One escape is surely the attempt to look for another orientation by *Re-positioning of Citizenship and Alienage (see Sassen, 2005)* or an approach under the heading of *Citizenship Denationalised (see Bosniak, 2000)*. However, although these are surely important points of bringing history back-in they are at the same time a-historical to the extent to which history is in these views concerned with introducing development as change, without establishing a fundamental link to understanding development as matter of emergence of some status from another. Such emergence rests on some elementary forms that exist as contradiction during the preceding phase, the contradictions contributing to this kind of development. This is getting clear when Bosniak writes that

> most such discussions presume that citizenship is appropriately (and necessarily) an enterprise located within the bounds of the modern nation-state, and treat any alternative conception as requiring special justification.
>
> (ibid.: 453)

Looking for a future alternative, though seeing the past as given – 'undeveloped' – status, a status that is at least in its fundamental structural pattern unchanged. Revisiting citizenship is then seen as

> acknowledgement of the increasingly transterritorial quality of political and social life, and the need for such politics where they do not yet exist.
>
> (ibid.: 450)

and as

> commitment to a vision of citizenship that is multiple and overlapping.
>
> (ibid.)

However, this forgets a general contentment of looking at citizenship: the commonly assumed notion of citizenship is that it is inextricably linked to the nation state; another issue is that it is seen as bound – or even defined – by rights, tasks and obligations. And rightly it is stated that nationality is not least based on these rights, tasks and obligations.

We find the same flaw in some respect of the *Tragedy of Commons* as presented by Garrett Hardin *(Hardin, 1968)*. First, it has to be appraised that Garret Hardin makes one essential contribution which is indeed frequently forgotten: the demand for developing a non-technical perspective for political debates, thus claiming that the technocratisation of politics leads into a dead end – this is frequently also claimed with respect when it comes to the argument that 'pure economic requirements', understood as practical constraints, have to determine politics and actually de-substantiate political decisions. Notwithstanding this, two points have to be raised.

First, Hardin's argument has not only a particularly moralist undertone but in the way in which it is brought forward it is also based on an elitist approach, aiming on the principal control over people by a others on grounds of their superiority rather than looking for standards that are and can be developed from collective insights *(expressed especially clear for instance in an interview: Hardin, 1990)*.

This leads to the second and more fundamental flaw, namely that he actually starts from the premise that the society and those societal conditions that he criticises are taken for elemental and irrevocable. As Audun Sandberg reminds us, however,

> *[c]ommons are basically collective rights, or more precisely 'property rights held in common by a social group'.*

(Sandberg, 1998: 1)

With reference to Paolo Grossi *(Grossi, 1981)* he points out that

> *[i]t is important to remember that this element in the 'modernization project' is quite old and was, to a large extent, ideologically motivated: the goal of 'progress and human well-being' was also linked to individual freedom in the possession of things. Other ways of owning than full individual ownership (dominium)were seen as obstacles to development and had to be eradicated.*

(Sandberg; op.cit.: 96)

It is clear that Hardin's argument is doddery, looking for the justification of a system that he immanently criticises as not appropriately reflecting human nature. The problem Sandberg mentions, namely that

> *commons were institutions that belonged to the pre-modern world, where the basic idea was not enclosure, but the true Genossenschaft where people were bonded to each other in co-proprietorship. While optimal for legitimate collective decisions related to the sustainable harvest and maintenance of a re- source, this 'bonding' of the individual has been interpreted in later centuries as an unjustified limitation of individual freedom*

(ibid.: 97)

is surely one that needs further debate.[1] One point in question is surely around the standard presumption of (classical) economics, namely that growth is without presupposition put forward as core and general goal of the entire economic process *(see for instance North, 1994)* is context made by Elinor Ostrom *(Ostrom, 2000)* who points out that

> [t]he debate about the relative merits of private and common property has been clouded by a troika of confusions that hinder scholarly communication. Different meanings are assigned to terms without clarifying how multiple aspects relate to one another. The source of confusion relates to the differences between (1) common property and open-access regimes, (2) common-pool resources and common property regimes, and (3) a resource system and the flow of resource units. All three sources of confusion reduce clarity in assigning meaning to terms and retard theoretical and empirical progress.
>
> (ibid.: 335)

Though both, Ostrom and North are highlighting the importance of learning and even social learning, the understanding of what learning is about and how it is socially performed is substantially different.

State and Economy

Much ink had been spilt over the relationship on the one hand between nation (state) and citizenship and on the other hand between (nation) state and the economy. However, little had been worked on aiming to bring the three together. It is proposed to develop an understanding of citizenship by elaborating this category as fourth moment of the equation. When being used as definiendum – looking for its relational location in this triangular concept – it evolves from there simultaneously as definiens and we are hopefully able to gain a clearer understanding of what the commons to which citizenship relates is actually about. We now have to overcome as well the limitation of the triangular structure that is frequently underlying Western thinking and usually utilised as means of constituting dichotomising, exclusionary notions.[2]

---

[1]   In connection with his work at the University of Eastern Finland, the present author is taking up work on this issue in the framework of an international research project of which he is the leader.

[2]   We can see this for instance in proposals of entities built on this triangular fashion: On the one hand they suggest dealing with 'non-statement' – as in third sector research organisations are characterised as non-governmental and non-profit and non-unorganised-peer groups (or similarly as Quasi-entities as

Developing this further as matter of deploying society as complex mechanism of (re-)production, it is advisable to start from turning attention to the notion of rights – not only but also because it is seen by many as constitutive for defining citizenship.

Point of departure for this undertaking is the perception that a major flaw in the citizenship debate is emanating from a one-sided interpretation of citizenship as political institution rather than seeing it as matter of a wider understanding of society-building. Moreover, the investigation of society-building itself tends to argue from today's perspective and is thus inherently linked to an interpretation that is build on a separation between economy and society *(see also Gerstenberger, 1990/2006:491 and passim)*. There is indeed good reason for doing so – definitely if we start from modernity, but also if we look at the ancient political (though pre-state) systems. The reasonably common threat of debates on state building is on the one hand the *polis,* on the other hand the *republic* especially of the ancient Greek.[3]

Even if they had been indeed by and large 'political entities', it has to be underscored that they had been very much equally economic entities. Developing a clearer understanding we have to restate that the understanding of economy and the economic process is distinct from today's general understanding in three respects:

- first of all, we have to acknowledge the centrality of household economy as entity for subsistence based reproduction;
- as such it is very much concerned with the (re-)production of the entire life (in substantial terms and also in terms of range, i.e. from childhood to old age;
- division of labour – within the household – plays a major role and with this management is an immediate part of the process of production itself, going beyond its distributive function.

There is surely the huge danger of obscuring these patterns in a romanticising way. However, though definitely not completely, the understanding of economy and society had been in some sense still one of subsistence economies.

QUANGOs); on the other hand they are seen as gap-fillers, tending to float in between these different 'extreme points'. See as well Herrmann, without date)
3   For the time being the underlying Eurocentrism is left aside.

This meant not least that law – in the widest possible understanding of different regulatory rules – had been a matter of directly 'managing the entire life'. What we would today suggest as management had been only one aspect; the other crucially important aspect had been concerned with the exchange process as immediate part of the productive process: a matter of regulating resources, distribution of products and not least the role of individuals within these processes, developing within the communicative processes their social identities and personalities.

Connecting from here to the wider approach, the economic or probably it is better to say: (re-)productive process is about conflating moments or dimensions.

- First, we are dealing with the power-appropriation dimension – this aspect is developed later in this book *(see pp. 213 f; see also: Herrmann/Dorrity, 2009)*.

- Second, we are dealing with the dimension of societality and individuality. Although this is of course also the commonly raised question of social responsibility and cohesion and development of personalities and responsible behaviour, it is in the present perspective necessary to look at the wider framework, namely the fact that any conditional perspective is in itself inadequate as long as it remain in its own realm, without being complemented by a constitutional perspective. This is not least made clear by the attention Marx gives to the idea of an organic totality: the analysis of the mode of production as combination of productive forces and relations ('objective factors') and the way in which people socially relate to each other and the environment ('subjective factors'). This had been expressed in the German Ideology by saying that

[t]he production of life, both of one's own in labour and of fresh life in procreation, now appears as a double relationship: on the one hand as a natural, on the other as a social relationship. By social we understand the co-operation of several individuals, no matter under what conditions, in what manner and to what end. It follows from this that a certain mode of production, or industrial stage, is always combined with a certain mode of co-operation, or social stage, and this mode of co-operation is itself a 'productive force.' Further, that the multitude of productive forces accessible to men determines the nature of society, hence, that the 'history of humanity' must always be studied and treated in relation to the history of industry and exchange.

(Marx, 1845: 43)

16

We can translate this into social quality jargon as matter of the relationship between conditional factors, the constitutional factors as 'activating them' and the normative factors as guiding this process.

Looking at the following compilation the meaning gets clear for the meta-level and equally for the level of analysing concrete soci(et)al structures and processes.

	CONSTITUTIONAL FACTORS	CONDITIONAL FACTORS	NORMATIVE FACTORS
SHOWING	Processes	Opportunities & Contingencies	Orientation
FACTORS	Personal (Human) Security Social Recognition Social Responsiveness Personal (Human) Capacity	Socio-Economic Security Social Cohesion Social Inclusion Social Empowerment	Social Justice (Equity) Solidarity Equal Valuation Human Dignity
ASSESSMENT	Qualified by Profiles	Measured by Social Quality Indicators	Allowing Judgement
MAIN DETERMINANTS	Each factor is an outcome of processes concerning the formation of a diversity of collective identities, strongly influenced by the interplay of processes of self-realisation across two main tensions and therefore also situated in one part of the quadrangle of the conditional factors.	Each factor is mainly influenced by aspects of the interaction between the two main tensions and is, therefore, especially situated in one part of the quadrangle of the constitutional.	Each factor is influenced by the dialectic relationship between conditional and constitutional factors and is therefore providing a thread, welding the different factors together.

Table 1: Social Quality as Matter of an Organic Totality

This goes also back to two moments that are centrally discussed in world systems theory – and had been already mentioned above. The one is the integrity of society – independent of possibly overwhelming systemic contradictions; the other is subsequently also the need for an appropriately holistic approach of social science analysis, overcoming the division as well captured by Immanuel Wallerstein, articulating in an interview

> this bigger question: I'm simply insisting on the fact that we are experiencing everything in a singular mode, We live in a singular world, so the historical social system should be analyzed as a single arena – I don't see where the state ends and the market starts, or where the market ends and civil society starts.

> (Schouten, 2008)

The other moment links into Christopher Chase-Dunn's analysis of capitalist globalisation, outlining:

> The historical development of the modern world-system can be understood in terms of the evolution of certain key institutions that have been shaped by tremendous struggles: commodity production, technology and techniques of power. The struggles have included conflict among contending powers and between the core and the periphery over the past six centuries as Europe rose to hegemony and capitalist globalization expanded in waves of commodification and integration.

> (Chase-Dunn, 2005 (a): 176 f.)

This suggests that we go in some respect beyond Immanuel Wallerstein's perspective of capitalism where he sees it only as process of continuous consumption by which the flow of resources varies in its direction and which causes a permanent tension between the different players and – in the long run – a shift of power relationships *(see Wallerstein, 2004)*.

Wallerstein himself actually insists on seeing

> social reality ... not [as] the multiple national states of which we are citizens but something larger, which we call a world-system. We have been saying that this world-system has had many institutions – states and the interstate system, productive firms, households, classes, identity groups of all sorts – and that these institutions form a matrix which permits the system to operate but at the same time stimulates both the conflicts and the contradictions which permeate the system.

> (Wallerstein, 2004: x)

This is goes beyond the consumptionist interpretation mentioned before and it is definitely a quite different notion as for instance that ventured by Paul Krugman and Anthony J. Venables who suggest also a – even dynamic – core-periphery model, however substantiate this in the sphere of circulation *(see Krugman/Venables, 1995).*

The wider conception follows the definition given by Christopher Chase-Dunn on another occasion, contending the complexity by writing:

> *World-systems are systems of societies (international systems) that are strongly linked to one another by interaction networks (trade, alliances, warfare, migration and information flows). Thousands of years ago these were small regional affairs, but they have gotten larger, merged with one another and the big ones have engulfed smaller ones. This process of network expansions has eventuated in the single global macrosocial system of today. One important meaning of the globalization is the expansion and intensification of large-scale interaction networks. At the same time that macrosystems have become spatially larger, the societies and intersocietal systems that make them up have become more complex and hierarchical. And the dynamics of systemic expansion may have qualitatively changed as new institutions, especially markets and financial systems, have emerged and become predominant.*
>
> *(Chase-Dunn, Christopher, 2005 (b): 2)*

This means that we have to look for the patterns that fully acknowledge that

> *[t]he hegemonic sequence is not a simple cycle that takes the same form each time around. Rather, as Giovanni Arrighi (1994) has so convincingly shown, each 'systemic cycle of accumulation' involves a reorganization of the relationships among big capitals and states. And the evolutionary aspects of hegemony not only adapt to changes in scale, geography and technology, but they also must solve problems created by resistance from below (Silver 2003; Boswell and Chase-Dunn 2000). Workers and farmers in the world-system are not inert objects of exploitation and domination. Rather, they develop new organizational and institutional instruments of protection and resistance. So the interaction between the powerful and less powerful is a spiral of domination and resistance that is one of the most important driving forces of the developmental history of modern capitalism.*
>
> *(Chase-Dunn, 2005 (a): with reference to Arrighi, 1994; Silver, 2003;Boswell/Chase-Dunn, 2000)*

It is of special importance to acknowledge this as the terms core and periphery as concepts

> *do not refer to countries. We use it that way as shorthand, to say things quickly, but it's not exact. Core-periphery is a relationship of production: there are core-like processes and peripheral processes, and they both exist in all countries. ... . A key element here is monopolization versus competition: the more competitive a product is, the more peripheral it is, because the less money you can make on it. The more monopolized a product is, the more core-like it will be, because you can make more money on it. So if given kinds of production spread out to more countries, that's because they have become less profitable within the original loci of production, not because these countries to which the processes spread are successfully 'developing.'*

> *(Schouten, 2008)*

This strongly brings back the question of locating power in a wider sense, of rights, however now allowing to think them in their connotation of reflecting mere different dimensions under the very same notion of citizenship as matter of a mechanism of (re-)production rather than or as *definens* of membership in different ways.

An important additional aspect is in this context the exploration of the state. Although it is commonly accepted that the state as we know it today is in historical terms only a recent contraption, actual reference is usually made in a rather a-historical fashion, suggesting this figuration – as state – as somewhat eternal pattern. As such, it goes hand in hand with other affairs of social life, aiming on concretising and/or specifying the understanding. Some of these strives are recognising specific factors as core characteristics[4] – this may be a general or a temporary classification; others are of a more general character, looking at usually temporary characteristics, very much derived from certain historical stages civilisatory principals or patterns.[5]

Since recently there is as well a debate that can in some respect be considered as being new and linked in different ways with (forms and parts of) globalisation. For instance we find issues that engage– in

---

[4] These may be functional moments or specific organisational traits as for instance corporatism or the features of a 'captive state' *(Monbiot),* the 'competitive state', the 'welfare state' or the like

[5] E.g. the 'ancient' state or the 'church state' (the 'welfare state' may possibly also claim some relevance here)

particular in the context of EUropean integration – with issues around bypassing the nation state *(see e.g. Herrmann, 1998; Herrmann, 1997;Jachtenfuchs, 1995).* On the other hand, and more recently, we find not least in the works by Saskia Sassen the thesis of the de-nationalisation of the state *(see for instance Sassen, 2007).*And following Charles Tilly, it is indeed questionable to see nationality as a strictly given liaison to the state. Introducing his opus magnum, he contends that

> *[s]tates have been the world's largest and most powerful organizations for more than five thousand years. Let us define states as coercion-wielding organizations that are distinct from households and kinship groups and exercise clear priority in some respects over all other organizations within substantial territories. The term therefore includes city-states, empires, theocracies, and many other forms of government, but excludes tribes, lineages, firms, and churches as such. Such a definition is, alas, controversial; while many students of politics use the term in this organizational way, some extend it to whatever structure of power exists in a large, contiguous population, and others restrict it to relatively powerful, centralized, and differentiated sovereign organizations – roughly to what I will call national state.*

(Tilly, 1990: 1 f.)

There are good reasons in favour of such wide definition, seeing the nation state as particular and distinct form of the state in general. However, this may well be also more confusing rather than elucidating. It speaks in favour insofar as it draws attention to more 'functional' elements of what we are talking about rather than leaving the definition to an underlying and not outspoken concept – that of nationality. However, it lacks elucidating power as it overstretches the meaning by actually focusing on a given understanding of the state rather than starting from making out possible specific functional requirements that make a 'state' necessary but also that allow to transcend the concept of statehood as such. Retrospectively this remark suggests highlighting the difference of the form of past 'statehoods'; in prospective it insinuates the search for alternative mechanisms – and moreover: possibly fundamentally changed conditions, replacing those that made a state necessary and possible. Then, we are not (primarily) looking for denationalisation, a multivalent state or multivalent denationalisation; rather the question is to which extent and moreover in which particular way should we maintain speaking of the state? – This does not suggest that history reached a stage where the state in the common understanding is already now replaced by something else. However it does suggest that we are facing a development that goes beyond simple structural shifts.

So, in the following a brief outline will be suggested, looking at two questions: first the question of power as civilisatory issue and the role of the state; second the issue of historical changes of capitalism and the question of re-feudalisation.

Power as Civilisatory Issue and the Role of the State

Trying to develop a closer understanding of current global societal changes, it is proposed to start from two main perspectives on the state, namely the classical definition given by Max Weber and the perspective as emerging from a classical Marxist perspective.

In the text on *Politics as Vocation,* Max Weber reiterates that

> [s]ociologically, the state cannot be defined in terms of its ends. There is scarcely any task that some political association has not taken in hand, and there is no task that one could say has always been exclusive and peculiar to those associations which are designated as political ones: today the state, or historically, those associations which have been the predecessors of the modern state. Ultimately, one can define the modern state sociologically only in terms of the specific means peculiar to it, as to every political association, namely, the use of physical force.

> *(Weber, 1919: 77)*

And shortly later he specifies that

> [t]oday ... we have to say that a state is a human community that (successfully) claims the monopoly of the legitimate use of physical force within a given territory. Note that 'territory' is one of the characteristics of the state. Specifically, at the present time, the right to use physical force is ascribed to other institutions or to individuals only to the extent to which the state permits it. The state is considered the sole source of the 'right' to use violence. Hence, 'politics' for us means striving to share power or striving to influence the distribution of power, either among states or among groups within a state.

> *(ibid.: 78)*

And in *Economy and Society* we read under the title

> *17. Political and Hierocratic Organizations*

> A 'ruling organization' will be called 'political' insofar as its existence and order is continuously safeguarded within a given territorial area by the threat and application of physical force on the part of the administrative staff. A compulsory political organization with

continuous operations (politischer Anstaltsbetrieb) will be called a 'state' insofar as its administrative staff successfully upholds the claim to the monopoly of the legitimate use of physical force in the enforcement of its order. Social action, especially organized action, will be spoken of as 'politically oriented' if it aims at exerting influence on the government of a political organization; especially at the appropriation, expropriation, redistribution or allocation of the powers of government.

(Weber, 1921: 54)

However, this leaves the problem open from where this legitimacy is borrowed.[6] In this respect, Marxist writing brings us at least in a first step further by making clear reference. Bob Jessop grasps this by highlighting that

Marx emphasizes the concrete-complex articulation of the economic and extra-economic conditions for the 'expanded reproduction' of specific class relations and what this implies for the reordering of what are always relative advantages in the class struggle. In this sense he also describes avant la letter the stakes, strategies, and tactics involved in what Gramsci would later term 'wars of position' and 'wars of manoevre'.

(Jessop, 2008: 86)

This should be reflected against the background of the view in the strict sense given by Frederick Engels, and commonly seen as standard, namely pointing out that the state is (i) the instrument of the ruling class – extending the economic power position of the ruling class into the political realm and serving as instrument to suppress and exploit of the other classes and (ii)performing as 'total ideal capitalist' and actually emerging from there as total real capitalist *(see Engels, 1884)*. In a wider understanding, and allowing more for recognising the contradictions, Nicos Poulantzas and Patrick Camiller we can see it as

[t]he condensation of a relationship of forces between classes and class fractions, such as these express themselves, in a necessarily specific form, within the State itself. In other words, the State is through and through constituted-divided by class contradictions.

(Poulantzas/Camiller, 1978/2000: 132)

---

6   There is of course much in Weber's writing on the legitimate rule – however, this at this stage this does not bring us any further as the argument is developed fro within the mechanism itself, i.e. suggests a reflexive structure.

However, leaving the question aside that territoriality is actually no topic of this definition, there is at least in these bold orientations a shortcoming – and even contradiction – entailed: This approach allows in its classical understanding state formation only within the capitalist framework – and thus limits the conceptualisation. This may be taken as deliberate step – but then it has to be made explicit.

So far, taking the two approaches together, we may actually say that definitions of the state aim on bringing together the two dimensions of (i) power[7] and (ii) territoriality together.

The notion of territoriality is also mentioned by Saskia Sassen – and one may well get the impression that she conflates nationhood and territoriality *(see e.g. Sassen, 2007:73; see in this context as well chapter 3 of Sassen, 2008).*

If we return to saying that the Marxist definition entails a shortcoming or contradiction, making these flaws explicit can actually help us to get a clearer understanding of what the state is about. In order to develop such an understanding, the following brief perspective offers an interpretation that tries to bring three dimensions closer together in a developmental perspective: the perspective (i) on power, (ii) territoriality and (iii) on how it is related to economic structures and class division/division of labour. A simple phasing may be proposed by looking at the following 'societal eras':

---

[7] In one case unspecified and simply defined in terms of varying legitimateness, in the other case specified by strict reference to class-interests and class-ruling.

Tributary Societies

POWER		TERRITORIALITY		ECONOMIC STRUCTURES; CLASS DIVISION/DIVISION OF LABOUR	
internal	external	sovereignty	resources/dependency	subsistence orientation and time	accumulation/mono-polisation orientation
mechanical[8] solidarity, limited role of power over others	n.a. due to nomadism and a large meaning of segmentary differentiation	n.a. due to nomadism	n.a. due to nomadism – resources taken in direct appropriation of the immediate environment in a non-competing way	hunting and gathering dominant, coordination oriented towards internal distribution and exploitation of the immediate environment – in the short term	not relevant

NON-STATE SOCIETIES

No major requirement of 'organic' mediation

Table 2: Power, Territoriality and Economics in Tributary Societies

---

[8] Here and in the following the terms mechanical and organic are used in more or less casual interpretation of the Durkheimian understanding.

Slave Societies

POWER		TERRITORIALITY		ECONOMIC STRUCTURES; CLASS DIVISION/DIVISION OF LABOUR	
internal	external	sovereignty	resources/dependency	subsistence orientation	accumulation/monopolisation orientation
Strongly politically based power, oriented towards control of slaves	limited expansionist	strong, even aiming on autarky, encouraged by dominant segmentary differentiation	Limited resource dependency due to the orientation on by and large sustainable management of existing resources in a non-competitive manner	agricultural products strong, though beginning internal competition based on management of existing, readily available resources, beginning of 'managing time'	limited

POLIS SOCIETIES

strict inclusion/exclusion rules with a combination of mechanical and organic rules, however in this combination not requiring a mediation by a separate body

Table 3: Power, Territoriality and Economics in Slave Societies

Feudal Societies

| POWER | | TERRITORIALITY | | ECONOMIC STRUCTURES; CLASS DIVISION/DIVISION OF LABOUR | |
internal	external	sovereignty	resources/dependency	subsistence orientation	accumulation/monopolisation orientation
strongly politically based, control of hierarchy; however, the hierarchy can to some extent be seen as perpetuating and self-regulatory so that a state as 'external power' had not been strongly necessitated (self-regulating 'Court Society')	strongly politically based and expansionist	strong and expansionist	though autarkic orientations continued playing a role, expansionist patterns played an increasing role as matter of resource enhancement and emerging as issue for markets – in consequence emergence of 'inter-territorial' resource imbalances' and 'inter-territorial competition'	largely agricultural and tool produce, for a minority production of luxurious goods	limited though slowly emerging; however: competition for 'best land'

EMERGING STATE SYSTEMS

no major mediation due to strict 'mechanical status attribution' and defined property relations, defining exclusion/inclusion/attribution not least on a hereditary basis

Table 4: Power, Territoriality and Economics in Feudal Societies

Developing Capitalist Societies

POWER		TERRITORIALITY		ECONOMIC STRUCTURES; CLASS DIVISION/DIVISION OF LABOUR	
internal	external	sovereignty	resources/dependency	subsistence orientation	accumulation/monopolisation orientation
economic basis of power gaining prevalence and building a hegemonic system of superiority of statehood that stands (seemingly) outside and over of the polity	strongly economic based and expansionist, though applying very much arguments of cultural hegemony	strong and geared towards establishing 'statehood supremacy'	oriented towards developing internal resource basis and mechanisms of improving their management and exploitation, not least by marketisation; increasing 'inter-territorial' and then 'international' resource competition and a distinct manifestation of 'world systems competition'	enhancing production of services and increasing meaning of financial markets and financing services, strongly linked into the emerging political system and 'culture'; huge gap between mass consumption as subsistence economy and elite consumption	accumulation of financial assets and only slowly emerging development of a productive basis
EMERGING STATE SYSTEMS					
especially nationally emerging organic mediation requirement on the basis of a shift towards enlightened economic power (re-) distribution					

Table 5: Power, Territoriality and Economics in Developing Capitalist Societies

Capitalist Societies[9]

POWER			TERRITORIALITY	ECONOMIC STRUCTURES; CLASS DIVISION/DIVISION OF LABOUR	
internal	external	sovereignty	resources/dependency	subsistence orientation	accumulation/monopolisation orientation
economically rooted and characterised by its ambiguity between control and securing legitimacy ('stick and carrot') state as distinct and differentiated politico-economic structure	in principal expansionist though very much coined by the global position within the core-periphery relations	strong and protectionist	depending on the position in the global order and the specific resource-availability and dependency – overall distinct world-systems competition with in many cases extreme resource inequalities and dependencies	based on producing industrial goods, though increasingly luxurious goods consumption getting increasingly 'needs independent' depending on wealth strong class segmentation, only on the edges dissolving class structures[10]	strong tendency towards concentration and centralisation. Small firms (SMEs) playing an ongoing role as 'independent sector'

NATION STATE SOCIETIES

nationally distinct pronounced need for organic mediation in order to tame increasing contradictoriness and for the management of the same – though this occurs in many cases in form of 'active reticence' ('night watch state')

Table 6: Power, Territoriality and Economics in Capitalist Societies

---

9   And it is in this latter case then where we can speak in strict sense of a state.

10   'Class' is here taken as wide classification, referring to the class in the strict sense but also to ethnicity, gender, urban-rural divide and the like. 'On the edges dissolving' refers in one perspective to the grouping, in another respect to certain 'characteristics' of life as certain leisure time activities, outfit, life style elements ... Of course, there is something artificial, highly analytical in such a proposal.

State-Monopolist Societies[11]

POWER		TERRITORIALITY		ECONOMIC STRUCTURES; CLASS DIVISION/DIVISION OF LABOUR	
internal	external	sovereignty	resources/dependency	subsistence orientation	accumulation/monopolisation orientation
oppressive hegemonial as state-monopolistic complex	oppressive hegemonial as state-monopolistic complex	strong and expansionist	depending on the position in the global order and the specific resource-availability and dependency; very distinct and usually stable inequalities of resource availability and control, backed and stabilised by political power	based on producing industrial goods, though increasingly luxurious goods consumption getting increasingly 'needs independent', in part 'socialised mass consumption', strong class segmentation, though on the edges dissolving class structures[12]	By and large concluded concentration and centralisation with relative rigid internationally structured division of labour and control of power Small firms (SMEs) playing an ongoing role as dependent sub-sector
				INTERNATIONAL STATE SOCIETIES	

national and international state mediation as specific productive force in its own right (''-industrial complexes'[13])*

Table 7: Power, Territoriality and Economics in State-Monopolist Societies

---

11 And it is in this latter case then where we can speak in strict sense of a state.

12 'Class' is here taken as wide classification, referring to the class in the strict sense but also to ethnicity, gender, urban-rural divide and the like. 'On the edges dissolving' refers in one perspective to the grouping, in another respect to certain 'characteristics' of life as certain leisure time activities, outfit, life style elements … Of course, there is something artificial, highly analytical in such a proposal.

13 With a specifically strong role for the military-industrial complex.

Globalised Capitalist Societies[14]

POWER		TERRITORIALITY		ECONOMIC STRUCTURES; CLASS DIVISION/DIVISION OF LABOUR	
internal	external	sovereignty	resources/dependency	subsistence orientation	accumulation/monopolisation orientation
Power dispersion and profiling extremes: on the one extreme violent oppression, on the other hand 'consumerist cultural hegemony'	strong role as matter of global positioning – however more as matter of functional units or cultural capital	n. fully a. – territoriality is dissolved as meaningful category and transferred to functional units and relationships on the one hand and 'lived spaces' on the other hand	strongly oriented towards developing 'cultural' and 'social' capital' and building on mobilising functional dependencies	service and consume oriented; hugely oriented on production and consumption patterns beyond subsistence rates	To a large extent concluded concentration and centralisation – though permanent redeployments play an important role in respect of property and small firms play increasingly a role as dependent suppliers and subcontractors. perforated in mentionable degrees by niche productions (may be starting points for new industries, monopolies...)

GLOCALISED FUNCTION-REGULATIVE SYSTEMS

mediation requirements and patterns shifting towards distinct de-territorialised and de-nationalised functionally defined entities and strategically defined relationships

Table 8: Power, Territoriality and Economics in Globalised Capitalist Societies

---

14 And it is in this latter case then where we can speak in strict sense of a state.

Of course, these tables can only provide a very rough outline. At least a few remarks may be added in respect of the most recent patterns *(see as well the section* Shortened Circuit, *pp. 62 ff.).* In the view of the present author it should be emphasised that the denationalisation/ deterritorialisation issue – very much a development that is inherent in the capitalist structure *(see Steinberg, 2009)* – is fundamentally an issue that reflects a functional shift. Resources – their concentration, distribution and redistribution – are now not primarily relevant in terms of the reproduction of territorial politico-economic powers. Rather, the focus is now on functional entities and also functional networks. In other words, it is about securing the relative independence of differentiated systems (e.g. financial markets, bureaucracies, (sub-)cultural entities etc etc.) and the links between them that function as strategic entities in their own right.[15]

Importantly, we find also a growing role of nongovernmental organisations – on the one hand as integrative factor, being themselves drawn into the maintenance of systemic processes, on the other hand as geyser of possible alternatives *(see e.g. Earles in this volume, Kratzwald in this volume; pp. 95 ff. and 175 ff. respectively).*

At the centre of all this we are talking about self-regulating functional entities, reflecting the 'functional definition' and fastening the social hegemony, i.e. class dominance. This hegemony gains dominance to some extent as somewhat 'incontestable position' by which the contestation of the system itself easily shifts towards struggles engaged with lifestyle issues rather than with fundamental systemic issues. However, the other way round one may also say that these struggles about lifestyle issues gain the character of fundamental contestations, reflecting the shifts within the mechanisms of the reproduction of the economic system itself – reflecting the shift in the systemic reproduction towards peripheral instances. To the extent to which not production itself but extension of foregoing and succeeding mechanisms gains at least temporary dominance, we have to consider the increased importance of such politico-systemic shifts also. However, that this hegemony is nearly

---

[15]   Cass R. Sunstein issues this in various respects in connection with the use of information technology and the tendency of supporting the emergence of self-referential circles, quoting Putnam who says "Real-world interactions often force us to deal with diversity, whereas the virtual world may be more homogeneous, not in demographic terms, but in terms of interests and outlook. Place-based communities may be supplanted by interest-based communities." (Putnam, 2000: 178, cited in Sunstein, 2007: 48)

incontestable and the dominant class position so strong is due to (i) the completion of the hegemonic power interpenetrating ever more spheres of life. David Harvey speaks of 'the web of life' and etches

> *[i]f it is invidious to view daily life and the lifeworld as something 'outside of' the circulation of capital, then we have to concede that everything that now occurs in the workplace and in the production-consumption process is somehow caught up within capital circulation and accumulation. Almost everything we now eat and drink, wear and use, listen to and hear, watch and learn comes to us in commodity form and is shaped by divisions of labor, the pursuit of product niches and the general evolution of discourses and ideologies that embody precepts of capitalism. It is only when daily life has been rendered totally open to the circulation of capital and when political subjects have their vision almost entirely circumscribed by embeddedness in that circulation that capitalism can function with affective meanings and legitimacy as its support.*

(Harvey, 2006: 82)

A further factor is (ii) the possibility to allow in certain areas an increasing self-control and regulation and at the same time an increasing oppression. This takes the form of self-oppression for instance by building 'gated communities of all classes' and 'self-exploitation of all professions'. In practice, we see this in various and hugely contradicting patterns, as for instance the ascendance of hugely specialised and professionalised service industries and at the same time niche-production especially in the service sector; the increasing gap between different degrees of affluence and at the same time some general trends towards post-materialist values, independent of material wealth; the growing divide also in spatial terms – as confrontation between the rich and poor regions within regions and between regions, however going hand in hand with decisive spatial mingling: for instance we find extremely wealthy groups and also regions/cities in the so-called 'developed world' and likewise extremely impoverished areas within the so-called developed world and we find equally meaningful the growth of new wealthy professional groups going hand in hand with low-paid jobs at their very side; or, to name a last example we find strict ethnical and racial segregation and next to it the most heterogeneous multicultural centres. Saskia Sassen points on an aspect that is of great importance here, not least showing pointing on the inherent link, articulating with view on large cities that *[t]he expansion of the high-income workforce in conjunction with the emergence of new cultural forms has led to a process of high-income gentrification that rests, in the last analysis, on the availability of a vast supply of low-wage workers. In turn, the consumption needs of the low-income population in large cities are partially met by manufacturing and retail establishments which are small, rely on family labor, and often fail to meet minimum safety and health standards.*

(Sassen, 2007: 116)

Significantly this opens the view on informalisation with the two overlapping aspects, the one being concerned with labour relationships and material concerns – the huge field of precarity laying in front of us *(see e.g. for a variety of aspects the work in the framework of the European Network Social Uncertainty, Precarity, Inequality);* on the other hand it is not only about increasing insecurity *(see on this aspect Sassen, passim)* but also the informalisation of the life styles in the widest sense.

Though Sassen seems not to agree this is well in line with world systems theory – we may recall the explanation by Immanuel Wallerstein who explicates that the core-periphery relationship is not about any regional distribution, but about the agglomeration of specifically defined capital and productive resources (see p. 20). Seen in this light, the elaboration by Sassen is actually very much a confirmation of world-systems-theory.

– Surely, one may ask to which extent this is a new pattern. Perhaps the actually new moment is only a paradoxical one: that its character today is much more distinct, stark and subtle at the same time. It is here where Saskia Sassen surely makes an important contribution when she draws out attention on

the global city as one strategic instantiation of multiple localizations

(Sassen, 2007: 118)

where it is necessary

to reconstitute [discontinuities] as borderlands rather than dividing lines

(ibid.: 110).

It is of utmost importance to emphasise the complementing relationship between economic and political processes – one may even say that we arrive at another confirmation of the concept of political-economy or a merger of the political and economic realm. Saskia Sassen makes us especially aware of the political side the emergence of new constellations, writing:

> *This interpretive stance brings with it a methodological concern about including informal, or not yet formalized, institutional arrangements and practices in the analysis of change. That which has not yet gained formal recognition can often be an indicator of change, of the constituting and inserting of new substantive logics in a particular domain of the social-economic, cultural, political, discursive, subjective – which is thereby altered even though its formal representation may remain unchanged, or, alternatively, altered even though it remains informal, or is not yet formalized. These informal logics and practices, I argue, can be shown to have contributed to historical change even though they are often difficult to recognize as such. The fact that informal logics and practices are one factor in historical change also con- tributes to the lack of legibility that is frequently a feature of major social changes in the making.*

> *(Sassen, 2008: 12)*

In this context we have to confront ourselves also with a fundamental shift, concerned with the subject-object understanding *(s. e.g. Trevillon, 1999)*. This shows that the gentrification and drawing of stricter lines on the one hand goes on the other hand along with processes of frazzling at the borderlines – processes that can be found within and between the systems.

The width and also depth of the problem is also getting obvious when we look at a further facet of

> *the paradoxical nature of the global village concept … . this 'global paradox' is usually described purely in economic terms … . But this economic/organizational paradox contains a second cultural one, which is less amenable to the tenets of 'progress theory'. As organisations become smaller and potentially more diverse in terms of their orientation to particular specialist niches in the world market, they also come to resemble one another more and more in terms of their internal characteristics. So, tendencies towards both pluralism and self-expression can be matched by tendencies towards a degree of conformism which is usually associated with the allegedly defunct mass production culture of the Fordist age.*

> *(ibid.: 66)*

At this stage it is probably fair to say that one of the major questions has to be concerned with conflict-theoretical issues and aspects of theories of power. The point that is pursued is based on the assumption of frequent shifts in the relationship between the political and economic realm. Not withstanding the principal stance of the fundamentally economic foundation of the political system, we should not fail to look closer at the definition of economy as societal process. As such we find a seemingly paradoxical movement: only to the extent to which the economy is developing as an 'independent area', claiming as such overall power over and within society, we find also the emergence of a seemingly independent political power as 'mediating instance' – in particular the dissolution of the 'integrated socio-economic functioning' with the emergence of capitalism *(see above)* requires such distinct institutional setting. Coming from a developmental perspective we can follow Giovanni Arrighi, Kenneth Barr, and Shuji Hisaeda who mark an important point of change.

> *And yet, change begat change only up to a point. The capitalist nature of the underlying objective of industrial expansion was both its main foundation and its main limit. Just as the commercial expansion of Dutch capital in the seventeenth and early eighteenth centuries was based on, and limited by, a reversal in the relationship between 'profit' and 'power,' so the industrial expansion of British capital in the nineteenth century was based on, and limited by, a reversal in the relationship between 'profit' and 'livelihood.' The reversal had two main aspects. One, underscored by Marx throughout his work, was the subordination of labor to capital in production processes (see especially Marx, 1976). The other, underscored by Polanyi (1957, especially chapter 3), was the subordination of the motive of gain in the regulation of social life.*

(Arrighi/Barr/Hisaeda: 117; with reference to Marx, 1976)

To extent to which we acknowledge such shift we can indeed assume that we face currently a reversal that follows the same argument. We see now the reintegration of societal functions under direct control of the economy. This, in consequence, changes the mechanisms that had been (and still are) state functions in the sense of undermining the regulative and mediating role of the 'state'. Rather than dealing with an 'independent state' or with a state-industrial complex we are now dealing – again – with an overall and encompassing economic structure. Alluding to Carl Schmitt's stance on the 'total state'*(see Schmitt, 1928),*reality may now turn towards an age of the total economy.

Looking at Carl Schmitt's approach, we are taught that

> *[c]ontemporary parliamentarism, based on delegate representation by party candidates, illustrated – at least on Schmitt's presentation[.] – a movement away from properly political representation. It did so by negating its necessarily personal or eminent character, and Schmitt claimed that the transformation of the modern state into a 'Leviathan' meant that it had actually come to symbolise a body that 'disappears from the world of representation.' This is because the theatrical Hobbesian Leviathan, which held the population awe, has been transformed by liberalism and capitalism into a simple machine.[.] As he suggested in the Verfassungslehre:*
>
> *'To represent means to make visible and present an invisible entity through an entity which is publicly present ... This is not possible with any arbitrary entity, since a particular kind of being (Sein) is assumed.'[.]*
>
> *(Kelly, 2004: 117 f.; with following references: Manin,1997; Pye: explicitly discusses Hobbes's 'theatrical' notion of representation. This relates to Schmitt's critique of political pluralism as well. See Schmitt, 1928: 209; Schmitt, 1930)*

This interpretation is of particular interest for the present argument as it highlights the contradictory character on which Carl Schmitt could build his argument – and on which, *cum grano salis,* the fear of a current turn towards an age of the total economy can rest as well. It is the trend of not simply distancing economic processes from social processes. Rather it is the double-turn: the new form of socialisation as complete interpenetration of the social with utilitarian thinking, going hand in hand with the complete dissolution of the economy into a space that is suggested as being positioned outside of the social sphere. We find as result of such equation the completion of self-alienation by which even governance, self-help, civic movement, participation, empowerment etc. are – not necessarily but potentially and easily – subordinated under such a total economy. And decisively this is now not anymore a matter of blunt force of material necessities but a matter of voluntary and/or non-recognised processes.

We arrive at an especially sardonic ascertainment, showing a somewhat Cartesian undertone. In his *Discourse on the Method of Rightly Conducting one's Reason and of Seeking Truth in the Sciences,* René Descartes highlights famously not only the credential of the existence in thinking*(ego ergo sum),* but also the reference to the good and right thinking as matter of following the reason set by eternal, i.e. divine law. Consequentlyhe suggests:

Following, from reflecting on the circumstance that I doubted, and that in consequence my being was not perfect as I clearly saw that it was a greater perfection to know than to doubt, I felt pushed to inquire whence I had learned to think of something more perfect than myself; and I saw immediately that I must expect this notion from some kind of perfect nature which in reality realised such perfection. As for the thoughts of many other objects outside of myself, as the sky, the earth, light, heat, and thousand others, I was less at a loss to know from where they came; for since I remarked in them nothing that seemed to render them superior to myself, I could believe that, if these were true, they were dependencies on my own nature, in so far as it possessed a certain perfection, and, if they were not true, that I held them from nothing, that is to say, that they were in me because of a certain imperfection of my own nature. But this could not be the case with the idea of an absolutely perfect nature, more perfect than myself; it had been obviously impossible to receive it from nothing; and, as it is not less repugnant that the more perfect an effect of it should be, and dependence on the less perfect, than that something should proceed from nothing, it was equally impossible that I could hold it from myself: accordingly, it remained however that it had been placed in me by a nature which was in reality more perfect than my own, and which even possessed within itself all the perfections of which I could form some idea; that is to say, in one word, which was God.

(Descartes, René, 1637: 117 f.; translation P. H.)

In other words, stating on the one hand the individual as 'independent actor', he then qualifies it by submitting him/her under this external power. This is exactly the pattern we can see today: the hyper-individualisation, the call for the reflecting and independent and conscious, self-responsible individual, limited though by the new quasi-divine order: the fetish of money, epitomized in and by the financial market (actors). This is in particular remarkable as we see in this current pattern a shift that is very similar to the one by Descartes inasmuch it claims an idealist starting point – the reflecting individual – and then leads us to a higher idealist real, namely that of divinity. In short: from real thinking to imagined thinking. In today's terms: from the real 'abstracting economy' that deals with exchange values rather than use values to the 'imagined abstracting economy' of exchange that deals with the imagination even of the exchange values, the mouse-click away replacing the prayer. – And actually this is not too far from calling for a smart economy and a new prince *(see pp. 49 f.)*.

Historical Changes of Capitalism –Renaissance Reiterated or on the Way to a New Statehood?

In recent years new forms of governance had been a central issue both on the political agenda and also the agenda of social and political science *(Commission of the European Communities, 2001; Commission of the European Communities, 2005; United Nations, [without date]; for the latter see e.g. University of Vienna. School of Governance [without date]).*

Although the topic had been frequently also explored in respect of the business world, it had not been taken up as matter of the economy itself. However, at the same time it cannot be denied that global governance is at stake. Does it mean more than thinking about governance in different parts of the world? Does it mean more than applying 'modern governance rules' as means of the work of international institutions? Finally – and this is here the question at work – does it mean to apply governance to globalisation itself?

Glancing over the growing literature there are no major clues on the substantial meaning of governance for globality or globalisation. Everything seems to be more oriented on

- widening the scope of governing in terms of space
- widening the range of governing in terms of the topics and
- recognising – and aiming to tackle – the increasing gap between the smaller and the larger units of soci(et)al bonds *(see for instance Ahearne/Pisani-Ferry/Sapir/Véron, 2006; Bonaglia/Braga de Macedo/Bussolo, 2001; Trichet, 2008).*

We may say as well that governance presents itself as answer on (i) the quantitative aspects of what Norbert Elias presented as *The Civilising Process (see Elias, 1939/2000)* and (ii) its inherent socio-political and socio-cultural consequences from the increasing length of chains of interaction.

Of course, globalisation is a complex socio-cultural-economic process. However, taking this statement seriously means to uncover the underlying economic process not in terms of different market systems (and the mechanisms that are in place to steer these processes). Rather, we are concerned with the more complex issue of socio-economic changes that are not primarily defined by the change of market relationships, the seeming re-emergence of what is claimed to be free trade principles. These are very important issues and it is not suggested by the present author that they should be underestimated. However, at stake is a fundamental change of the socio-economic mechanisms by way of changing power structures and the redefinition of the different elements of the process of the relationship between them. Importantly, the emergence of changing relationships means at the same time a change of the understanding of the elements themselves.

The following remarks are therefore employed by the broad aim to locate these issues in the wider framework of changes as they had been explored before. The guiding question then is if we find the shift towards governance as one item of a general change-agenda that is concerned with the 'de-statisation' by which old borders change, frazzle and dissolve and at the same time a new system emerges that had been tentatively called *Glocalised Function-Regulative System (see* Table 8: *p.31 and the remarks pp. 32 ff.).*[16]

Then, in more stern terms, the character of the social itself needs to be reconsidered by recognising it as immediate part of the process of production in a wider understanding, following Marx in his remarks in the *Grundrisse*. Furthermore, we have to observe closely the two dimensions: globality as state of a – at any point in time – given pattern of global power structures and globalisation as process of shifting powers, having its roots in the reshuffling of resources and requirements. Finally, looking at the contradictions behind this process we have to look for elaborating a four-dimensional perspective. The centrality of the development of a new mode of production has to be underpinned by the analysis of its socio-political foundation, i.e. by looking at the shift to some kind of 'global citizenry and citizenship' and global governance and by looking at the interlink between the economic and the socio-political sphere. – Surely, this remark does not claim to point on something fundamentally new. However, it is still a necessary statement when we consider the fact that it is too often fading away – also behind quests for politically responsible steering of globalisation issues.

---

[16] To be sure, I do not suggest that the 'state' does not play a role anymore – actually in many respects we have to acknowledge that it or elements that are commonly seen as core-defining moments plays an even stronger role – if we look at war-mongering of the US over the recent years we get a clear picture of the ongoing meaning of nationalism. However, this should not prevent us from of fully acknowledging some fundamental trends that concern the validity of moments that are usually considered as foundations of the understanding of the modern state.

It is proposed to revisit various aspects of current societal trends of today's reality in this light in order to develop at least a clear understanding of a configuration that is commonly understood as state. And looking at a way of developing a clearer question means not least investigating possible historical parallels.

Today we find in various respect societal features and patterns that may remind us – at least at first glance – at the times of earlier societies, in particular the time of the emerging early capitalism: the time of the *Renaissance* and *Ancient Régime* which is proposed as the crèche of modernisation, disemboguing into the later actual take-off during the period of enlightenment.

Seen from here the working thesis, namely that we are currently facing – on the global level – a shift of capitalism of which the core is not globalisation as such but a fundamental change of the mode of production that is equally ample as the emergence of modern capitalism. This formulation suggests that the change is not just about the mode of production in the strict sense but about the wider societal mechanism of (re-)production, including a change of the understanding and meaning of citizenship. Without elaborating them, important issues can be listed under following catchwords *(some features had been already developed earlier in this chapter, others will be looked upon in the various following chapters; and they will be also explored in Herrmann, forthcoming (c); Herrmann, forthcoming (b))*.

- A first aspect is the shift in the economic sphere, the dominance of the finance markets suggesting a more fundamental shift of the economic system by way of moving from production as 'manufacturing' towards distribution and exchange.

  Linked to this pattern of development we find shifts that come along in different terms, but should also be considered immediately under the heading of economics: privatisation of policing and the privatisation of welfare not only in terms of an increasing role of private for-profit-services but also in form of voluntary services *(see as well p. 63)*.

  The reader may be hinted towards the parallels between the extreme exclusion and at the same time regulation of vagabondage and begging and today's increasing 'management' of begging and exclusion, translating exclusion policies very much into issues of technical capturing of the social problem: for instance means of enforced labour market integration on the one hand and the anti-

41

begging legislation on the other hand – today meaning indeed today as pattern of very recent incidence.

- This has huge direct and indirect effects not simply in terms of the distribution and redistribution of wealth but perhaps even more groundbreaking consequences on (i) how wealth is generated and (ii) – in part expression of this – the class structure. We can observe in both respects an increasing tension. In the first case it is the enormous agglutination of absurd wealth and the mind boggling poverty*(see e.g. Heshmati, 2006: 61-107);* in the second case it is the coexistence of tightened sealing of politico-economic classes; on the other hand we are witnessing the dispersion of class borders in several areas – be it in terms of space or of life styles and values or be it in terms of formerly valid attributions like job security as characteristic for the members of the middle class, academics etc.

The patterns of production are hugely important as well in terms of the structure of property, the emergent niche production and the dissolution of traditional employment patterns.

- Technological shifts play different roles – being on the one hand conditions, enabling factors, however also emerging as result from the aforementioned momentums.

- Closely welded into the concurrence of technological developments in the context of the change of property structures, the mode of production, the new patterns of distribution are noteworthy developments on positioning labour inside and outside of the marketised system. Without going into detail, the following are especially significant: segmentation of labour markets and changes in the meaning of location – in some respect 'replacing' social segmentation, but also the re-emergence of stricter segmentation, the former working class districts now being the various new ghettoes: some being located within the centres and metropolis, some being hidden in sub-urban areas of being in – seen in a world-systems perspective–in regions of (semi-)peripheral status while on the other hand headquarter work is hugely concentrated in the new centres. It has to be also recognised that these new centres are to a large extent prone to short circles of rise and fall: financial centres, technological centres etc. *Cum grano salis,* the tiger economies show an important part of the dilemma: especially extreme amplitudes of crisis follow very short-lived and extreme rise.

- With this we find, of course, as well – be it on the micro- or on the macro-level – shifts of power relations, for instance:
  - o these may reflect the relation of power-patterns (e.g. the role played by 'different forms of capital', if taken in Bourdieu's understanding – due to this there may be power developing that is moving in some areas against the patterns of standard class structures),
  - o power locations (the strengthened role of local and community related power and also of international and supranational powers),
  - o power generation (power expressed by state institutions and in law being possibly replaced, complemented by or merging with 'non-statutory law' and other means and expressions of private power)
- In and linked to these various contexts, we find furthermore 'subjective reflections'. Religion and questions of faith, post-materialist values and charity *(see already p.41),* but equally hedonism and identity issues play in different respect and different fields and to different degrees important roles.
  Surely not contesting the importance and in some ways increasing meaning of class structure, we should nevertheless be sufficiently open to look at issues of redefining certain status elements in this context. In both respects, the objective and the subjective, life-world respect, we find some shifts that can give at least the impression of blurring borders but that surely show also objective shifts as the increasing insecurity and precarity of previously secured groups, with this shifts in status, relative opening of upstream mobility, alignment of life styles and others. This is surely not about restructured class divisions. However, to the extent to which we accept the thesis of a fundamental change of the economic mode as venture towards a new capitalism (and its possible resemblance with earlier historical patterns) we should consider the changes in terms of class restructuration also in a different light. Heide Gerstenberger's remarks in connection with the historical analysis of England, are possibly telling. She looks at the shifts and emergence of new estates and classes and in this context as well at the extreme borderlines of inclusion/exclusion as

vagabondage *(Gerstenberger, 1990/2006: 123 ff.).* One aspect is in the present context especially remarkable:

With the increase of the population and the – though not generally but in some regions hugely – changed economic and social forms of the profitable utilisation of land property 'abandonment' emerged as permanent problem for those who had been working towards the constitution of order – and who did have the means of doing so. Which methods should be used for this purpose had been hugely disputed.

(ibid.: 133 – translation P. H.)

With this retrospect we can present current debates on reshuffling social over in the light of what is later issued as overall challenge of finding a new mode of social appropriation *(see pp. 60 ff.).*

- And one important moment of such movements is concerned with the issue of developing actor perspectives: the increasingly important debate on responsibility and the subject – as subjectivity and also actor – is going far beyond individual attributions and shows immediate meaning on the level of local and global action.

- In various respects we can see a re-emergence of the role of communities and localities – be it as empirical question or as issue of political contest and support. One strand is concerned with the wide range of communitarianism and social capital – a hugely diverse and contradicting array; another strand may be seen as matter of 'community citizenship' *(see Phillips/Berman, 2001; Berman, forthcoming; in terms of political developments concerned with acknowledging the status Australian Aborigines and Torres Strait Islanders as 'state within a state' are a case of special interest; see e.g. Reynolds, 1996; Australian Human Rights Commission, 2009; Reynolds, 1996/2000).*

- But we should see in the very array of debate also the emergence of new configurations which may be seen as social constructs of location-independent spaces. To some extent these are detectable as networks, not least digital networks which constitute their very own 'network societies' but furthermore with this specific regulative systems with legal and legislative character independent from the state. The most pronounced and probably also developed example are the regulative instances of the Internet *(see Kohl, 2007; Svantesson, 2007).* Another area can be seen in the development of 'global law' of which the United Nations body is only a small and probably the least important part – due to its weakness of juridical self-assertion*(Koehler, 1987, passim)*. However, this is not least also a matter of the subject area that is full of conceptual and definitional disputes and very open to specific socio-cultural frameworks. In other areas, global law may well be easier to be advance and Gunther Teubner comes to the conclusion that

[t]he emerging global (not inter-national!) order is a legal order in its own right which should not be measured against the standards of national legal systems. It is not – as is usually understood – an underdeveloped body of law which has certain structural deficiencies in comparison to national law. Rather, its peculiar characteristics as fully fledged distinguishes it from the traditional law of the nation states. These characteristics can be explained by differentiation within world society itself. While global law lacks political and institutional support on the global level, it is closely coupled with globalized socio-economic processes.

(Teubner, 1996: 4)

He outlines substantial shifts especially on four levels, namely the orientation of boundary setting not along the line of territoriality but by invisible communities and networks; the sources in self-organised processes within certain functional fields'; the lack of independence and self-reference of the aw-making process itself, and thus the openness to influences coming from different interest-groups; and finally the unity of law not as matter of a coherent legal codification but as abstract form of intercultural negotiation *(see op.cit.)*.

Presumably more important – if only as predecessor for further development in this area – are 'functional social spaces' as for instances closed digital networks that are – for certain political areas, economic sector (finance sector/banking) or topics– closed for members and, importantly – defining their own strict rules. Their special importance has to be seen in their potentiality of being germs to new legislatures: governments without territorial reference and with a 'selected membership'. The criteria for selection may well be open. However, we may find here as well rather strictly regulated new 'communities' as for instance in terms of corporate networks: having their own rules and moreover: claiming to impose these rules not only on their members but also on wider societal areas by getting involved into 'stakeholder processes' *(on some general issues: Bauer, 2007 (a); Bauer,*

Rudolph, 2007 (b); dealing with concrete areas of relevance: Kentor, 2005; Nollert, 2005; in the overall context also: Castells 1996, 1997).

- A crucially important aspect in the present context – when we look at the shifts between political and economic foundation of power – is the fact that we are currently facing such a shift in the power basis.

Heide Gerstenberger advances that the emergence and development of the bourgeois state *('buergerliche Staatsgewalt')* has to be interpreted as a matter of forming a power without subject *(Gerstenberger, op.cit.)*. We can indeed find many reasons for such perspectives – in one way. However, such interpretation neglects the inconsistence and ambivalence of the process itself. On the one hand we find the confirmation of such thesis in the fact of an increasing separation of power from the persona of the king as Gerstenberger frequently issues throughout her book *(see Gerstenberger, 1990/2006)*. It is important to note this as objective process, as the development of an objective kind. However, there is another objective development which links into the overall pattern – underlying and emerging from it, namely the emergence of the 'modern subject' – *bourgeois* and *citoyen*. An illustrative presentation especially on the second meaning, the *citoyen,* is given by Michael Mascuch, pointing out that

[t]he value – moreover, the paramountcy – for individualism of the autonomous agency of self-determination is inscribed in the concept of individual responsibilities and reciprocal rights, to which all persons who identify themselves as self-creating beings willingly and equally subscribe. Indeed the tacit act of subscription to such rights and responsibilities, the core of modern citizenship, is understood as a version of self-creation, which is consonant with individualist self-identification. Additionally, as the philosopher Charles Taylor has explained, the enjoyment of the rights of self-creation in modern individualist societies also entails as a correlate a specific personal agentive capacity, that of being, in his formulation, a 'respondent.'

(Mascuch, 1996: 20)

It is a development that has also deep socio-cultural roots, explored by Christel Meier who elucidates that

[b]oth reasons of self-explication, justification and essemple e dottrina are due to the reference to the speaker, the auctor, fixed on the societal

horizon by the determination of their impact; it is not concerned with the free expression of the autonomous author. The individual substantiates his role as speaker in the public-social space with an authorisation.

(Meier, 2004: 207 f. – transl. P. H.)

But of course the more decisive aspect is that hand in hand with the emergence of the individual as economic subject we find the emergence of the individual as legal subject, i.e. as institution that is now in some peculiar way independent of society:

it constituted a unity of rights and duties, and on the social level, an institutionalised reciprocity

(Luhmann, 1981: 51; quoted in: Verschraegen, 2002: 265)

The more or less extensive exploration is meant to highlight the fact that we find many of today's debates also in this respect paralleled: The new economic developments and sweeping structural changes that we currently witness are not only showing effects on the individuality, personality and the understanding of sociability but find to some extent also there roots in these changes which – not denying their constitutional character – are nevertheless positioned on the level of the superstructure. – Indeed, this is about dialectics.

Interesting as side note is a pointer on new developments on this topic today that provide some provocative stimulus for further thoughts on this topic – the tile of the work by Helga Nowotny and Giuseppe Testa has to suffice: *The Vitreous Genes. On the Invention of the Individual in the Molecular Era (Nowotny/Testa, 2009).*

Looking at the underlying thesis of the present contribution, i.e. focusing on the interpretation of the current recurrence of identity politics, the newly emerging centrality of faith, religion, ideological debates (at least in their orientation on ways of life) etc. as being founded in the movement of structural economic changes: seen as shift within the economy towards areas that are peripheral to the actual value production in the strict sense we can see from another side a kind of new 'Renaissance'. Then the formation of political power regains a certain stronghold, partially supplanting the dominance of the economic power in its strict meaning, however most importantly and paradoxically only needed in order of establishing another time the final triumph of the economy as soci(et)al subject, or, taken from before, the triumph of the total economy, as it had been called alluding to Carl Schmitt's 'total state' *(see p. 36)*. The political configuration – if we continue calling it state or not is not decisive – may then be interpreted as postmodern dictatorship by a self-proclaimed master race, intellectual elite of new philosophers of enlightenment or as opportunity of initialising a process of actually regaining political power – within the tensional field of differentiated dimensions and directions of appropriation *(see in the following pp. 59 ff.)*. Looking at the movement between de-subjectivation and re-subjectivation of the state in the *longue durée* as matter of a developmental law can at least shade another light on patterns of current policies, strongly leaning towards clientelism, privatisation also of the power apparatus – not as matter of abolition or erosion of economic developmental law but as their confirmation, i.e. as way of generating space for new developments of the productive force. This may be a matter of qualitative or quantitative development and it may be very different in its social meaning. It is exactly this question that makes matters going beyond the purely technical instances.

It is the 'ceremonial governance' that finds today its seeming popularisation in the form of branding that allows everybody – at least in the sphere of appearance – to participate in new forms of ruling n a consumerist world.

- Citizenship, statehood, nation – these are some major issues at stake and that can be seen in a wider referential framework, namely the search for a 'good order' or 'good society'. However, as such it is not a matter of moral concerns – as it had never been such a matter of morality. Instead it is a matter of searching and rebalancing the reach and scope of processes of appropriation with their 'overlapping dimensions of space and people'. Citizenship, statehood and nation are then not least of interest as matters of redefining legal frameworks but also redefining means of regulation.

So it is the question of what, where and how in their togetherness as new dimension of defining 'statehood'. Here, the questions of new paternalism, clientelism, rules of social heritage of positions versus the call for near to divine vocation of individuals for charismatic leader positions are on a micro-level the complement to the call for new responsibilities for sustainable growth by world leaders, the search for a new history rather than the dismal of history and the call for smart societies and '(moral) virtue instead of (monetarised) value'. The call for new Machiavellian princes is on both sides – the right and the claimed left – a politically dangerous reply as long as it positions itself as benevolent request to a political economy that remains unexplored – and unchanged. – Debates in (social) policy,calling for virtue, putting forward that

[t]he Greek word arete is translated as 'virtue' and means the quality which entitles any institution or individual to be called good. ... It is virtue that makes an individual both good and social

(Powell, Fred: 2001: 96; see as well Powell, 2005)

are surely benign from their subjective background. But – especially if they go hand in hand with highlighting greed as major issue of the current economic crisis – they are at most dangerous romanticism, at worst and certainly in analytical perspectives they are not much more than a naïve call for new charismatic leadership under the rule of an intellectual elite claiming secular divinity – heaven on earth.

It can be without embroidery assumed that in general these issues are typical for eras of fundamental societal changes, being concerned with redefining borders. Coming another time back to Saskia Sassen, she sees this topic as well as central to the work on her *Sociology of Globalization,* stating that

[if] there is one theme that captures aspects of all I have discussed, it is the notion of borders.

(Sassen, 2007: 213)

Linking to this statement it can be in the present contribution qualified by saying that the borderline which is at stake when it comes to defining 'the state' and its development is the border between politics and economics, better to say: their specific role in the constitutional process of power *(see further on this topic below pp. 59).*A decisive moment of such processes is that the structure of constituting citizenship, i.e. the point of reference for it underlies a permanent fundamental change. Moreover, the meaning of citizenship itself is changed.

Interim Conclusion: A Methodological Challenge

From here we can name four fundamental requirements that should serve as guidance of any further analytical work. These had been already developed in another context *(see Herrmann, (d))*. They are about the requirement for recognising processuality, mutuality, relationality, and contradictoriness.

- *Processuality* means understanding the historical processes as for instance outlined by Leonid Grinin as

  notion that generalizes an intricate complex of internal transformations and actions of various historical subjects, as a result of which important societal changes and integration, continuous enlargement of intersocietal systems take place, transition to the new levels of development is going on, and in general (taking into consideration the present results and future perspectives), humankind gets transformed from a potential unity into an actual one.

  (Grinin, 2006: 13)

  The challenge of understanding the full meaning of this historicity arises from the fact we have to look at history with the three different dimensions outlined by Fernand Braudel and already mentioned earlier *(see p. 9)*. Taking this serious means that we have to be conscious about applying the perspective of the presence as well on the past, in the same way as we apply the principles of the past as means of understanding the presence – dialectics in history is then also very much about inter-temporary relationships: expectations by actors formed by their past and expectations coined by where they want to go to.

- *Mutuality* is the interference of structures and actors, shading a different light on societal formations as we are now not aiming on understanding different structures but also actual systems of soci(et)al practice. This links to some extent into debates as they are brought forward by Anthony Giddens, but more importantly to Margaret Archer and it this has to be seen closely as matter of emergence and maintenance of figurations as they are discussed by Norbert Elias.

- *Relationality* refers to the fact that we actually have to focus on the social – its emergence, maintenance and development itself. Importantly this cannot be understood as matter of social values in any abstract sense. Rather, we have to develop an understanding of

50

the nominal dimension of the social as it finds its expression in the definition brought forward by the social quality approach as it had been presented above.

- Finally, *contradictoriness,* is expressed in the fact that all this develops around the ways people are dealing in every day's life with appropriateness and power, the latter as matter of ability (empowerment) and control (being controlled and controlling others).

This brings us to the point where we have to reconsider the development of statehood and economy from the perspective from a secular long-term perspective. Again, though in other words, the thesis is that we find a shift of both, (i) the state shifting more and more towards being an instrument of economics rather than being itself part of a wider form of economic organisation (precisely an intermediary for the management of distinct and to some extent independent) subsystems) and (ii) the economy shifting towards an immediate societal actor. – We may say as well that we are confronted with a re-merger of the immediate entity of politics and state.

In order to develop a better understanding, we can refer to the two closely interwoven processes of accumulation, based on 'production beyond immediate consumption' and individualisation and with this the redefinition of the social as part of an increasingly utilitarian system of thought. Two important points that will not be further explored on this occasion are (i) that production moves beyond immediate consumption not only in terms of the productive/economic circles but in terms of the of the actual ultimate aim of the economic process that is – more then ever – solely based on producing the 'consumptive needs' that it aims to serve. One may say it depends on producing the consumers – an *absurdum* if we listen to politico-economic instances that claim supply would follow demand. The other point in question is closely linked and concerns (ii) the redefinition of the social as part of an also socio-cultural system of thought that is guided by purely utilitarian hegemonic project.

Importantly the developing pattern is not just a matter of privatisation of appropriation and – going hand in hand with this – a perverted socialisation of power. Rather, we see an underlying pattern of 'de-socialisation' or, to be more precise: the mediatisation of the social in form of emerging long chains of interaction with the –though not inevitable – capped mechanisms of control. Especially the works by

Norbert Elias on the process of civilisation helped us to understand these mechanisms in a wider perspective.

However, having said this we should avoid any hasty judgement: this is not only an evitable advance. It is also a process that has – individual and social – advantages. One of the points in question is that even private accumulation has usually the by-product of what may be called 'social spill-over effects', leading to social enrichment or to the indirect enrichment of individuals who are not immediate profiteers. It is also true that the process of de-socialisation is very much (i) in any case not complete and (ii) very much a pattern of developing different patterns of socialisation. On the first we may refer to the work by Audan Sandberg *(see Sandberg, 1998)*who maintains the claim of a specificity of the Nordic model, in which a 'commons-attitude' continues to exist. We may also refer to the wide-ranging literature disputing the *Loss of the Commons (not least the only recently extensively recognised work of Elinor Ostrom, e.g. Dols̆ak/Ostrom, 2003; Ostrom, 1990)*. On the second point I refer especially to the social quality approach *(see for general information: European Foundation on Social Quality)*.

In any case, at stake is in actual fact – again – the already mentioned issue of (i) the power-appropriation dimension and (ii) the dimension of societality and individuality *(see p. 16; also p. 213)*.

Re-Feudalisation and Globalisation: Reaction or Savour

The question remains if – and if so: in which sense – this may be a progressive development that has a similar meaning as the development described by Karl Marx when he wrote about the historically progressive role of the bourgeoisie, stating:

> *The bourgeoisie, during its rule of scarce one hundred years, has created more massive and more colossal productive forces than have all preceding generations together. Subjection of Nature's forces to man, machinery, application of chemistry to industry and agriculture, steam-navigation, railways, electric telegraphs, clearing of whole continents for cultivation, canalisation of rivers, whole populations conjured out of the ground – what earlier century had even a presentiment that such productive forces slumbered in the lap of social labour?*

> *We see then: the means of production and of exchange, on whose foundation the bourgeoisie built itself up, were generated in feudal society. At a certain stage in the development of these means of production and of exchange, the conditions under which feudal society*

produced and exchanged, the feudal organisation of agriculture and manufacturing industry, in one word, the feudal relations of property became no longer compatible with the already developed productive forces; they became so many fetters. They had to be burst asunder; they were burst asunder.

Into their place stepped free competition, accompanied by a social and political constitution adapted in it, and the economic and political sway of the bourgeois class.

(Marx/Engels, 1848: 489)

And Frederick Engels brings this to the point when he writes about Marx' defence of Free Trade, referring to

an ever recurring cycle of prosperity, glut, crisis, panic, chronic depression, and gradual revival of trade, the harbinger not of permanent improvement but of renewed overproduction and crisis; in short, productive forces expanding to such a degree that they rebel, as against unbearable fetters, against the social institutions under which they are put in motion; the only possible solution: a social revolution, freeing the social productive forces from the fetters of an antiquated social order, and the actual producers, the great mass of the people, from wage slavery.

(Engels, 1888: 521)

To begin with, we need centrally in any case an explanation of the current changes in broad political-economic terms, reflecting the long term, secular developments and also the fundamental character of a change of the entire societal structure where social and economic changes (and their interpretation) are inherently linked rather than 'interdisciplinarily' bound together. This argues not least against somewhat voluntarist, politically lead state theoretical or power theoretically reflections. The latter would suggest following a line of eclectic state theories as for instance brought forward by St. Augustine, summarised by Anton-Hermann Chroust by saying

Justice is 'but a habit of the soul which imparts to every one the dignity due to him', yet always with reference to the common good. Its origin proceeds from nature. For reasons of the common utility (or good), some of its different aspects (or contents) turn afterwards into custom; and finally this notion of justice is sanctioned by the fear of the law and by religion. Nature (the eternally fixed and stable order of things) is law, which is not the product of man's personal opinion, but something implanted (in man) by a certain innate power.' (Chroust, 1944: 198; with reference to Aquinas (app. 1256-1259): quaest. 31)

Instead following such line, I suggest devoting particular attention on four major shifts.

- The re-emergence of an economy that is centrally built around financing mechanisms and thus exchange and trade focused. Economically this points centrally on two aspects, namely overvaluation of goods and services and under-valuation of labour. This translates into a huge disparity concerning affluence and poverty and with this also into a parasite system that undermines in medium and long terms its own foundation, being in permanent search for new productive arrays. The latter is the ground that we witness – at first glance – a tremendous productivity which is, however, grounded in a substantial lack of productivity to the extent to which 'values' are only assessed as exchange values rather than being strongly linked to use values.

- This is made possible and enforces technological loops as foundation of the mode of production. An example *par excellence* is the development of at least some aspects of the information technology that generates it own (and with this its customer's) 'needs'. Software and applications are to such an extent boosted that they require new hardware – without fundamentally changing the quality of the 'technical work'. In turn the new – and actually underutilised – hardware encourages the development of new software and applications and all this moves towards a vicious cycle. However, this statement requires immediate qualification. Although it is justified to say 'without fundamentally changing the quality of the 'technical work', major alterations of work are consequence of these developments, translating the technical loop into a new eclipse of reason, now one that is instrumental in that it translates thinking and behaviour into subordination under these technical terms. Research, to take one example, is not about free exploration of the subject matter but about following technically set links. Of course, there had been always issues around any free exploration – the limitation of freedom and equally its abuse; however, they had been themselves explored disputed politically[17] rather than technically 'solved' *(see in this context Herrmann, forthcoming (a); Holmquist/Sundin, 2010).*

---

[17] and with this stuck in range of problems of elitist power within academia and as well the political control of contested knowledge.

- Change of settlement structures – as a step to hyper-urbanisation in form of emerging metropolis and mega cities – are another point of huge importance, going far beyond the meaning of infrastructural issues. Of special importance is the need of focussing on new sources of generating wealth and power, to some extent independent of territoriality and nationality, natural resources and others; but important now with view on specifically changed combinations of qualifications, income-expectations, available infrastructure, technologies etc. – different in terms of newness not so much in their pure actuality but in their combination.[18]

- Taken together, these three factors feed into a reconsideration of social movements, emerging now against globalisation – being qualified as anti- and alter globalisation movements, but also very much being an issue of local movements that feed directly into global process though this may not always be immediately obvious. One important point is as well the blurring of borders between institutional political development and developments outside of the institutions. An imperative contradiction has to be highlighted as we find with many of these movements protectionism going hand in hand with border-busting activities, parochialism going hand in hand with globalist orientations.

Taking this together, we can understand the world systems approach here as methodological and also heuristic moment that allows understanding

- socio-economic complexity
- its developing character
- as it finds its origin in contradictions within the economic system and also between the economic and the social development.

A major point in interpreting the different elements – each in their own right and in their interaction – is the question Fernand Braudel puts forward as the fundamental question of civilisation, using his words from the book already referred to in the beginning of this small essay:

The great problem for tomorrow, as for today, is to create a mass civilisation of high quality. To do so is very costly. It is unthinkable without large surpluses devoted to the service of society, and without the leisure that mechanization will no doubt soon be able to offer us. In

---

[18] labour force, infrastructure etc. – all these had always been important. New is the specific combination needed.

the industrialised countries, such a future can be envisaged not too far ahead. The problem is more complex in the world as a whole. For, just as economic growth has civilization more accessible to some social classes than to others, it has similarly differentiated various countries in the world.

(Braudel, op.cit.: 21)

This surely is at one level a 'simple social policy question': the matter of achieving 'just distribution'. However, it is also a question for an ever-changing understanding of civilisation itself as it is concerned with the understanding of justice– as one of the cornerstones of the entire process – that is by far from being clear. It is proposed to understand it in very bold terms as a systemic pattern based on the specific interplay of social inclusion, socio-economic security, social cohesion and social empowerment – the factors or dimensions that are highlighted by the Social Quality Approach as conditional factors. We can then say that we are looking – understanding social quality as project of civilisation[19] – at the three general questions guiding societal development'

- Who is included?
- What is the framework into which inclusions takes place?
- In which way is inclusion designed?

The two challenges ahead, to which in the following only a tentative outline will be provided, are as follows: first, how can we apply this in a meaningful way when it comes to the single factors that are/had been presented as being of vital importance*(see before pp. 41)*. The second challenge is to follow up on the question how we can link this into the analysis of economic changes. Here we have to emphasise that – somewhat parallel to Braudel's distinction of different social times – we have to distinguish also between different 'social economies'[20] – in some ways this debate had been already undertaken in earlier times by looking at the concept of 'socio-economic formations' *(see e.g. Küttler, 1976; IMSF (Hrsg.), 1981).*

---

[19] See one of the definitions of civilisation used by Fernand Braudel, seeing it as "neither a given economy nor a given society, but something which can persist through a series of economies or societies, barely susceptible to gradual change. A civilization can be approached, therefore, only in the long term, taking hold of a constantly unwinding thread ..." (Braudel, op.cit: 35)

[20] Obviously, the term social economy is here not linked to any of the customary understandings.

For the time being – later the two challenges will be taken up again *(see pp. 70 ff.)*– four points are suggested as being of utmost importance.

First, with Doreen Massey we have to look in a new way at space, namely by highlighting its relational character. Looking at

> *the reconceptualisation of spatial identities*

she underscores

> *An understanding of the relational nature of space has been accompanied by arguments about the relational construction of the identity of place. If space is a product of practices, trajectories, interrelations, if we make space through interactions at all levels, from the (so-called) local to the (so-called) global, then those spatial identities such as places, regions, nations, and the local and the global, must be forged in this relational way too, as internally complex, essentially unboundable in any absolute sensem and inevitably historically changing[.].*

> *(Massey, 2004: 5; with reference to: Massey, 1994; Amin, 2002)*

The point here is that we have to turn away from a simplistic notion of linking nation, territory and state. Rather, we have to search for a more complex understanding that reflects (i) different dimensions of relations (and with this structures and processes in their simultaneity) and (ii) fully acknowledges the immediate, non-hierarchical relevance of the different aggregate levels of these relations.

Second, based on resurgence of the dominance of finance capital we have to investigate n economic analysis if and to which extent this part of a temporary wave of escaping the productive circle due to over-accumulation or a fundamental shift, preparing a new circle of – possibly qualitatively different – 'productivity' and/or a new mode of production?

Third, looking closer at the first point, we have to re-interpret space not only in the strict sense but have to go a step further, looking at the redefinition of political space as well. As step into this direction – and admittedly a huge challenge – it is proposed to look for a functional definition of a new 'state' hood as newly emerging dimension. This picks up – and tries to make new sense – of the old debates on the emergence of a configuration that has a specifically far-reaching scope, characterised by the following fundamental and general moments:

- We are dealing with an entity that is fundamentally characterised by its institutionalisation which includes the execution of 'legitimate power', notwithstanding the understanding of legitimacy – it can well be a matter of simple force but remains as such specifically incontestable. Here is not the place to discuss further the character and difference of a state based on the rule of law *(Rechtsstaat)*and a just system – surely two entirely different things.

  Important is that the entity we are looking for is characterised as relative firmly defined enclosure.

- Though this may take again different forms, this entity is characterised by its orientation along the interests of an economically ruling class. At this stage it will be left open if and to which extent an 'economically ruling class' can actually mean as well an 'economic rule on the basis of political power'.

  So far, the two moments presented before are very following positions of both the classical Marxist approach and the Weberian approach. However, the latter interpretation can only be maintained if we disregard the Kantian slant that is underlying Weber's thinking.[21]

- With this, this entity presents itself as economic force in its own right – again this can take different forms. Direct economic activities (i.e. state enterprises) play a role as do services and infrastructure provisions by the state; an important point of reference can be seen in Wagner's law according to which industrial growth is accompanied by an increase in public expenditure*(Wagner, 1893);* this means in turn an exponential growth of an 'independent economic force'. Though this is not necessarily a productive force, it is a force that develops its own and from a certain point inherent dynamic.

- Important is to go beyond an instrumentalist or mechanical[22] deduction of political power and position of such entity. In which way ever the concrete relationship between the political and the economic dimension will be defined, there is always the feature of

---

[21] Surely a stratagem, only suggested allowing for a formally reasonable understanding of legitimacy which in this way is surely problematic then from a Marxist position at least as far the latter goes beyond the Hegelian approach.

[22] Including voluntarist

the relative validity and acknowledgement of a normative system that allows such system to emerge and to be maintained – even if we emphasise that in the last instance it is depending on an economic and material basis respectively. With this we may refer to broad and formalist functionalist and structuralist views as for instance claimed by David Easton as one extreme to the strong political notion of Gramsci's stance of 'wars of position' and 'wars of manoevre' as part of which hegemonies are defined.

In this context we may come back to what had been briefly named before under the catchwords of de-subjectivation and re-subjectivation of power. This means that we can use as further point of reference for the definition we can assume a certain degree of homogeneity. This is far from being a matter of any kind of 'unitarianism' – it is a matter of any kind of fundamental consensus under the supremacy of a hegemonic class. In which way this is achieved can be left open again. It may be worthwhile to remember that legal systems are not anything else than specifically defined normative systems – and thus reflecting just one particular form of force that stands well aside, complementary, in addition or against other normative, enforcement and negotiation systems.

- A further momentum has to be seen in the external relationship, namely the fact that – despite existing or possible competition – the regulative order in question is as such also acknowledged from other systems in exactly this capacity. 'Other systems' refers in particular to systems with a similar 'political remit', in the commonly used jargon: other states. This is not primarily the acknowledgement of the in any given case defined constituency but a matter of recognising the competence of 'equal ruling'.

In any case, centre stage is not entering or reviving the debate about the state in the traditional sense. At the core of the present interest is the investigation of an overarching mechanisms or configuration

- that brings two moments centrally together, namely the search for an instance

  o that acts as configuration of overarching socialisation
  o and overarching regulation

overarching in terms of mechanisms that are not limited by directly manageable space, relations etc. but securing the operativeness of the systemic character beyond the borders of immediate reach.

- and that is also – and not least – momentous as instance that is able to deal with fundamental, i.e. antagonistic and systemic conflicts.

The present author is well aware of the numerous problems of such definition – it leaves the definitions and links to classes, economic formations and the reach and scope of such configuration rather open. This is surely a flaw that needs to be addressed in further work. At this stage, however, it seems to be acceptable to leave it for some time to an iterative process.

Fourth, enlightenment – as new rationality and at the same time development of a 'new value basis' is another factor to be taken into account. The inverted commas refer to the fact that we are obviously facing a long avenue along which this new thinking developed. And they refer to the fact that this new thinking was, of course, part of a complex soci(et)al development of appropriating the social and natural environment, which made new thinking and ideologies possible and required them at the same time. The most important characteristic of this process is its inherent and systematically contradictory character which had been reflected in the contradiction of the formation of the modern state with the two dimensions of de-subjectivation and the ground of the emerging subject as mentioned earlier *(see pp. 46 ff.)*. In general terms, it is the contradiction between on the one hand rationalisation as means allowing change and intervention in the form of conscious activity – meaning a huge step away from what we may call the 'behaving human being' to the 'human actor' – and on the other hand rationalisation as process of segmentation and fragmentation, allowing – if we take a metaphor – the investigation of the sequencing of genes but losing the overall genetic code out of sight.

Looking at these four moments, the overall problem behind the present question is – so the thesis – that we find in a broad historical perspective an ongoing shift – a kind of rocking motion – between the dominance of mechanisms of integration, on the one hand an economically based and economically directed mode; and on the other hand we find an economically based mode, however geared towards political control. The latter has to be understood (i) as political in the strict sense, i.e. as matter of control by direct intervention and regulation or (ii) as being concerned with establishing a lifewordly oriented hegemony. – Of course, it has to be noted that such distinction and separation can only be taken as analytical, offering a heuristic tool rather than being a matter of 'real significance' in the strict sense. However, by using this distinction as instrument it is possible to interpret historical development as contested array with two dimensions. The one dimension is the strive for absolute expansion; the other dimension is the concern for relative expansion. Using the term 'expansion' has to be considered with care as it always has or can have very different content. And in which way ever it is used – as matter of material wealth, cultural appropriation, knowledge amplification ..., all this is possibly a matter of not only quantitative but also of qualitative relevance. Moreover, one may hypothesise that we even find a shift where expansion by one societal group/class reaches limits because of the self-limiting character: striving for a mode of appropriation that is exclusive. Overcoming this inherent limitation requires an new orientation – and with this a qualitative shift of the how and what of appropriation.[23]

In various different realms this has been discussed throughout social science since its development, or one may say that it is even a driving force standing behind social science altogether: division of labour versus holistic and equalising, sustainable forms of socially useful activities; concentration and centralisation versus equalising and distributive developments; rational and planned development versus value-oriented, organically growing movements and the like, externally derived and as eternally valid defined values versus values developed by soci(et)al personalities in their daily life.

Then, what appears to be historical similarity or even a repetition of history, comes into a perspective of an entirely new meaning, providing a framework for some kind a teleology – however, not as matter of externally and eternally given and defined pattern but as contested realm with permanently changing actual content. And *teleological* should not delude to the assumption that we are dealing with any 'straight process of progress' nor with a conclusive and customary process of 'just inclusion'. This is especially true as it is – in its overall perspective – a process that is concerned with different dimensions as social inclusion, spatial inclusion, time extension, coherence development, functionality and others.

---

[23] Only in a side remark to be mentioned – and hugely problematic in various terms we could consider here the *'International Initiative Beyond GDP' (see http://www.beyond-gdp.eu/)* – one initiative amongst several others, showing at least some awareness in broad circles of the ruling classes that some kind of shift is needed in the question of defining and measuring 'progress'.

To the extent to which this is an acceptable approach we can see from here a close link to the power-appropriation perspective that had been presented above *(see pp. 16, 213)*.

Shortened Circuit

In interesting point, showing one of the problems is a development that we may call shortened circuit. We can exemplify this by looking at a recent example. It starts with

> *[]the Fed Govt ... considering forcing Australian ISPs to retain data on how Australian citizens are using the internet, such as their sent and received email and browsing history.*

> *(LeMay, 2010)*

In today's time one could even say – cynically –that this is not really remarkable. The reason for not being remarkable is simply that indeed the planned practice can justifiably refer to EUropean procedures as laid down in the European Union's Data Retention Directive (European Parliament, 2006). However, without going into detail one should not pause to think further. We have to recognise this very much – though not alone – as one of the many consequences of George W. Busch's War on Terror (by any means much more than an ideological phrase, only casually being used: Chairman of the Joint Chiefs of Staff, 2006) – going hand in hand with many other measures like tightening of airport security and the like. However, the actually notable point is that the same forces that are claiming to fight fundamentalism are also supporting the stated enemy. One example is Fethullah Gülen's Grand Ambition (see Sharon-Krespin, 2009; Schwartz, 2010; Ibrahim, 2009; cf in this context also Amin, 2007)

This looks like an extreme example – an example that is staged on a global level. However, a comparable example can be seen on the level of municipalities and cities. Two comprehensive essays –On the Way Towards the Neo-Feudal City, (Ronneberger, without date [1998]) and Preventive Urban Discipline: Rent-a-cops and Neoliberal Glocalization in Germany (Eick, 2006) respectively – present the situation in rather impressive descriptions, writing about the shift from the 'idea of solidarity' towards the concept of 'competitive federalism'.[24] Ronnenberger states

---

[24] Original: 'Idee der Solidargemeinschaft' and 'Wettbewerbsföderalismus'

> *Going hand in hand with the crisis of Fordism we find also here a differentiation and heterogenisation of the national system of cities into internationally competitive, prospering metropolitan regions on the one hand and stagnating or shrivelling cities on the other hand. As the disparities of social spaces cannot be anymore balanced by centrally lead transfer payments local models of development gain importance.*

> *(Ronneberger, op.cit.: 1)*

One might even say that the idea of city as space of living is – at least in some respect – replaced by the concept of the city as productive force. This justifies the view that

> *central to these hypotheses about the organizaional architecture of the global economyis the proposition that this economy contains both the capabilities for enormous geographic dispersal and mobility and pronounced territorial concentration of resources necessary for the management and servicing of that dispersal.*

> *(Sassen, 2007: 27)*

And of course, there are huge implications then for the idea of citizenship also. On the one hand this means a policy shift towards capitalisation and marketisation of cities and in particular their centres, going hand in hand with a privatisation as matter of the loss of their public character *(see already p. 41)*.

> *Such archipelagos of a controlled experience and adventure suggest the atmosphere and image of a traditional open space in the city which is commonly seen as space of communication, public and spectacle. The traditional public spaces – street, square and park – are in the meantime, at least in the USA, replaced by the large shopping and leisure complexes.*

> *(Ronneberger, op.cit.: 2 f.)*

Decisively, these spaces are now subject of privatisation also in respect of achieving and maintaining 'security'. Although by far not all employed in such commercial centres, the enormous growth of private security forces may give some idea.

Jahr	1970	1974	1978	1980	1990	1997	1998	1999
Unternehmen	325	335	472	542	835	1.600	2.100	2,500
Beschäftigte (11)	47.400	50.300	56.700	61.700	105.000	250.000	260.000	k. A.
Umsatz, Mio.	314	573	709	10141	2.289	3.900	5.1	5.4

Table 9: Employees and turnover of private security services in the FGR 1970- 1999[25]

Fahrzeug-/ Schiffsbewachung	Messe-/ Museumsdienste	Psychiatrische Anstalten	Neu: Bewachung/ Management:
Absperrdienste	Notrufzentralen	Urlaubsdienste	Facility Management
Arbeits-/ Gesundheitsschutz	Separat-Bewachung	Veranstaltungsdienste	Asylbewerberheime/ Abschiebegefängnisse
Werkschutz	Geldbearbeitung	Arbeitssicherheit	Alarmverfolgung
Überwachte Schlüssel-aufbewahrung	Türöffnungs-/ Schlüsselfunddienst	Ausspähung/ Sabotagedetektion	Elektronischer Raumschutz (privat)
Ausbildung	Objektschutz	Baubewachung	Fahndung
Parkraum-bewirtschaftung	Personen-begleitschutz	Pförtner-/ Telefondienst	Gefängnisbau/ -management
Datensicherheit	Altennotruf	Fluggastdienst	Radarkontrolle
Aufzugbewachung/ -notruf	Liegenschafts-bewachung	Technische Meldung	Umweltschutz/ "Ranger"
Diskothekenschutz	Erfolgskontrolle	Begleitdienste	Videoüberwachung

---

[25] *Jahr* – year; *Unternehmen* – enterprises; *Beschaeftigte* – employees; *Umsatz* – turnover

Sicherungsposten bei Gleisbauten	Sicherheitsanalsyse/ -beratung	Geld-/Werttransporte	Sicherheitsdienste im ÖPNV
Kaufhausdetektive	Parkplatzeinweisung	Sicherheitsdiens-transporte	Zweiter Arbeitsmarkt
Kurier/Transport-dienste	Liegenschafts-bewachung	Bundeswehr-bewachung	"City-Streifen"/ Security Points

Table 10: Activity Areas of Private Security Services (selection)

(from: Workfare City, without date; see already early Hitzler/Peters, 1998:; more recently and showing an important aspect of the problematic, namely the low income: Von Gersdorff, 2008)

The Confederation of European Security Services summarises in a more recent report – for the EU 25

> *The private security sector in the 25 EU Member States has experienced significant growth in the last three decades, both in terms of the number of companies and in the numbers of private security personnel. Today, the private security workforce more or less matches the public police workforce in most EU Member States and in some Member States they even outnumber the public police. In relation to the population it can safely be stated that the representation of the private security sector averages a 1/500 ratio.*

> *(Confederation of European Security Services, without date (2004): 13)*

Volker Eick contextualises this, pointing out that

> *literature has broadly observed that the strengthening of market competition, the selling of the public infrastructure, the proliferation of market logic throughout the public sector, and 'free' trade are international trends in urban economies.*

> *(Eick, op.cit.: 68; see in this context also: Eick, 2002:)*

This can be seen in the context of an overall shift in between different modes of social integration. Eick makes us aware of the work by Bob Jessop who presents four different *Strategies to Promote or Adjust to*

Global Neoliberalism,[26]in the following the précis offered by Jessop is reproduced:

Neoliberalism

1. *Liberalization – promote free competition*

2. *Deregulation – reduce role of law and state*

3. *Privatization – sell off public sector*

4. *Market proxies in residual public sector*

5. *Internationalization – free inward and outward flows*

6. *Lower direct taxes – increase consumer choice*

Neostatism

1. *From state control to regulated competition*

2. *Guide national strategy rather than plan top-down*

3. *Auditing performance of private and public sectors*

4. *Public-private partnerships under state guidance*

5. *Neomercantilist protection of core economy*

6. *Expanding role for new collective resources*

Neocorporporatism

1. *Rebalance competition and cooperation*

2. *Decentralized 'regulated self-regulation'*

3. *Widen range of private, public, and other 'stakeholders'*

4. *Expand role of public-private partnerships*

5. *Protect core economic sectors in open economy*

6. *High taxation to finance social investment*

---

[26] rather than three as stated by Eick.

Neocommunitarianism

1. *Deliberalization – limit free competition*

2. *Empowerment – enhance role of third sector*

3. *Socialization – expand the social economy*

4. *Emphasis on social use-value and social conhesion*

5. *Fair trade not free trade; Think Global, Act Local*

6. *Redirect taxes – citizens' wage, carer's allowances*

(Jessop, 2002: 14)

As pointed out by Ronneberger, a decisive moment is that despite the ongoing importance of the productive sector

> *organising consumption is increasingly important for the economic and social structures of society.*
>
> *(Ronneberger, op.cit.: 3)*

We see especially here an increasing denotation of new communitarian strategies which is similarly important as the before mentioned 'securitisation-strategy' – moreover it is going hand in hand with the same. This takes two forms: gentrification and ghettoisation. In connection with the security-discourse we may go even so far seeing some form of inversion: the ghetto is now the elitist encapsulation – Eick speaks of prosperity enclaves, Ronneberger von archipelagos. The majority lives – still – outside of such enclaves and archipelagos respectively. However, there is also an undeniable trend that such enclaves are increasingly 'normality' – and this brings us back to the core issue of the present exposition: the establishment of new forms of socialisation, aiming on answering the challenges as they are arising with the suggested new mode of production *(this fits neatly into the picture of new 'private princedoms of ruling also as exhibition of a specific habitus)*.

Before coming back to the more fundamental question, a short remark on a more mainstream perspective on this topic may do suffice – a perspective that is approaching the topic from a reasonably enlightened point of view of governance and 'critical managerialism'. Seen from there all these developments are about the question posed by Joel F. Handler.

A common theme throughout the decentralisation debates concerns the role of the ordinary citizen. Local control, as well as the market, is justified in terms of enhancing the power of the citizenry – they are closest to the elected official or administrator or they can vote with their feet. ...

Decentralisation, deregulation, and privatization are moves toward local control. This book asks the question: what are the consequences of these moves for citizen empowerment? Will ordinary citizens – clients, patients, teachers, students, parents, tenants, neighbors – have more or fewer opportunities to exercise control over decisions that affect their lives?

(Handler, 1996: 4 f.)

However, a major problem with the way in which the question is posed is the understanding of empowerment. Handler defines it correctly as

a relationship

(ibid: 19)

but then he continues, saying that

[a]n individual can be empowered vis-à-vis another individual. Groups can be empowered politically. Here, we are concerned with the empowerment of subordinate people in public programs or services – with the relationship between clients, patients, workers, students, and parents with agencies, usually but not always public? We ask: How do agencies respond to clients, and why? How do clients respond to agencies?

(ibid: 19)

The flaw with this perspective is that Handler goes not far enough in radicalising empowerment, giving it more of a social perspective.[27] Agreeing that empowerment is a relational issue, it has to be further elaborated that this is not sufficiently characterised by pointing on a bipolar relationship, dealing with the power-(im-)balance between the two poles (between individuals and institutions, between groups and institutions, between distinct groups etc.. Rather, at the core we find a relationship that spans across the entire field of individuals (as personalities), peer- and 'hostile' groups, institutions in vicinity and the

---

[27] Actually, after reading Handler's text I would have made this more radical myself in the disquisition on Empowerment – processing the processed *(247 ff.)* which is a separate chapter of this book.

large societal context – and all this under consideration of the different social time frames.

Still remaining within this framework, we can make a step further – another time with reference to Bob Jessop who makes an extremely important point by highlighting the *inherently* contradictory character of the now dominant liberalism. The contradictions follow from the different perspectives – namely the ideological, the economic and the political perspective – that liberalism epitomises and from which an internal contradiction emerges.

> *Ideologically, liberalism claims that economic, political and social relations are best organised through formally free choices made by formally free actors who seek to advance their own material or ideal interests in an institutional framework that, by accident or design, maximises the scope for formally free choice. Economically, it endorses expansion of the market economy – that is, spreading the commodity form to all factors of production ... and formally free, monetized exchange to as many social practises as possible. Politically it implies that collective decision making should involve a constitutional state with limited substantive powers of economic and social intervention, and a commitment to maximizing the formal freedom of actors in the economy and the substantive freedom of legally recognized subjects in the public sphere.*

> *(Jessop, 2002: 106)*

Seen from here, we are in the current situation confronted with inherent systemic conflicts – the contradictory character of liberalist capitalism itself; but we are also concerned with the inherent search for the forces that point beyond this system – the need of system maintenance over time.

We see also another time *(see already p.56)* that the entire socio-economic and civilisational shift is only to some extent a question of distribution – just as Braudel says:

> *Whether in boom or slump, economic activity almost always produces a surplus. The expenditure, or squandering, of such surpluses has been one of the indispensable conditions for luxury in civilisations and for certain forms of art.*

> *(Braudel; op.cit.: 20)*

And – *nolens volens* – against this background

> *civilisation reflects a redistribution of wealth. (ibid.)*

But the answer – and even the way in which an answer is looked for – is still very much open and contested. Nevertheless, and this may come for many along as provocative, we have to acknowledge that there surely is a 'search for alternatives' as well by those who do only want to maintain the status quo.

Outlook – Challenges Ahead

We are in at least three cases concerned with a re-distributional question; however we have to acknowledge at the same time that the fundamental orientation guiding the question is quite different.

First, the different levels, or to employ the term Braudel uses when classifying different times: the different planes, of the distributional question follow very much the classification into (a) – not least national – short-term economic cycles, (b) the in particular international relations of production and (c) the not least supranational developments of the mode of production.

Only a heuristic proposal is presented in the following – and further work will be needed to come to sound conclusions – the later contributions in this volume may give already some evidence. The basic idea is to link different distributional 'models' into the social quality architecture *(s. e.g. pp. 17 f.)*, highlighting the dimensions that are specifically destined by the different modes – this is presented in the following three tables:

CONSTITUTIONAL FACTORS	CONDITIONAL FACTORS	NORMATIVE FACTORS
Processes	Opportunities & Contingencies	Orientation
Personal (Human) Security **Social Recognition** Social Responsiveness **Personal (Human) Capacity**	**Socio-Economic Security** Social Cohesion **Social Inclusion** Social Empowerment	**Social Justice (Equity)** **Solidarity** Equal Valuation Human Dignity

Table 11: Intra-Systemic Redistribution

CONSTITUTIONAL FACTORS	CONDITIONAL FACTORS	NORMATIVE FACTORS
Processes	Opportunities & Contingencies	Orientation
Personal (Human) Security Social Recognition **Social Responsiveness** Personal (Human) Capacity	Socio-Economic Security **Social Cohesion** Social Inclusion **Social Empowerment**	**Social Justice (Equity)** **Solidarity** Equal Valuation Human Dignity

Table 12: inter-systemic redistribution

CONSTITUTIONAL FACTORS	CONDITIONAL FACTORS	NORMATIVE FACTORS
Processes	Opportunities & Contingencies	Orientation
Personal (Human) Security Social Recognition **Social Responsiveness** Personal (Human) Capacity	**Socio-Economic Security** **Social Cohesion** Social Inclusion Social Empowerment	**Social Justice (Equity)** Solidarity **Equal Valuation** Human Dignity

Table 13: Super-Systemic (Global) Redistribution

Against this background we may see this – with all reservations – as shortened circuit of historical processes, concerned with the problematique of *Gemeinschafts-Gesellschafts*-relationships as they had been repeatedly brought up in social science *(see for instance my own discussion of the topic: Herrmann, 2009).*

References

Agnoli, 2002: Das Negative Potential. Gespräche mit Johannes Agnoli by Christoph Burgmer; Freiburg: ça ira Verlag

Ahearne, Alan/Pisani-Ferry, Jean/Sapir, Andre/Véron, Nicolas, 2006: The EU and the Governance of Globalisation; prepared in the framework of the Finish EU Presidency; http://www.unescochair.uns.ac.rs/sr/docs/ahearne2006Globalisation.pdf

Amin, Ash, 2002: Ethnicity and the Multicultural Cit. Living with Diversity; in: Environment and Planning A; 34: 959-980

Amin, Samir, 2007: Political Islam in the Service of Imperialism; in Monthly Review, December; http://monthlyreview.org/1207amin.htm - 08/07/2010 06:38

Aquinas, St. Thomas (app. 1256-1259): De Diversis. Quaestionibus, quaest. 31

Arrighi, Giovanni, 1994: The Long Twentieth Century: Money, Power, and the Origins of Our Times. London: Verso; Silver, Beverly, 2003: Forces of Labor. Cambridge: Cambridge University Press

Arrighi, Giovanni/Barr, Kenneth/Hisaeda, Shuji, 1999: The Transformation of Business Enterprise; in: Arrighi, Giovanni/Silver, Beverly J., 1999: Chaos and Governance in the Modern World System; Minneapolis/London: University of Minnesota Press: 97-150

Australian Human Rights Commission, 2009: Our Future in Our Hands – Creating a Sustainable National Representative Body for Aboriginal and Torres Strait Islander Peoples. Report of the Steering Committee for the Creation of a New National Representative Body, Sidney: Australian Human Rights Commission

Babones, Salvatore J., 2006: Conducting Global Social Research; in: Chase-Dunn, Christopher/Babones, Salvatore, 2006: Global Social Change: Historical and Comparative Perspectives; Baltimore: The Johns Hopkins University Press: 8-30

Bauer, Rudolph, 2007 (a): Die 'Bertelsmannisierung' der Bürgergesellschaft; in: Krauß, E. Jürgen/Möller, Michael/Münchmeier, Richard (Hrsg.), 2007: Soziale Arbeit zwischen Ökonomisierung und Selbstbestimmung. Kassel: kassel university press: 485-501

Bauer, Rudolph, 2007 (b): Kommerz statt Kommune. Bertelsmann(-Stiftung) und Kommunalpolitik; in: Wernicke, Jens/Bultmann, Torsten (Hrsg.), 2007: Netzwerk der Macht. Der Medial-Politische Komplex aus Gütersloh. Marburg: BdWi-Verlag: 291-316

Berman, Yitzhak, forthcoming: Social Conflict between State and Community: The Revival of Jewish Community in Israel [working title]; in: Kalaycioglu, Sibel/Celik, Kezban/Herrmann, Peter (eds.), forthcoming: Religion and the Loss of Confidence. Social Policy in Today's World [working title]; New York: Nova

Bertelsmann Stiftung, without date (a): CSR Einblick; http://www.bertelsmann-stiftung.de/cps/rde/xchg/SID-7EE86B4E-F32305F0/bst/hs.xsl/87048_99456.htm - 27/06/2010 1:24 a.m.

Bertelsmann Stiftung, without date (b): What is CSR?;
http://www.bertelsmann- stiftung.de/cps/rde/xchg/SID-7EE86B4E- F32305F0/
bst_engl/hs.xsl/87048_99456.htm - 27/06/2010 1:25 a.m.

Bonaglia, Federico/Braga de Macedo, Jorge/Bussolo, Maurizio, 2001: How
Globalisation Improves Governance; OECD-Development Centre;
http://www.oecd.org/dataoecd/41/48/2675871.pdf

Bosniak, Linda, 2000: Citizenship Denationalised; in: Indiana Journal of Global
Legal Studies; 7: 447-548

Boswell, Terry/Chase-Dunn, Christopher, 2000: The Spiral of Capitalism and
Socialism: Toward Global Democracy. Boulder: Lynne Rienner

Braudel, Fernand, 1987: A History of Civilizations; Translated by Richard Mayne:
New York: Penguin Books, 1993

Castells, Manuel, 1996: The Information Age: Economy, Society and Culture, Vol. I:
The Rise of the Network Society; Cambridge, MA/Oxford, UK: Blackwell

Castells, Manuel, 1997: The Information Age: Economy, Society and Culture, Vol.
II: The Power of Identity, Cambridge, MA/Oxford, UK: Blackwell

Castells, Manuel, 1997: The Information Age: Economy, Society and Culture, Vol.
III: The End of the Millennium; Cambridge, MA; Oxford, UK: Blackwell

Chairman of the Joint Chiefs of Staff, 2006: National Military Strategic Plan for the
War on Terrorism; Washington: 1 February 2006;
http://www.defense.gov/qdr/docs/2005-01-25-Strategic-Plan.pdf - 11/06/2010
9:20 a.m.

Chase-Dunn, Christopher, 2000: The Spiral of Capitalism and Socialism: Toward
Global Democracy. Boulder: Lynne Rienner

Chase-Dunn, Christopher, 2005 (a): Social Evolution and the Future of World
Society; in: Journal of World-Systems Research; Special Issue: Globalizations
from 'Below' and 'Above'. The Future of World Society; Herkenrath,
Mark/Koenig, Claudia/Scholtz, Hanno/Volken, Thomas: 171-192; JWSR.UCR.
edu; vol XI. No 2:
http://jwsr.ucr.edu/archive/vol11/number2/pdf/jwsr-v11n2-chasedunn.pdf -
10/06/2010 9:15 a.m.

Chase-Dunn, Christopher, 2005 (b): Upward Sweeps in The Historical Evolution of
World-Systems; http://irows.ucr.edu//papers/irows20/irows20.htm - 10/06/2010
8:58 a.m.

Chroust, Anton-Hermann, 1944: The Philosophy of Law of St. Augustine; in: The
Philosophical Review, 53/2 (March); Published by: Duke University Press on
behalf of Philosophical Review Stable URL:
http://www.jstor.org/stable/2182025; Accessed: 23/06/2010 03:52; 195-202

Commission of the European Communities, 2001: European Governance A White
Paper; Brussels, 25.7.2001 COM(2001) 428 final; http://eur-lex.europa.eu/
LexUriServ/site/en/com/2001/com2001_0428en01.pdf - 10/06/2010 4:57 a.m.

Commission of the European Communities, 2005: Communication from the Commission to the Council, the European Parliament, the European Economic and Social Committee and the Committee of the Regions: The Commission's Contribution to the Period of Reflection and Beyond: Plan-D for Democracy, Dialogue and Debate; Brussels, 13.10.2005 COM(2005) 494 final http://www.cor.europa.eu/migrated_data/communication_planD_en.pdf - 10/06/2010 4:54 a.m.

Confederation of European Security Services (CoESS), without date (2004): Panoramic Overview of the Private Security Industry in the 25 Member States of the European Union. Part 3; linked from http://www.coess.org/studies.htm - 19/06/2010 8:26 a.m.

Descartes, René, 1637: Discours de la Méthode pour Bien Conduire sa Raison, et Chercher la Vérité dans les Sciences; Paris: Éditions de Cluny, 1943

Dolšak, Nives/Ostrom, Elinor, 2003: The Commons in the New Millennium: Challenges and Adaptation; Cambridge, Mass.: MIT Press; Ostrom, Elinor, 1990: Governing the Commons: The Evolution of Institutions for Collective Action; Cambridge/New York: Cambridge University Press

Earles, Wendy, in this volume: The New Business of the Third Sector within a Market Society – As Consumable, Elite Few and Distant Broker

Eick, Volker, 2002: Integrative Strategien der Ausgrenzung: Der exklusive Charme des Kommerziellen Sicherheitsgewerbes; in: Hamburger Institut für Sozialforschung (Hrsg.), 2002: Ausgegrenzte, Entbehrliche, Überflüssige; Hamburg: Hamburger Edition

Eick, Volker, 2006: Preventive Urban Discipline: Rent-a-cops and Neoliberal Glocalization in Germany; in: Social Justice: A Journal of Crime, Conflict, and World Order, 33/3: 66-84; http://media.web.britannica.com/ebsco/pdf/24/24179059.pdf - 12/06/2010 8:54 a.m.

Elias, Norbert, 1939: The Civilizing Process; Vol. I. The History of Manners, Oxford: Blackwell, 1969; Vol. II. State Formation and Civilization, Oxford: Blackwell, 1982; The Civilizing Process. Sociogenetic and Psychogenetic Investigations. Revised edition of 1994. Oxford: Blackwell, 2000

Engels, Frederick, 1884: The Origin of the Family, Private Property and the State; in: Marx Engels. Collected Works. Volume 26: Frederick Engels 1882-89: London: Lawrence&Wishart: 129 ff.

Engels, Frederick, 1888: Protection and Free Trade. Preface to the Pamphlet: Karl Marx, Speech on the Question of Free Trade; in: Marx Engels. Collected Works. Volume 26: Frederick Engels 1882-89: London: Lawrence&Wishart, 1990 524 ff.

European Foundation on Social Quality: www.socialquality.eu

European Network Social Uncertainty, Precarity, Inequality: http://www.supi-project.eu/index.php - 17/06/2010 4:11 a.m.

European Parliament, 2006: Directive 2006/24/EC of the European Parliament and of the Council of 15 March 2006 on the Retention of Data Generated or Processed in Connection with the Provision of Publicly Available Electronic Communications Services or of Public Communications Networks and Amending Directive 2002/58/EC; in: Official Journal of the European Union; L 105/54-63; 13.4.2006

Gerstenberger, Heide, 1990/2006: Die Subjektlose Gewalt. Theorie der Entstehung Buergerlicher Staatsgewalt; Muenster: Westfaelisches Dampfboot

Grinin, Leonid, 2006: Periodization of History. A Theoretic-Mathematical Analysis; in: History and Mathematics. Analyzing and Modelling Global Development; Edited by Leonid Grinin/Victor C. de Munck/Andrey Korotayev; Moscow: KomKniga: 10-38

Grossi, Paolo, 1981: An Alternative to Private Property. Collective Property in the Juridical Consciousness of the Nineteenth Century; Chicago: Chicago University Press

Handler, Joel F., 1996: Down from Bureaucracy: The Ambiguity of Privatization and Empowerment; Princeton: Princeton University Press

Hardin, Garrett, 1968: The Tragedy of the Commons. The Population Problem has no Technical Solution; It Requires a Fundamental Extension in Morality; in: Science, 162: 1243-1248

Hardin, Garrett, 1990: Interview with Garrett Hardin on Human Nature and the Tragedy of the Commons. As Interviewed by Nancy Pearlman. Conversations on Population. Program 802. 1990; Los Angeles: Educational Communications; Interview/clip; http://www.youtube.com/watch?v=g8yOamWq3a0&feature=r elated - - 13/06/2010 2:19 a.m.

Harvey, David, 2006: Spaces of Global Capitalism. Towards a Theory of Uneven Geographical Development; London/New York: Verso

Herrmann, Peter, 1997: Sozialpolitik in der EU; Berlin/Rheinfelden: Schaeuble

Herrmann, Peter, 1998: EC-Integration and the Paradox of Modernity. Revised Version of a Presentation on the Conference European Integration in Mannheim, Germany; in: Herrmann, Peter, 1998: European Integration between Institution Building and Social Process. Contributions to a Theory of Modernisation and NGOs in the Context of the Development of the EU; New York: Nova Science: 33-62

Herrmann, Peter, 2009: Gemeinschaft der Gesellschaft – die Suche nach einem Definitionsrahmen für Prekarität; in: Hepp, Rolf (ed.): The Fragilisation of Socio-structural Components/Die Fragilisierung Soziostruktureller Komponenten; Bremen: Europaeischer Hochschulverlag: 76-107

Herrmann, Peter, forthcoming (a): Global Publishing – Global Recognition: Arrogance and Imperialism versus Openness and Debate; in: Herrmann, Peter, forthcoming (c)

Herrmann, Peter, 2012 (b): God, Rights, Law and a Good Society. Overcoming Religion and Moral as Social Policy Approach in a Godless and Amoral Society; Bremen: Europaeischer Hochschulverlag

Herrmann, Peter, forthcoming (c): Searching for Global Social Policy – Economy, Economics and Governance [working title]

Herrmann, Peter, 2011 (d): The Lifespan Perspective in Comparative Social Policy Research: a Critique of Gøsta Esping-Andersen's Model of Three Welfare States and its Implications for European Comparisons in Social Pedagogy; in Kornbeck, Jacob/Rosendahl-Jansen, Niels, 2011: Social Pedagogy for the Entire Lifespan, I; Bremen: Europaeischer Hochschulverlag: 29-49

Herrmann, Peter, without date: Nearly Straightforward – Some more Fundamental Differences between Organisations of the Sector; http://socialpolicy.ucc.ie/defining_the_third_sector.htm - 11/06/2010 12:41 a.m.

Herrmann, Peter/Dorrity, Claire, 2009: Critique of Pure Individualism; in: Dorrity, Claire/Herrmann, Peter [eds.], 2009: Social Professional Activity – The Search for a Minimum Common Denominator in Difference; New York: Nova Science: 1-27

Heshmati, Almas, 2006: The World Distribution of Income and Income Inequality: A Review of the Economics Literature; in: Journal of World-Systems Research; XII, 1, July; http://jwsr.ucr.edu/: 263-286: 61-107

Hitzler, Ronald/Peters, Helge, 1998: Inszenierung, Innere Sicherheit: Daten und Diskurse; VS Verlag

Holmquist, Carin/Sundin, Elisabeth, 2010: The Suicide of the Social Sciences: Causes and Effects; in: Innovation. The European Journal of Social Science Research, 23: 1, 13 — 23; DOI: 10.1080/13511611003791141 URL: http://dx.doi.org/10.1080/13511611003791141

Horkheimer, Max, 1947: Eclipse of Reason, New York, Continuum

Ibrahim, Raymond, 2009: Islamist Perfidy and Western Naivety. Which Is More Lethal?; in: Middle East Forum; http://www.meforum.org/2496/islamist-perfidy-western-naivety - 11/06/2010 11:08 a.m.)

Jachtenfuchs, Markus, 1995: Theoretical Perspectives on European Governance; Mannheim: Mannheimer Zentrum für Europäische Sozialforschung, AB 3

Jessop, Bob, 2002: Liberalism, Neoliberalism, and Urban Governance: A State-Theoretical Perspective; in: Brenner, Neil/Theodore, Nik (eds.), 2002: Spaces of Neoliberalism: Urban Restructuring in North America and Western Europe; Malden et alt.: Blackwell: 105-125

Jessop, Bob, 2008: State Power: A Strategic-Relational Approach; Cambridge: Polity

Kelly, Duncan, 2004: Carl Schmitt's Political Theory of Representation; in: Journal of the History of Ideas; 65/1 (Jan); University of Pennsylvania Press: 113-134 [Stable URL: http://www.jstor.org/stable/3654285; - 17/06/2010 07:23]: 117 f.

Kentor, Jeffrey, 2005: The Growth of Transnational Corporate Networks 1962-1998; in: Journal of World-Systems Research; XI, 2, December; Special Issue: Globalizations from 'Above' and 'Below' – The Future of World Society http://jwsr.ucr.edu/: 263-286

Koehler, Peter A., 1987: Sozialpolitische und Sozialrechtliche Aktivitäten in den Vereinten Nationen. Baden-Baden: Nomos

Kohl, Uta, 2007: Jurisdiction and the Internet: A Study of Regulatory Competence Over Online Activity; Cambridge: Cambridge University Press; Svantesson, Dan Jerker B., 2007: Private International Law and the Internet; AH Alphen aan den Rijn: Kluwer Law International

Kratzwald, Brigitte, in this volume: Precarity and Responsibility – Techniques of Governing the Neoliberal 'Consumer-Subject'?

Krugman, Paul/Venables, Anthony J., 1995: Globalization and the Inequality of Nations; in: The Quarterly Journal of Economics, Vol. 110, No. 4 (Nov.): 857-880; The MIT Press (Stable URL: http://www.jstor.org/stable/2946642); 04/06/2010 22:08

Küttler, Wolfgang, 1976: Theoretische Grundlagen und Methoden historischer Analyse von Gesellschaftsformationen; in: DZfPh, 1976, Heft 9: 1079 ff.; IMSF (Hrsg.), 1981: Ökonomische Gesellschaftsformationen. Theorie und Geschichte; Frankfurt/M.. 1981

LeMay, Renai, 2010: BREAKING: Govt wants access to your emails, browsing history; in: APC Magazine and APCMag.com; 11 June, 2:32 PM; http://apcmag. com/govt-may-record-users-web-history-email-data.htm - 6/11/10 8:21 AM

Luhmann, Niklas, 1981: Subjektive Rechte: Zum Umbau des Rechtsbewusstseins für die Moderne Gesellschaft; in: Luhmann, Niklas, 1981: Gesellschaftsstruktur und Semantik. Studien zur Wissenssoziologie der modernen Gesellschaft. Vol.2; Frankfurt/M.: Suhrkamp

Manin, Bernard, 1997: The Principles of Representative Government; Cambridge

Marx, Karl, 1845: The German Ideology; in: Karl Marx. Frederick Engels. Collected Works. Volume 5: Marx and Engels: 1845-1847; London: Lawrence&Wishart, 1976

Marx, Karl, 1976: Capital. Vol. I: Results of the Immediate Process of Production: Harmondsworth: Penguin Books, in association with New Left Review: 948-1084

Marx, Karl/Engels Frederick, 1848: Manifesto of the Communist Party in: Karl Marx. Frederick Engels. Collected Works. Volume 6: Marx and Engels: 1845-1848; London: Lawrence&Wishart, 1976

Mascuch, Michael, 1996: Origins of the Individualist Self: Autobiography and Self-Identity in England; Stanford: Stanford University Press: 20; with reference to Taylor, Charles, 1985: The Concept of a Person; in: Human Agency and Language. Philosophical Papers, 1; Cambridge: Cambridge University Press: 97-114

Massey, Doreen, 1994: 'A Global Sense of Place', in Space, Place and Gender. Cambridge: Polity Press, pp. 146-156

Massey, Doreen, 2004: Geographies of Responsibility; in: Geografiska Annaler. Series B, Human Geography, 86/1. Special Issue: The Political Challenge of Relational Space: 5-18; Blackwell Publishing on behalf of the Swedish Society for Anthropology and Geography; Stable URL: http://www.jstor.org/stable/3554456; Accessed: 20/06/2010 06:36

Meier, Christel, 2004: Autorenschaft I 12. Jahrhundert. Persoenliche Identitaet und Rollenkonstrukt; in: von Moos, Peter (ed.), 2004: Unverwechselbarkeit. Persoenliche Identitaet und Indentifikation in der Vormodernen Gesellschaft; Cologne: Boehlau: 207-266

Nollert, Michael, 2005: Transnational Corporate Ties: A Synopsis of Theories and Empirical Findings; in: Journal of World-Systems Research; XI, 2, December; Special Issue: Globalizations from 'Above' and 'Below' – The Future of World Society http://jwsr.ucr.edu/: 289-314

North, Douglass C., 1994: Economic Performance Through Time; in: The American Economic Review; American Economic Association (Ed.); 84/3 [June]: 359-368; Stable URL: http://www.jstor.org/stable/2118057 - 12/06/2010 22:55

Nowotny, Helga/Testa, Giuseppe, 2009: Die gläsernen Gene. Die Erfindung des Individuums im Molekularen Zeitalter; Frankfurt/M.: Suhrkamp

Ostrom, Elinor, 2000: Private and Common Property Rights; in: Bouckaert, Boudewijn/De Geest, Gerrit (eds.), Encyclopedia of Law and Economics, Volume I. The History and Methodology of Law and Economics, Cheltenham, Edward Elgar: 332-379; http://encyclo.findlaw.com/tablebib.html - 13/06/2010 7:33 a.m.; here: http://encyclo.findlaw.com/2000book.pdf - 13/06/2010 7:31 a.m.

Peters, Anna (projectmanagment), without date: Case Study. German Telecom and 'Schools Online' (SaN)'. Connecting German Schools to the Internet; Guetersloh: Bertelsmann Foundation http://www.bertelsmann- stiftung.de/cps/rde/xbcr/SID-CC1ABE86- 14D912AC/ bst/csrTeaching_CaseStudy_DeutscheTelekom.pdf; 27/06/2010 1:05 a.m.

Phillips, David/Berman, Yitzhak, 2001: Social Quality and Community Citizenship; in: European Journal of Social Work; 4/1; Oxford: Oxford University Press: 17-28

Polanyi, Karl, 1957: The Great Transformation: The Political and Economic Origins of Our Time; Boston: Beacon Press

Poulantzas, Nicos/Camiller, Patrick, 1978: State Power, Socialism; London: Verso, 2000

Powell, Fred, 2001: The Politic of Social Work; London et altera: Sage

Powell, Fred, 2005: Speeches. Autumn Conferrings 2005; http://www.ucc.ie/en/Conferrings/Speeches/ConferringCeremonies2005/Title,23 931,en.html - 23/06/2010 4:04 a.m.

Pye, Christopher, 1984: The Sovereign, the Theater, and the Kingdome of Darknesse: Hobbes and the Spectacle of Power; in: Representations, 8/91

Reynolds, Henry, 1996: Aboriginal Sovereignty. Reflections on Race, State and Nation; Leonards: Allen&Unwin

Reynolds, Henry, 1996/2000: Indigenous Social Welfare: From a Low Priority to Recognition and Reconciliation; in: 97-109 – with a wide range of documents annexed; in: McMahon, Anthony/Thompson, Jane/Williams, Christopher (eds.), 1996/2000: Understanding the Australian Welfare State. Key Documents and Themes; Croydon: Macmilllan Education Australia/Tertiary Press

Ronneberger, Klaus, without date (1998): Auf dem Wege zur Neofeudalen Stadt. Text of Presentation 'Rote-Ruhr-Uni-Series'; http://www.rote-ruhr-uni.com/cms/IMG/pdf/Ronneberger_Stadt.pdf - 11/06/2010 1:20 p.m.

Sandberg, Audun, 1998: Against the Wind: On Reintroducing Commons Law in Northern Norway; in: Mountain Research and Development, Vol. 18, No. 1 (Feb., 1998), pp. 95-106 Published by: International Mountain Society; Stable URL: http://www.jstor.org/stable/3673871 - 12/06/2010 21:49

Sassen, Saskia, 2005: The Re-Positioning of Citizenship and Alienage: Emergent Subjects and Spaces for Politics; in: Globalizations; Routledge: 2/1: 79-94 – DOI: 10.1080/14747730500085114

Sassen, Saskia, 2007: A Sociology of Globalization; London: Norton

Sassen, Saskia, 2008: Territory, Authority, Rights: From Medieval to Global Assemblages; Princeton: Princeton University Press

Schmitt, Carl, 1928: Constitutional Theory; Translated and edited by Jeffrey Seitzer. Foreword by Ellen Kennedy; Durheim/London: Duke University Press, 2008

Schmitt, Carl, 1928: Verfassungslehre

Schmitt, Carl, 1930: 'Staatsethik und Pluralistischer Staat,' Kant-Studien, 35, 28-42

Schouten, Peter, 2008: Theory Talk #13: Immanuel Wallerstein on World-Systems, the Imminent End of Capitalism and Unifying Social Science. Theory Talks; http://www.theory-talks.org/2008/08/theory-talk-13.html [04.08-2008); assessed 05/06/2010 9:42 a.m.

Schwartz, Stephen, 2010: Islamist Gülen Movement Runs U.S. Charter Schools; in: Middle East Forum, March 29; http://www.meforum.org/2628/islamist-gulen-movement-charter-schools - 11/06/2010 11:04 a.m.

Sharon-Krespin, Rachel, 2009: Fethullah Gülen's Grand Ambition. Turkey's Islamist Danger in: Middle East Quarterly Winter 2009; http://www.meforum.org/2045/fethullah-gulens-grand-ambition - 11/06/2010 10:59 a.m.

Steinberg, Philip E., 2009: Sovereignty, Territory, and the Mapping of Mobility: A View from the Outside; in: Annals of the Association of American Geographers; 99, 3, 467-495

Sunstein, Cass R., 2007: Republic. Comm. 2.0; Princeton: Princeton University Press

79

Teubner, Gunther, 1996: 'Global Bukowina': Legal Pluralism in the World Society; (ed.), 1996: Global Law Without a State; Aldershot; Brookfield, USA: Dartmouth, 1997: 3-28

Tilly, Charles, 1975: Reflections on the History of European State-Making; in: Tilly, Charles (ed.), 1975: The Formation of National States in Western Europe; Princeton/London: Princeton University Press: 3-83

Tilly, Charles, 1990: Coercion, Capital and European States, A.D. 990-1992; Cambridge: Blackwell

Trevillon, Steven, 1999: On Being a Social Worker. Globalization and the New Subjectivities; in: Chamberlayne, Prue et altera (eds.), 1999: Welfare and Culture in Europe. Towards a New Paradigm in Social Policy; London/Philadelphia: Jessica Kingsley: 63- 80

Trichet, Jean-Claude, 2008: The Governance of Globalisation. Speech by Mr Jean-Claude Trichet, President of the European Central Bank, at the Bocconi University and Corriere della Sera International Forum 2008, Milan, 12 May 2008: http://www.bis.org/review/r080513a.pdf

United Nations, (without date): Governance and Institution-Building; http://www.un.org/en/development/progareas/governance.shtml - 10/06/2010 5:02 a.m.

University of Vienna. School of Governance (without date): References; http://vigo.univie.ac.at/index.php?id=15537 - 10/06/2010 4:49 a.m.

Verschraegen, Gert, 2002: Human Rights and Modern Society: A Sociological Analysis from the Perspective of Systems Theory; in: Journal of Law and Society; 29/2; Oxford: Blackwell: 258-281

von Gersdorff, Andrea, 2008: Zwischen Boom und Billiglohn; Welt online; http://www.welt.de/welt_print/article2520631/Zwischen-Boom-und-Billiglohn.html - 19/06/2010 7:41 a.m.

Wagner, Adolph 1893: Grundlegung der Politischen Ökonomie. Teil I: Grundlagen der Volkswirtschaft, (3. Auflage), Leipzig: C.F. Winter'sche Verlagshandlung

Wallerstein, Immanuel, 2004: World-Systems Analysis. Introduction; Durham: Duke University Press

Weber, Max, 1919: Politics as Vocation; in Max Weber: Essays in Sociology. Edited, with an Introduction by H.H. Gerth and C. Wright Mills; London: Routledge: 1991: 77-128

Weber, Max, 1921: Economy and Society; Berkeley, Los Angeles, London: University of California Press, 1956/1978

Workfare City – without date: Statistics; Freie Universität Berlin, John F. Kennedy Institute for North American Studies, Department of Politics; http://workfare-city.lai.fu-berlin.de/index.php?id=94&no_cache=1&sword_list[]=security - 19/06/2010 7:56 a.m.

Organisations and social groups – Tertiarisation and sectorisation in modern societies

Peter Herrmann

Abstract

The following reflection discusses the thesis that the overall role and function of third sector organisations is not mainly caused by mechanisms of organisational mechanisms of adapting to structural mechanisms of institution building. Rather such processes are largely explainable by reviewing the societal development. Decisive on this level is the shift in the economy from the primary, to the secondary and finally the third sector (i.e. agricultural, productive, service sector respectively). Reaching largely the service provision as (phenomenologically) dominant economic activity has major consequences on organisations of the third sector, its overall role in society and the reflection of social stratification in organisational structures.

However, the paper argues as well that the traditional mechanisms and especially the class structure is by no means obsolete in the debate and replaced by the contingent, project-based lines of processes of building societies.

NGOs and classes – foundation of meaning between sector overlaps

For many times classes and even social strata as well as organisations had been said dead. However, time and again we find the contrasting argument stressing the meaning and even increasing role of both, classes and organisations. And indeed, there is to some extent a link between these views since, of course, classes move from being entities as such to be entities by themselves – a strong argument of the historical and dialectical materialism pointed on the fact that only on the second level, classes become a real power in society. Moreover, the philosophical and political argument was that only as organised power classes have a real and active historical role to play.

Nevertheless, even if there has always been a strong link between classes, the process of organising and organisations there had been a debate in social sciences as well that organisations lead a kind of life in themselves. The argument was that the structures of organisations as such have a role on their own to play and that those who join organisations and even those who actively run them are only functional for specific structural laws of social and societal processes.

As far as the second strand is concerned we can point on the works of Daniel Bell *(cf. Bell 1973)* and – from a completely different angle – Robert Michels *(Michels, 1915)*. While the first argued that organisational structures are, in fact, far more important for the functioning and shape of societies than social processes as people and groups relating one to another and social stratification the second made out a kind of iron law.

This law is part of an extensive elaboration and debates. It says – as a supposed general law of social and societal development – that we find mechanisms in organisations at work which result in a process of alienation of 'the organisation' from 'its' original goals. However, as this formulation and the use of inverted commas already suggests it is not correct to take this as law of social and societal development. Rather in this understanding it is a law of human behaviour and/or/respectively institutional mechanisms. – There is, of course, only a gradual dividing line between this and 'the social'.

Though, even if it is difficult to separate these different dimensions of the social, attention has to be paid to factors of original social and particularly societal mechanisms. This comes especially in recent developments to the fore where

- NGOs are individually and as sector being specifically recognised by state institutions, are being integrated in the statutory system of service delivery and, moreover, being acknowledged in their role as participants in the process of policy preparation and decision making. Even if mechanisms of this kind had been in place already for a long time two distinctive aspects point at the specific meaning of the current situation, i.e.

  a) already the quantitative and qualitative leap marks it as a new, distinct phase;

  b) in particular on the international and even supranational level we find – to some extent this is the background of the before mentioned leap – the setting up, new development and shifts in governance structures. Looking at developments in the framework of EUropean integration, the wider Europe of the Council of Europe, the system of the United Nations and to some extent – emerging and yet only visible as a root setting pattern – even in the frame work of the G8 civil society is well recognised

82

as important part which has to be taken into account and which has to be, furthermore, strengthened as integral element of the overall structuration. In respect of this developing and changing understanding of governance patterns we can even speak of the process of building up a social contract as consciously lead process. Being aware of the danger of being misunderstood we can see the 'building of a society from the scratch'.[28]

- Actually to some extent immediately in connection with the before mentioned point – we find the emphasis of a supposed diminishing meaning of classes, and moreover 'social boundaries and, vice versa, social distinction as constituting feature of society building. We nearly can say that in such views on so-called post-modern society building classes and strata are replaced by individual contingency and an open space of individualised options – not least sociologists as Beck, Giddens and Foucault and the like *(one for many: Giddens/Lash/Beck, 1994)* stressed this factor. In the same string of arguments we find – even earlier – the transformation of 'classical' theories of social stratification *(see Bourdieu, 1979; Vester et altera, 1993)*. Moreover, 'societal models' with supposedly new founding or defining features had been developed alongside these arguments – the German sociologist Schulz claimed the development of a society oriented on events *(cf. Schulz, 1992)* and the ex-German chancellor Kohl spoke even of a leisure society.

This translates into cohesiveness as a mechanism of contingent flows of 'project based social contracts' as result for the building and processing organisations on the one hand and individualism as foundation of social cohesion on the other side. However, it translates paradoxically at the same time into a high degree of formalisation. In this view the suggested end of history *(Fukujama, 1992)* is complemented by an end of ideologically founded organisations. Organisations emerge as skeleton for any short-term action. As such, these entities lead a life of their own. Seen in this light we should not draw a contradiction between early, and in fact very 'modernistic' views of society as society of organisations *(cf.*

---

[28] Of course, this is a process, determined by previous structures and strongly lead by different and in many times even contradicting ideas, interests, power relationships and factual forces of influence and implementation. Thus the characterisation of a conscious process has to be qualified.

Bell, 1973) and – supposed to be postmodern[29] – interpretations of society as open spaces of individual contingent action.

The sector concept – different angles. Theses of departure

Taking this as point of departure we can ask if there is a specific societal leap which causes the shift of organisational development from being part of a 'civil entity' as somewhat distinct societal element (for instance expressed in the term of a third sector, the idea of the triangular constitution of society by the state, the market and the 'private sector' and the like.[30] The idea is that, rather than finding a development as described beforehand, we find a changed appearance and meaning of constituting stratificational and organisational patterns in the context of the shift in the overall meaning of economic sectors, i.e. the primary (= 'agricultural'), secondary ('industrial') and tertiary (= 'service') sector. Basically, the relationship between these two concepts of sectors – the 'economic' and the 'social sectorisation' – has never been analysed. My thesis is that the development away from the primary sector to the tertiary sector is accompanied by the socialisation of even more spheres of action. Many tasks of life had been – taking a historic perspective – up to recently largely undertaken in the private sphere even if they had been, in fact, social tasks. Of course, we could already see in other regimes the shift of formerly private tasks which had been differentiated e.g. from the ancient Greek oikos and established as public, i.e. social sphere. Nevertheless, 'the private' had always been seen as the 'core of society building' – we all know about the central role which had been ascribed to the family. In the long-term development this strict split between the private and the public had been levelled down. Many of before 'privately' undertaken activities had been socialised and became 'public' tasks as well. Actually we could say that in tendency a fourth sector – the

---

[29] To formulate it in this way is based on the difficulty – or impossibility – to find a common denominator in defining post-modernity and in fact it is the yet unanswered question if we ever reached a modern society.

[30] Only in passing we mention the nevertheless important point of restrictions in all these approaches *(cf. Part I – conceptual equipment in: Salamon/Anheier, 1997)* and, in fact, the fact that all this debate goes back already far into philosophical debates – already in ancient Greek history, for example, we find ideas elaborated by *Aristotle on the* philía, the associational mode, which is set apart from the societal level and the – even at that time – contradicting relationship between different 'sectors' – at the time lead by the idea of 'the private' and 'the public' as discussed by Plato.

family which existed aside the state, the market and the voluntary sector – ceased to exist in objective terms as core of social reproduction.

Now this means as well that the split between social strata, namely between classes overlapped with a second split, i.e. the one of differentiated tasks. For this it is important to underline that these tasks – as childcare, education, care for the elderly and disabled, fulfilment of reproductive provisions (up to cooking, cleaning etc.) – had been shifted into the public sphere.[31] Meaning at the first glance a de-differentiation (bringing the different tasks under one – now – public roof) the second view gives a quite distinct picture. The public sphere differentiated and further differentiates itself. We can see this in the distribution of different roles between genders.

It is not necessary and possible to elaborate this here – even if it has to be said that there remains the necessity to develop this idea more in detail. What remains, anyway, is the fact that there is a strong superimposission between two lines of soci(et)al differentiation. We can refer to the one as socio-economic differentiation between social groups/strata and to the other one as societal-economic differentiation referring to 'sectors' in one or the other sense. Of course, there is a wide overlap between them, of course there is as well in both a similarly important division between publicity and privacy. Nevertheless, this increasing visibility and depth of the fundamental structuration of society by two basic mechanisms causes a process of blurring the formerly dominant position of classes. For organisations, in particular nongovernmental organisations this means that they are moving from a pattern of intermediary organisations to one of double-intermediary organisations.

On the phenomenological level we are dealing, in consequence, with quantitatively and qualitatively far more organisations, thus perceiving a picture of a society which organises itself along 'project-based' patterns. Actually, rather than indicating a diminishing meaning of organisations in society we find an increasing meaning. Furthermore, the stability is given by a permanent renewal and turn-over of this organisational pattern: The same interests are again and again starting point for the development of new organisations or the personal renewal of existing

---

[31] Of course, we have to be aware that this is a process which is by no means completed. Especially social factors play a major role and what is for some time already socialised for one group is still a mainly private task for other strata. – For many times this includes a different 'social interpretation of the meaning' of the same factual conditions.

ones. Finally, we find an ongoing class bias of these organisations. Even if based on a single-issue background, based on the ongoing socialisation of previously 'private' tasks,[32] the class bias is the permanent noise in the background. And to speak of a noise in the background does by no means point in the direction of a 'secondary meaning'. Actually, the development of NGOs and the way they fit themselves into the prevailing societal and institutional system shows too well the strong structural effects – as founding principle and in regard of their shape and impact alike. It is, however, to some extent hidden by variety respectively multiple number.[33]

The tertiarisation of the third sector

Nevertheless, there is a strong point which has a far reaching effect on NGOs and means in fact a far-reaching pressure on them, alienating them – in tendency –from their class basis and moreover from their original goals in general. As stated the social economy shifted from the primary to the secondary and later to the tertiary sector of production. In fact today's 'products' are to a large extent 'services'. As well known the split of societies in classes is based on the notion of production. The development of social structuration in terms of classes and stratification in this context has to be further developed – any kind of refusal of the ongoing meaning of classes and even social stratification has to be viewed with suspicion. And the same is true for making out 'new classes' as constitutional elements, namely seeing the working class replaced by any kind of a 'service class' – we have to leave it with this remark for further investigation and debate.

What is interesting here is the following paradox. With the socialisation of tasks of reproduction, their positioning in the public sphere (i.e. the acknowledgement as 'public tasks' and their transfer into 'services') they gain the status of products rather than remaining solely aspects of reproduction. Thus, they gain a new character, namely the immediate link – and split – between productive activities on the one hand side and reproductive activities on the other hand is to some extent abandoned.[34] For the foundation and development of NGOs this means that their

---

[32] According to the previous remark it is surely better to speak of hidden social tasks, privatised tasks or family tasks.

[33] Rather than complexity – the latter would justify to speak of a diminishing meaning.

[34] Abandoned, indeed; it does in no way cease to exist!

existence is not anymore oriented on the secondary sector and its reproduction. Instead, they gain – as 'new productive sector' – a status on their own, being at least on the phenomenological level independent, relational to the productive sector, existing in a separate sphere.

I

We can see this very well in the Scandinavian countries. Roles and tasks which had been traditionally[35] linked to the families and 'private' activities had been socialised and in part transferred to the public sector, in part carried out by QUANGOs and NGOs. What is important here is that socialisation meant and means at the same time a 'publication'. This process entailed a change in the role of women as well as in the societal positioning of the respective tasks. Rather than being appendage of the productive system they came to the fore and had been 'productive' on their own. Overall, the delivery of services had been included in the valuation via the market system. This does not say anything about the actual way of the provider structure – even as statutory or voluntary services they had been established as part of the market system, simply because they had been part of the 'public'.[36] In the strict sense and under the given circumstances the status had not been one of reproduction anymore. Rather they had been concerned with the 'production of welfare'. One and perhaps the most important indicator is the employment of women in the field of statutory services, which parallels with the increasing meaning of NGOs providing comparable 'welfare goods' *(Luhndström/Wijkström, 1997; Ministry of Social Affairs and Health [ed.], 1998)*

II

Part of this – and this is well observable at least in all member states of the EU – is the orientation of NGOs along statutory and governmental administrations. Insofar as the respective organisations are concerned with service provision as part of the wider market system (as it had been described before) they are embedded in the determination of prices by the market system – even if it is paid for by the state, i.e. by public finances. Again, we find a shift away from the second, the productive

---

[35] We have to be aware that even the Scandinavian welfare state and the strong position of women is only a recent development.

[36] In theoretical terms it would be necessary and possible to connect this theses to the Marxist elaboration of the fetishism of goods, and in addition, the approach of alienation under the condition of the market society, based on the valuation of goods.

sector into the direction of the tertiary, the service sector. And since this shift as such takes place from 'reproduction' of the productive system to the 'production of services' we find a partial detachment from the original productive system. Not the immediate needs of the productive system are decisive. Instead the services, their financing and the regulation and 'shape' follow distinct patterns, corresponding 'own' laws and requirements. The long-lasting debater on bureaucratisation can be taken as indicator. Furthermore, there is some good rationale to consider the influence of science, paving the way for innovation.

III

However, it is this not simply a mechanism which follows 'institutional laws' – or to use a common terminology: follows laws of organisational development. Rather it is the detachment from the productive basis. We see this in several cases by the fact that meanwhile many 'voluntary initiatives' and NGOs are initiated by statutory and government bodies, namely and importantly by the European Commission. From the early 1990[s] already the *European Anti-Poverty Network (EAPN)* had been an organisation which had been initiated by the European Commission; it had been put on its own feet, enjoying an extensive freedom of leading strings, nevertheless being still largely financed by the European Commission. Other individual networks followed – even if there always had been differences in scope and mode. Meanwhile this development arrived on a new stage, namely the Commission's attempt to steer the whole sector by using a few key organisations, founded and funded as nongovernmental networks, responsible for themselves respectively for their own member organisations. The *Platform of social NGOs* is an outstanding example. And just currently this trend is being highlighted by

(a) plans to set up a new network – the name will be *AGE, the European Older People's Platform (cf. AGE, 2000; Marking, 2000; see as well European Commission, 1999)* and

(b) plans to centralise and concentrate funding mechanisms, especially by changing the shape of programmes, developing them to large scale programmes rather than financing a large number of small projects *(cf. Wellinghoff-Salavert, 1999: 14 ff.)*.

We find initiatives as well on various national levels – for the time being a long-lasting debate in Ireland seems to have come to an end as the Government just published the White Paper (while writing the delivery didn't took place; the Green Paper was aimed on questions *on the community and voluntary sector and its relationship with the state*

[Department of Social Welfare, 1997]). In the United Kingdom the development just begins – since about one year – a broader debate takes place, in a way initiated by the statement of Tony Blair who 'made it clear that he expects the voluntary or third sector to play an important role in the implementation of the Third Way, the policy framework that serves as the guiding principle for his administration' *(Blair, 1999; quoted from Anheier, 2000: 1)* In Germany we find strengthened efforts around questions of these issues, not least the foundation of the Commission on the future of the civil-society activities/civil engagement *(Enquete Kommission zur Zukunft des buergerschaftlichen Engagements)* and the launch of the foundation for the promotion of civil society in Berlin. But what easily is being overlooked is that this process of 'decentralisation' actually is at the very same time a process of concentration. This strategy of a promotion of 'the sector as such' means that in fact the respective individual organisations are forced into a position which is much more centralised then it had been ever before. In fact, this way of centralised acknowledgement has in consequence the paradox effect that promotion of the sector forces the individual organisations into a unmanageable competition between each other. – They are dealing on a business basis rather than on a basis of ideology *(cf. Deutscher Verein für oeffentliche und private Fuersorge: 1994)*.

This, in fact, is a much more social and societal background for changes in patterns of NGOs. In a longer time span they developed from nongovernmental organisations and as such nagging organisations to necessary for government organisations and are now on the way to establish themselves as nailed by government organisations, nailed on the grounds of competition law, nailed against the requirements of a sectorised economy.

Conclusion

At the end of the day it should never been forgotten, however, that the described trend is still mainly being derived from the original productive sector. Instead of repeating the classical and neo-Marxist analysis of the state *(cf. Poulantzas, 1974)* it is sufficient just to remind of the fact that the state is based on and functioning in the interest of the productive system and the capitalist mode of producing added value. And NGO's are – in one way or another – based on nothing else than the 'added value' of one of the main classes: profit or deductions from wages.

The for many times suggested 'contingentisation' of the previously strongly organised and 'structurated' society and the diminishing meaning of classes and social strata – due to the very same processes of opening previously closed patterns of structuration vanishes in the light of the arguments from above behind a shift between sectors and the overlap of distinct, yet related sectors respectively soci(et)al spheres, namely

- classes and social strata

- the economic sectors, i.e. the agricultural, productive and service providing sector

- the social sectors, i.e. the private, the market, the statutory/state and the nongovernmental sector

- the private and the public.

Paradoxically, the decommodification means vice versa a commodification of 'the social'. This again hides and opens the class bias of the overall process. Goods of general interests and in particular social services are taken out of the immediate conflictual field of classes. However, as provisions that are subsumed under the currently dominant valuation of the market the services – and thus the respective providers – are immediate elements of the classical antagonisms of the capitalist system.

Insofar the reference to the original productive system, i.e. the creation of value, is different for the provision of services in the market system, the statutory system, and the nongovernmental, voluntary system respectively. And furthermore the accessing users are different as well. It is most likely that we find two determinants here. The one is regulating access via price mechanisms, distributing quantitatively better services to the better offs (market provided services). For another group of better offs (educational bourgeoisie, to some degree 'philanthropists', few petty-bourgeois) the civil sector provides services, combining specific qualitative aspects with a sound material basis. This leaves a wide field of last resort services, to be provided by the state, which looks after those who cannot avail of [better] services. Obviously this reflects the class division of the given society – which is still a capitalist society and will be the very same – in the member states and in the EUropean Union as a distinct entity – if the current plans of EUropean integration continues in the same direction as they develop up to now.

An open question now is if and – if so – how we can meaningfully combine further research with the approach on class analysis as proposed by Pierre Bourdieu.

This might make it possible to find an answer on the question if and in which sense the more ideological aspects of the original meaning of nongovernmental organisations respectively the sector, such as vanguards, improver/advocates and value guardians *(cf. Kramer, 1981: 9)* can be maintained. The other way round on this basis it could be studied what exactly the social structural basis is for the shift of NGOs to reduce their performance on that of service provision. One assumption in this regard would be that with a widening class bias and attempts of juggling with different dimensions of societal sectors, respectively soci(et)al spheres, namely

- classes and social strata
- the economic sectors, i.e. the agricultural, productive and service providing sector
- the social sectors, i.e. the private, the market, the statutory/state and the nongovernmental sector
- the private and the public.

is a predetermination for such a shift. The actors (not the organisation) get stuck in a trap between different boundaries and that justifies speaking of nailed by government. In fact, rather than widening governance structures they are being limited by the reduction of nongovernmental action in a limited frame embedded into the tertiary, service providing sector.

In this light, the suggestion that welfare has a productive function is only true insofar as it fulfils a reproductive role. As soon as this is forgotten and it is said that it has a productive role on its own *(cf. Pintasilgo, 1996 and European Commission, 2000, where again it is stated that 'The Lisbon Summit highlighted the essential linkage between Europe's economic strength and its social model. It also addressed the European Union's weaknesses. Importantly, it agreed on the parameters of Europe's economic and social agenda for the next decade. To take this forward, a guiding principle of the new Social Policy Agenda will be to strengthen the role of social policy as a productive factor.' [ibid.: 5])* the point of departure for nongovernmental work is further undermined.

This points on a final question arising from the theoretical approach of sector diversion as determinant of NGOs – actually it is the reactualisation of an old and ongoing question, now put into a new light. This question is How is the development of NGOs being determined by the character of the individual organisation as self-help oriented or oriented on the help for others? And furthermore we have to ask if organising is a special service[37] motivated on the assumption of aiming on rights and/or redistributive processes (for one-self and his/her equals, meaning self-help and/or help for others) or is it motivated by an orientation along general values of good will and any kind of producing a common good? Many old questions are raised, however set against a new background.

Sure, there is no immediate answer from here to the meaning of NGOs respectively civil society organisations in regard of the good society. What gets clear, at least, is that NGOs have lost much of their potential for change as soon as they follow the call of the service providing society and as soon as they accept or even ask for their reputation as service providers. Then, they are already part of the good society – and miss the opportunity to make the society better.

---

[37] Here the term service includes the services in the classical understanding as well as 'advocacy services', the 'service' of value guardianship and the like.

References

AGE, 2000: Europe's Older People's Platform set to become reality; in The Bulletin. July 2000. vol XV: Issue 3: 1 f. Eurolink Age [Ed.]; Brussels/London

Anheier, Helmut, 2000: Introduction; in: Helmut K. Anheier: Third Way – Third Sector. Proceedings of a policy symposium organised by the LSE Centre for Civil Society, June 7th, 1999: London: Centre for Civil Society at the LSE 2000

Bell, Daniel, 1973: The coming of the post-industrial society: A venture in social forecasting: New York: Basic Books

Blair, Tony, 1999: Keynote Speech delivered at the Annual Conference of the National Council of Voluntary Organisations; January 21st

Bourdieu, Pierre, 1979: La distinction. Critique sociale du judgement; Paris: Les editions de minuit; Paris

Department of Social Welfare, 1997: Green Paper on the community and voluntary sector and its relationship with the state; Dublin: Stationary Office

Deutscher Verein für oeffentliche und private Fuersorge, 1994: 'Wenn man die Ideologie weglaesst, machen wir alle das gleiche'; Eine Untersuchung zum Praxisvertstaendnis leitender Fachkraefte unter Bedingungen des Wandels der freien Wohlfahrtspflege; Frankfurt/Main: Eigenverlag des Deutsche Vereins für oefentliche und Private Fuersorge

European Commission, 1999: Towards a society for all Ages; promoting prosperity and intergenerational solidarity (COM(1999)221 final Brussels; http://europa.eu.int/comm/dgs/employment_social/key_en.htm – 10/9/2000

European Commission, 2000: Communication on the Social Policy Agenda; COM [2000] 379 fin.; Brussels, 28.6.

Fukujama, Francis, 1992: The end of history and the last man; London: Penguin Books

Giddens, Anthony/Lash, Scott/Beck, Ulrich: Reflexive modernisation: politics, traditions and aesthetics in the modern social order; Oxford: Polity Press, 1994

Kramer, Ralph M., 1981: Voluntary Agencies in the Welfare State; Berkley et altera

Luhndström, Tommy/Wijkström, Filip, 1997: The nonprofit sector in Sweden; Manchester/New York: Manchester University Press, 1997 [Johns Hopkins Nonprofit Sector Series, 11]

Marking, Christine, 2000: Creating a European Older People's Platform; 28/8/2000

Michels, Robert, 1915: Political parties. A sociological study of the oligarchical tendencies of modern democracy; New York: The Free Press/London: Collier-Macmillan; 1962

Ministry of Social Affairs and Health [ed.], 1998: Socius Finland 4/98; Helsinki

Pintasilgo, Maria de Lourdes, 1996: For a Europe of Civic and Social Rights. Report by the Comité des Sages chaired by Maria de Lourdes Pintasilgo. Brussels, October 1995 - February 1996. Final Report; (Brussels)

Poulantzas, Nicos, 1974: Les classes socials dans le capitalism aujourd'hui; Paris: Editions due Seuil

Salamon, Lester/Anheier, Helmut K., 1997: Defining the nonprofit sector. A cross-national analysis; Manchester/New York: Manchester University Press

Schulz, Gerhard, 1992: Die Erlebnisgesellschaft. Kultursoziologie der Gegenwart; Frankfurt/M.: Campus, 19977

Vester, Michael et altera, 1993: Soziale Milieus im gesellschaftlichen Strukturwandel. Zwischen Integration und Ausgrenzung: Koeln: Bund

Wellinghoff-Salavert, Joline, 1999: Unité Liberté de Mouvement des travailleurs et lutte contre le racisme de la Direction Générale Emploi et Affaires sociales; in: Lignes budgétaires de la Commission européenne en faveur de la lutte contre le racisme. ENAR – European Network Against Racism; Brussels: December; 14 ff.

The New Business of the Third Sector within a Market Society – As Consumable, Elite Few and Distant Broker

Wendy Earles

Abstract

Organising that is separate from state and market organising is variously called voluntary, nonprofit, not-for-profit, informal or grassroots and increasingly third sector at the more formalised scale of organising. Such third sector organising is deemed to involve people working together to serve or advocate for self or others beyond profit and coercion and is considered to support civil society.

Considerable analytical and political energy has been expended in recent decades in many jurisdictions to create the third sector as a policy entity alongside the state and market. Some claim that the third sector is being created, from the seemingly disparate array of principles and logics outside of those of the state and the market, in order for it to be governed. Such political creation of the third sector has occurred within the dominance of an economic paradigm and can been a considerable distraction from the triumph of such market-based principles and logics. No less energy has been expended on creating the third sector as a social space with a value-base and logics outside of those of the state and the market, but perhaps with less demonstrable results.

Classic representations of third sector positioning depict the quadratic of 'the market', 'the state', 'the third sector' and a fourth sector (such as community, households, families, or informal sectors) and their relations, variously arranging them as separate but relating, overlapping or parts of a whole. An alternate depiction of a market paradigm positioning for the third sector is posited and explored through a number of tentative accounts of manifestations or indicators of such new 'positioning' of actors and change directions. Three major flows of change are considered: from the informal sector via the third sector to market; from the third sector via the state to market; and from the state via the informal sector to the market.

Such demonstration begins to highlight some of the new 'business' of the third sector as a consumable for social entrepreneurs; as elites of business-like large providers; and as distant brokers for the state. These flows from, to and through the third sector both demonstrate the dominance of economic thinking and the precarious nature of the third sector as created 'partner' within the national political realm. Such an approach lifts our gaze to focus on transformative flows in change rather than the instrumentalism of particular changes, from a focus on changes in the third sector to third sector space as a conduit for wider change.

Introduction

The nature and positioning of the third sector has consumed considerable analytical energy over the past few decades. Such analysis seeks to articulate core shared essences or elements 'within' and key differences 'without' the third sector, or what Alcock (2010) notes as endogenous or exogenous approaches to third sector definition.

The way we attempt to define the third sector should reflect our thinking about the dominant paradigm from within which the sector operates and draws its practice options not just the sector itself. 'The political', 'the social', and 'the economic', as systems, behaviours, consciousness and culture, condition the meaning and practice of sectors of (re)production such as the third sector, the state, the market and the informal sector (represented as households, families and community organising). Such sectors are products of political, geographical and cultural contexts and historical dynamics (Alcock 2010).

To date, third sector thinking has been dominated by 'the political' through consideration of state-third sector relations and the top-down creation of the 'third sector' within policy and political structures and discourses (see for example Alcock (2010) for an account of such 'third sector' emergence and contestation within the United Kingdom from earlier discourses of 'voluntary action'). Alcock (2010) claims that the third sector 'is being created and imposed by the politicians and policy-makers who wish to govern it (2010: 17). Over a decade earlier, Leat (1998) went as far as describing this as third sector myth-building.

An alternative thinking is more embedded within 'the social' and is taken up by Van Til (2009) in his call for a wider endogenous definition within the third sector silo. Such exploration he argues is needed given the changes within each of four silos: governments' withdrawal from welfare, the end of 'good' work in business, breakdown of informal support systems, and increased partnership and sub-contracting in the third sector. Van Til (2009) considers the need to view the third sector as 'social space' as about more robust and more varied relationships in line with the work of Gecan (2002). He claims that we are yet to articulate a social conception of the third sector 'outside and distinct from biological, economic and political concerns' (2009: 1076).

The dominance of the 'economic' is acknowledged by Van Til (2009) in the 'triumph of corporation-defined values' (2009: 1072) and he asks what is lost by becoming too business-like and in the glorification of a 'less number of large elite-directed nonprofit businesses' (2009: 1074). Further analysis by Anheier (2009) acknowledges 'the economic' alongside the political and social perspectives. He outlines three broad perspectives in the complex policy dialogue around the third sector that determine trends in how the sector is perceived. In line with the growing economic importance of non-profit organisations as providers of services in developed countries, Anheier (2009) notes the impact of new public management and the mixed economy of care but he also notes the perspective of social capital and civil society directed at community and citizenship development. He adds a third perspective that of social accountability, with the third sector as instruments of improved governance. His analysis variously denotes the third sector as corporate providers, 'associative' integrators and 'instruments' of reform. He argues however that these positions for the third sector and third sector practice exist in the absence of an analysis of the role of business and the articulation of the 'kind of future society leaders have in mind' (Anheier 2009: 1090).

The analysis undertaken here starts from the space claimed for the third sector and classic representations of third sector positioning, articulates an alternate positioning based on the dominance of the market paradigm, gives tentative accounts that are indicative of such an alternate positioning, and suggests that all roads might indeed lead to the market. Such an approach responds to Evers (2010: 114) who highlighted that it is 'important to encourage debate about the meaning and role of markets for the third sector and civil society at large' as a response to the invasion of society by market logics and the real and presumed threats to or possibilities for civility.

The space claimed for the third sector

The third sector is considered to be comprised of voluntary and non-profit organisational forms (Evers/Laville 2004) and in some cases it is mistakenly equated with the much broader phenomenon of civil society. Third sector organisations can contribute to, or detract from, a stronger civil society through their practices (Eikenberry/Kluvers 2004: 136).

The logics of organising associated with the third sector are those of network, consensus and negotiation (Earles/Moon 2000). The principles considered to be driving this organising are association, mutuality, altruism, and democracy (Paton 2009). Eikenberry and Kluvers 2004 sum up these principles and logics as involving un-coerced association, relational networks and moral formation.

The fundamental goals, ideals or rationales for the third sector have been related to social provision and advocacy.

> *Nonprofit organisations are the expression of the determination of people to work together to provide a service or advance a cause for themselves and others. They do so free of government direction or desire for profit. (Lyons 1997: 24)*

Within and alongside this service and advocacy the third sector can contribute to the wider civil society agenda of participatory democracy through value creation and guardianship, socialisation and capacity-building, and representation and contestation outside of the state (Edwards/Foley 2001). Salamon (1997 in Eikenberry/Kluvers 2004) describes three ways that nonprofits achieve this, through service and advocacy, as value guardians and as builders of social capital. The third sector practice that arises can be diverse in nature and directed at multiple ends. Jordan et al (2001: 242) for instance identify that nonprofits develop grassroots movements, lobby governments, provide services, develop capacity and infrastructure, seek to influence the policy cycle and work to shape public opinion. The means for practice are varied but common inputs are volunteering and philanthropy.

Classic third sector positioning

Classic representations of third sector positioning depict the quadratic of 'the market', 'the state', 'the third sector' and sometimes a fourth sector (such as community, households, families, or informal sectors) and their relations, variously arranging them as separate but relating, overlapping or parts of a whole. In many depictions the third and fourth sectors are conflated and replaced with conceptions such as civil society (an action focus) or the informal sector (a level of organising focus). Much of the debate regarding a third and fourth sector relates to nation-based analyses of the third sector which can be narrowly focused on provider organisations (such as in the United States, see Van Til 2009) or more broader focused including grassroots organising, social movements and co-operative activity. Conflation leaves a triadic representation. The term 'informal' sector is used for the fourth sector in these depictions merely in order to have a simple way to emphasise such conflation or separation while still incorporating a less formal organising aspect. This also avoids the distraction of these debates plus to some extent those in relation to the use of the terms non-profit, voluntary and so on.

Figure 1 depicts the notion of separate but relating sectors. The state and market are ever-present in such representations and the third sector and other informal organising make up the third party in the triad.

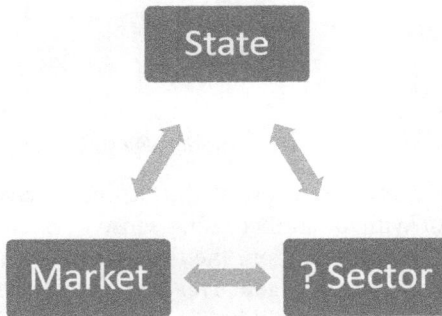

Figure 1: Separate but relating

Figure 2 recognises the blurring of boundaries between sectors. Again the state and market are always present. A third sphere can variously be the third sector or in some cases the fourth sphere such as the informal sector is included. The overlaps represent the 'hybridity' that such segmentation facilitates. Billis's (1989) now classic representation of overlapping worlds takes such an approach with the fourth world in this case titled the personal world. Forms of third sector hybridisation abound with new non-profit 'businesses' directed at other non-profits (for human resource and financial administration services), businesses with corporate social responsibility arms and quasi-non-government organisations as some examples.

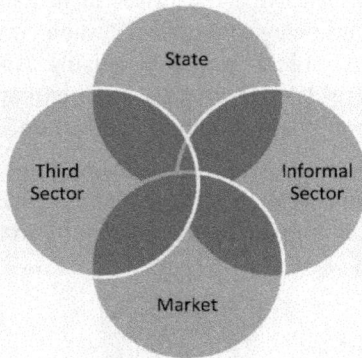

Figure 2: Overlapping

Figure 3 begins the re-integration of the distinct sectors into a whole. This can be with or without an increasing sense of overlap. In Evers and Laville's (2004: 17) representation, the third sector occupies the middle space and overlap is acknowledged. This begins to place the third sector as existing within the tension field between the others. This can be as the glue in one sense, or in another, the place/space where the actions of the others are manifested (or as non-profit practitioners are oft to say their mistakes are acted out). Such blurring of boundaries arises from complex interdependencies (Ostrander/Langton 1987).

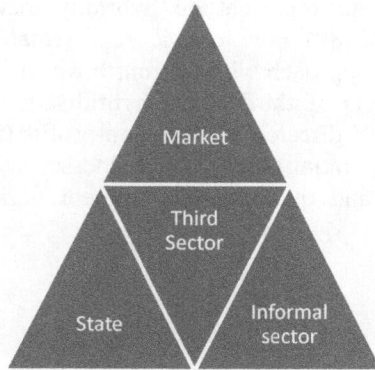

Figure 3: Parts of a whole

These representations treat the phenomena of state, market, third sector and informal sector variously as organisational forms, ways of organising, sets of principles and arenas for action (Table 14).

Differences	State	Market	Third	Informal
Forms of organising	Public agencies (Evers/Laville 2004) Government bureaucracy (Billis 1989)	Private Firms (Evers/Laville 2004) Business bureaucracy (Billis 1989)	Voluntary and non-profit organisations (Evers/Laville 2004) Civil society = Voluntary associations (Decker 2009)	Families and households (Evers/Laville 2004) Informal sector (Van Til 2009) Personal world (Billis 1989)
Logics of organising *(Dynamics)* *(Performative)*	Hierarchy and bureaucracy (Earles/Moon 2000)	Contract and competition (Earles/Moon 2000)	Network, consensus and negotiation (Earles/Moon 2000)	
Principles driving organising *(Values)*	Formality, regulation, coercion, and redistribution (Paton 2009)	Entrepreneurship, investment, accumulation, and competition (Paton 2009)	Association, mutuality, altruism, democracy (Paton 2009) Un-coerced association, relational networks and moral formation (Eikenberry/Kluvers 2004)	Kinship and consanguinity (Van Til 2009)

Practice through organising (Agency) (Arenas) (Action)			Develop grassroots movements, lobby governments, provide services, develop capacity and infrastructure, seek to influence the policy cycle and work to shape public opinion (Jordan et al 2001) Service and advocacy, value guardians and builders of social capital (Salamon 1997 in Eikenberry/Kluvers 2004) Provision and advocacy (Lyons 1998)	Socialisation and capacity-building (Eikenberry/ Kluvers 2004)

Table 14: Unpacking sectors

Unpacking difference has been a complex and multifarious occupation for many for some time. Table 14 seeks only to be illustrative of some accounts of difference and to draw attention to the parameters (rows) that are used to describe difference between sectors, and the assumed coherence within sectors (columns).

Debates still rage about the primacy of parameters (rows) in definition and abstraction with a drift from action to organising form dominating in more recent attempts to create the third sector as a legitimate actor in policy discourses (Alcock 2010). Similarly, Alcock (2010) identifies the fractured unity within third sector coherence (column) and the pragmatic approach of strategic unity. The utility and futility of such disintegration of the forms and means of (re)production are questionable with the increasing focus on hybridisation not just empirically but conceptually.

All of these representations however share a non-existent or non-disclosed paradigmatic context for this relating, overlapping, holism or tension field. Definitional debates, whether endogenous or exogenous in nature, in effect distract from such paradigmatic analysis. The debate can stay fixated on changing roles and boundaries or move to consider the hegemony of particular paradigms. Currently it is preoccupied by a focus on relations and the ideological doctrine of partnership (Casey/ Dalton/Melville/Onyx 2010).

Exploring an alternate depiction

An alternate depiction of the quadratic starts from a premise of the dominance of the market paradigm as means of (re)production and positions the state, the third sector and the informal sector within this market paradigm dominance (Figure 4). This repositioning takes as its focal point 'the Market' as all-encompassing paradigm and simultaneously centralises the market as actor in the space in-between the state, the third sector and the informal sector. Hence this depiction positions the market as not only actor but as dominate paradigm to a schema of actors and relations and seeks to create a new prism for refracting third sector practice and analysis of third sector change.

The original insight that drove this approach arose from considerations of Giddens' (1998) account of the Third Way which involved a democratisation of the family (related to but not the same as the informal sector), a strengthening of civil society (again related to but not the same as the third sector) and a reinvigorating of the public sector (some of the apparatus of the state). An acknowledgement of the market or any call for its reform could not be found in this change agenda, it was just not there and yet everywhere as omnipotent backdrop to the prescriptions for change called for in the other sectors. This insight alerted me to the need for paradigmatic positioning of any depiction of the third sector and its relations to other sectors (as taken up in Figure 5). This has more recently resonated with debates on the primacy of 'the economic' (Herrmann 2010, this volume).

The 'generalisation of the market' or the 'naturalisation of the economic' are becoming recurrent themes in analysis of change in political and social systems. The increased embeddedness of the economic within the state is manifest in neoliberal policies that facilitate the operation of the market, the process of globalisation and the expansion of information technologies. The market paradigm is deemed to act as a force for the emergence of new mechanisms of governance as reflections of new modes of accumulation.

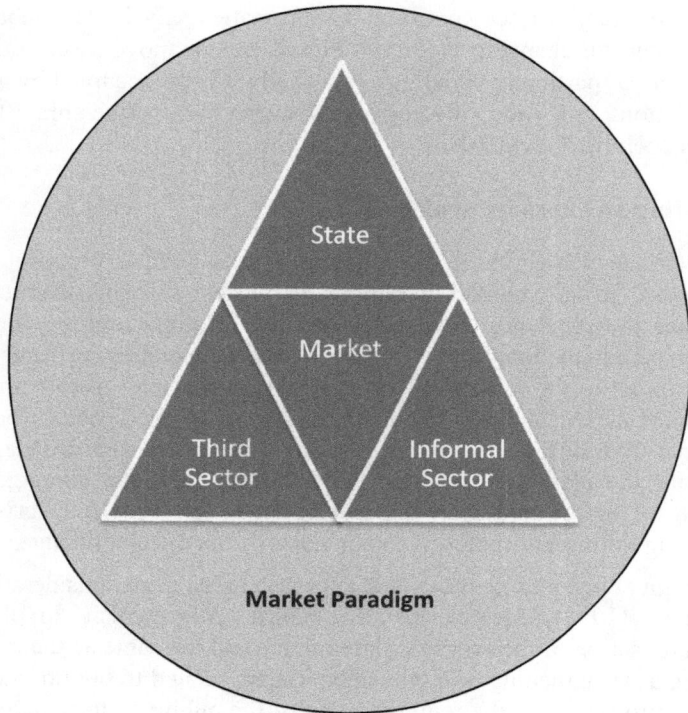

Figure 4: Market paradigmatic positioning

The infiltration of the economic in the social has progressed to claims that the economic now equals the social as a fundamental understanding of human beings as social actors (Herrmann 2010 this volume). The market paradigm is manifest in a shift in people's productive and reproductive relationships from society to self through individualisation of both actors and acts. It is also manifest through the market means of exchange which is deemed to have shifted from production as social relations to social relations (broad) as contracts (narrow) and hence the contractualisation of social relationships (Herrmann 2010 this volume).

Third sector analyst Evers (2010) relates these themes directly to the invasion of the third sector by market logics. He describes the existence of pure instrumental orientations which put economic value on volunteering and participation (such as social capital formulations), the dominance of managerial advice that focuses on core business and key performance measurement whereby reducing what is permissible to what is measurable, the increased notions of autonomy and choice though market-based freedoms, and the rise of the entrepreneurial spirit.

Much of the analysis has focussed on encroachments on third sector space which compel third sector organisations to become more 'market-like in their actions, structures, and philosophies' (Eikenberry/Kluver 2004: 133). Such encroachments come from both the market and the state.

> *Major public policy changes over the past few decades have played a significant role in nonprofit organizations' growing reliance on the generation of commercial revenue, as well as increased emphasis on performance-based contract competition. More recently, donors of the 'new pilanthropy' have exerted increased pressure on nonprofit organizations to be more market-like, while many nonprofit executives have embraced the social entrepreneurship model as a model of management. (Eikenberry/Kluver 2004: 133)*

This market-embeddedness (rather than the more limited view of marketisation), arising from a shift from production to distribution and exchange, creates increasingly long chains of interdependencies and increased limited understanding of how to control variables and the possibility of intervention and ultimately a loss of control over actual social processes (Herrmann 2010 this volume). In essence, the economic system destabilises the other systems' stakeholders, management and identity through powerful ideology-driven isomorphism.

Re-positioned actors and accounts of change

The alternate depiction of a market paradigm positioning for the third sector is explored through a number of tentative accounts of manifestations or indicators of such new 'positioning' of actors and change directions. The author is most familiar with the arena of third sector practice in social policy and the welfare and post-welfare states in so-called developed nations with liberal welfare states and these reflections are therefore captured by that familiarity and by geographic positioning in Australia. So third sector here is not expanded to the broader concept of civil society nor is it inclusive of the co-operative sector. The analysis of other arenas and localities can be, and no doubt are being, explored by others. Integration of such analyses is crucial.

This approach draws its humility and strength from the work of Castells (1989), who charges us to start with the analysis of the process of restructuring in its different (but specific) manifestations, in order to understand current change.

> *Each restructuring process leads to a new manifestation of the system, with specific institutional rules which induce historically specific sets of contradictions and conflicts developing into new crises that potentially trigger new restructuring processes. (Castells, 1989: 21)*

He further posited that only after such analysis can we look at specifying some of the likely consequences of restructuring for particular sectors.

> *Once they had taken place, they shaped societies, technologies and space in a particular direction which is now full of historical meaning. (Castells, 1989: 4)*

Three flows of change are considered: from the informal sector via the third sector to market; from the third sector via the state to market; and from the state via the informal sector to the market (Figure 5). These accounts cumulatively, with no claim for definitively, seek to provide insights into the influence of the dominant market paradigm.

These flows from, to and through the third sector both demonstrate the dominance of economic thinking and the precarious nature of the third sector as created within the political realm. Such demonstration begins to highlight some of the new 'business' of the third sector within a market society as a consumable for social entrepreneurs; as elites of business-like large non-profit providers; and as non-profit brokers for the state.

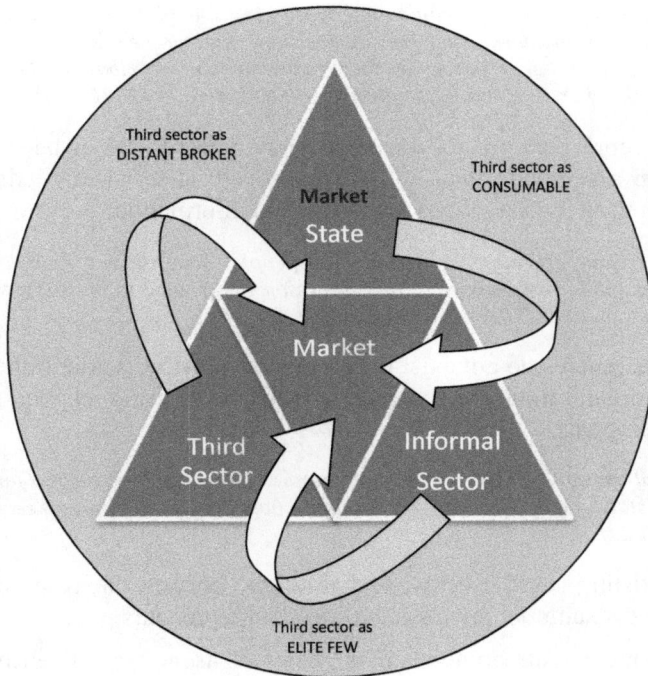

Figure 5: Flows of Change

From the state via the informal sector to the market: Third Sector as consumable

In the divestment by the state of responsibility for welfare (or non-take up of new social needs by the state in a post-welfare state era) there has been a shift to the promotion of social entrepreneurism to generate local action on issues. Inherent in entrepreneurial thinking according to some writers is the adoption of business-like practices (Zahra/Neubaum 2009) even if actioned through non-profit organisations.

Entrepreneurism as a concept empathises the individual; innovation and the ownership and pursuit of new ideas or opportunities; acceptance of risk in pursuing a particular outcome; and a brokerage role linking resources and needs.

> *Entrepreneurs were people interested in changing patterns of production by harnessing new technology, finding new sources of materials or better processes for production and distribution. They were the change agents of the economy. (Stewart-Weeks 2001: 27)*

Social entrepreneurs are presumed to work towards social benefit and there is an assumption they will spontaneously arise when needed and come with the necessary skills, expertise and information.

> *Social entrepreneurs are inside-out people – they find people in communities with ideas and find the resources needed to bring those ideas to market ... (Stewart-Weeks 2001: 25)*

Such entrepreneurs do not exist in an organisation-free world, rather they consume organisational infrastructure when organising is required to further their goals.

> *Social entrepreneurs are subversive people. They have little respect for the status quo or for institutional boundaries. (Stewart-Weeks 2001: 24)*

Hence existing third sector organisations become a resource for temporary consumption by transient social entrepreneurs.

In this context, entrepreneurism is manifest as active citizenship by individuals potentially in and through the third sector and civil society (Decker 2009). Some third sector organisations make space for such support to entrepreneurs offering funds management support or services (in some cases as fee-for service), co-location opportunities (as paid space in some cases) and branding (for legitimacy or identity with some form of later reciprocity) when required. Some third sector organisations make it their specialisation to foster such entrepreneurism by acting as brokers for linking entrepreneurs and organisations.

This trend to entrepreneurism can be aligned with a parallel trend of 'new volunteering' theorising which positions volunteers as self-interested individuals who contract episodically with others (including third sector organisations) to achieve their goals rather than volunteering as a collective activity enacted through existing organisations and shared goals (Hustinx/Handy/Cnaan, 2010 forthcoming; Ottoman/Snyder 2002). Volunteering involves *voluntary agency* (MacDonald and Warburton, 2003) which is the act of engaging deliberatively and is an expression of social capital in action. This voluntary agency does not occur in a vacuum it is a dynamic between the volunteer and an agency and can bring about change in both. Volunteers are themselves institutional agents and can transform the role and operations of an organisation. MacDonald and Warburton (2003) describe volunteers as *carriers of change* inferring that they can both maintain institutional order or create institutional order within the context of their organizational setting. This dynamic is influenced by normative perspectives held by both the volunteer (beliefs about self and ideological positioning) and the agency (as expressed in modes and discourses of operating).

Eikenberry and Kluver (2004) further unravel such social entrepreneurial thinking in the third sector through highlighting that individual non-profit executives take on the mantel of social entrepreneurs who play the market with mission in mind. Much of this entrepreneurism relates to filling the service demand or funding short-fall gaps through diversified funding sources often in partnership with business or in direct business ventures. In this scenario third sector organising can ultimately become an expendable commodity that is readily substitutable with for-profit logics and even legal status. Anheier (2009: 1089) alerts us to this increased commercialisation and possible trend of changing status to for-profits, particularly through mechanisms such as the mooted 'public benefit corporation' classification in the United Kingdom.

In this world of entrepreneurism the third sector becomes a consumable, a temporary vehicle for transient social entrepreneurs and 'new' volunteers who consume organisational infrastructure, or market/mission driven executives who transcend organisational form. The social ends pursued are individually-driven (even if altruistic) and the outcomes of previous collectivism (third sector organisations as artefacts) become disposable consumables in rapidly changing networks of entrepreneurial production.

From the informal sector via the third sector to market: Third Sector as elite few

In the individualising of funding and provision for welfare, individuals and families become consumers of service provision either directly from the for-profit or non-profit sectors, or by organising together to shape the type of service provision they are seeking. Waves of new individualised funding packages have seen the birth of small provider groups (Earles 1999). The struggle that small third sector organisations have with increasingly complex and onerous accountability regimes is well noted (as is the call for collective action by small organisations, see for example Suhood 2001). Many exist as separate organisations because of a fierce sense of identity that rests on a belief that they and they alone can meet the needs of their client or user group (Earles 2009). There are pressures towards third sector formalisation of this informal organising and wider professionalization of third sector organising. Small groups have been encouraged to incorporate and take on the trappings of associational life. Groups that were less formalised and engaged in advocacy often in the absence of other means for provision become incorporated in order to manage funding of social services for the state. In doing so they became bound by contracts and less able to advocate (Rawsthorne 2005). Many of these smaller 'organisations' (in reality little more than one funding agreement with the state rather that an independent organisation) are ripe for take-over by larger provider third sector organisations themselves on the road to greater professionalization. Hence each level becomes the engine of growth for the next and individualisation of provision becomes an indirect route to market-embeddedness.

This formalisation and professionalization of the third sector under the rubric of New Public Management (NPM) was well documented as the managerialisation of the third sector and welfare provision (Rees/Rodley 1995) and is not taken up here. In this setting third sector service and advocacy were products for consumers, and workers carried the burden of narrowly-defined scientific management practices (Ife 1997). These management practices gave rise to a generic management class or profession outside of, and independent from, individual third sector organisational mission. This class was committed to managerial solutions (such as more performance monitoring or organisational development) and the reduction of value to that which is measurable. The non-profit CEO with market skills, values and commensurate salary is now a reality.

This professionalization of management in an increasingly competitive environment generates a trend towards a management class that prioritises (economic) efficiency over/as mission, blends non-profit and for-profit (commercial revenue-raising) activity, actively seeks our relationship with for-profit entities, and vigorously pursues venture philanthropy. These trends often manifest as a quest for individual organisational growth through pursuing market share to ensure viability. The increased interest in the phenomenon of non-profit merger is readily apparent (see for example Austin, 2003; Kohm/La Piana 2003). The creation of exclusive non-profit provider cartels as new collectivism is another area of growing interest. In some areas, the generation of a sense of monopoly in provision in order to relate to the state's monopsomy in purchasing is the aim.

In this world of a managerialised third sector under a market paradigm, we experience the realisation of Van Til's (2010) claim of the formation of a 'less number of large elite-directed non-profit businesses' (2009: 1074). It is not the move to market-like actions, structures and philosophies (Eikenberry/Kluver 2004) that should draw so much attention but its ultimately impact on the number and nature of third sector organisations.

From the third sector via the state to market: Third sector as distant broker

In the divestment of provision from the state to the third sector or new provision via the third sector, third sector organisations became third party providers and fears were raised in relation to the statisation of the third sector and the creation of a shadow state (see Wolch's 1999 call for a decentering of the third sector as a response to statisation). The statisation of the third sector was seen as an indirect route to marketisation through the creation of a shadow corporatised state of quasi-nongovernment organisations and business-like third party non-profit providers (sometimes with the reality of 100% state-funded non-profit organisations). This is indeed old news from the 1980s and 90s in many developed countries and more recent or even current news in developing countries as market-based models of funder-purchaser-provider institutional arrangements, contracts as instruments of engagement and competitive tendering as systems for trade are rolled out almost context-free (Deakin/Walsh 1996). Such synchronisation on a global scale of third sector change was likely unprecedented. These changes were often lamented with reference to preferred alternative models of partnership. The current pre-occupation of much of the third sector at sector level within national context is partnership through compact development.

A further trend has developed where the third sector now acts as contractor or broker for the state taking on the role of purchaser to the state as funder (Baulderstone/Earles 2009). This can be in relation to individualised funding packages that have arisen from quasi-voucher service models or it can be in relation to area-based funding programs which seem to be experiencing renewed interest as a basis for fostering innovation and integrated service delivery. Contracting roles and associated lead organisation status as capacity-builders for the non-profit sector potentially create a two-tiered system of third sector organisations. This furthers the distance of provision from the state, creates more links in the chain of interdependencies between citizens and the state, and leaves new invisibilities in decision-making in some areas.

In this world of market-based brokerage, two futures can be envisioned, within one a few elite business-like non-profit organisations contracting with each other (a self-reinforcing system), within the other a few elite business-like organisations fostering the creation of new small non-profit organisations from community groups (potentially feeding the growth cycle discussed above). Within such models there is a requirement by the state that brokered provision is to become sustainable (beyond state funding) which generates a search for volunteers and philanthropic support often casting such endeavours into the realm of entrepreneurism and venture philanthropy (as discussed above) in effect closing the circle.

All roads lead to the market because it is everywhere

Salamon and Anheier (1996) identified eight crucial issues for third sector sustainability and adaptation: visibility, legitimacy, a paradigm of conflict, the move from agent to partner, the philanthropic base, accountability, professionalization and globalisation. While many of these are played out in the political sphere and are represented by the top down creation of the third sector as policy actor in partnership with the state (Alcock 2010), they are enacted under the dominant market paradigm.

As claimed earlier, the flows of change from, to and through the third sector described here both demonstrate the dominance of economic thinking and the precarious nature of the third sector as created 'partner' within the national political realm. We can argue about the existence of the third sector as a coherent entity, its distinctiveness from the state and the market, its problematic conflation with the broader arena of civil society organising, and the reality of partnership with the state, yet all of these can be distractions. However temporal the creation of the third sector as policy actor, from where it came and at whose bidding, it is a conduit for wider change.

A focus on flows of change within the market paradigm highlights not the marketisation of a somewhat static sector but sector space as fluid means of sustaining a market society. Such flows can create a market-world of organisation-free entrepreneurs, elite business-like organisations and self-generating distanced brokerage organisations that all act through or claim third sector space.

Others have taken-up the concerns about the role of the third sector in wider civil society and the impact of marketisation. They raise legitimate concerns, for instance,

> ... the commercialization of nonprofits influences their ability to contribute to this social capital ... if it weakens its social networks; makes its network of relationships less stable; reduces the size, diversity, or involvement of its governing board; or reduces its level of voluntary participation. (Backman/Rathberg Smith 2000: 355)

> Market-driven, social entrepreneurial nonprofit organizations may only enter into or continue activities that are profitable. (Eikenberry/Kluver 2004)

Such claims are only further realised by the flows of change described here.

This story simply offers one possible scenario of third sector space shaped, by somewhat contradictory flows of change within a dominant market paradigm, to a space comprised of a consumable resource, an elite few and distant brokers. The disintegration and substitutability inherent in the individualism of entrepreneurism, the agglomeration and inherent placelessness imbued by the dominance of business-like elite, and the instrumentalism and invisibility enacted in distant brokerage all threaten mission implosion for the third sector as created partner to the state.

Such a flow of change approach lifts our gaze to focus on transformative flows in cumulative change rather than the instrumentalism of particular changes, from a focus on changes in the third sector to a focus on third sector space as a conduit for wider change. It reminds us to change our analytical perspective and detect new mechanisms behind core categories (Herrmann 2010 this volume). These flows of change and indeed many others will no doubt interweave in practices to produce new market-based forms, logics and principles within and through third sector space. We cannot afford to live with rose-tinted view of what might be lost (if it ever was). We must focus now on what is manifest in emerging configurations of third sector space through a critical awareness of third sector practices that are underlain by a shift in power to economic actors and market order. To re-iterate Van Til's (2009: 1076) lament, we are yet to articulate a social conception of the third sector 'outside and distinct from biological, economic and political concerns'. In analysing such change we must remain cognisant of the dominance of the economic over the social and political in third sector space and even beyond to the economic as political and social system (Herrmann 2010 this volume).

References

Alcock, P. (2010) A Strategic Unity: Defining the Third Sector in the UK. *Voluntary Sector Review*, 1(1), 5-24.

Anheier, H. (2009) What Kind of Third Sector, What Kind of Society? Comparative Policy Reflections, *American Behavioural Scientist*, 52(7), 1082-1094.

Austin, M. (2003) The Changing Relationship Between Nonprofit Organizations and Public Social Service Agencies in the Era of Welfare Reform. *Nonprofit and Voluntary Sector Quarterly, (32), 97 - 114.*

Backman, E./Rathberg Smith, S. (2000) Healthy Organizations, Unhealthy Communities? *Nonprofit Management and Leadership*, 10(4) 355-373.

Baulderstone, J./Earles, W. (2009) *Changing relationships: how government funding models impact relationships between organisations. Third Sector Review*, 15 (2), 17-36.

Billis, D. (1989) *The Theory of the Voluntary sector: Implications for Policy and Practice.* London: Centre for Voluntary Organisation, London School of Economics and Political Science.

Casey, J./Dalton, B./Melville, R./Onyx, J. (2010) Strengthening government-nonprofit relations: International Perspectives on Compacts. *Voluntary Sector Review*, 1(1), 59-76.

Castells, M. (1989). The informational city: Information technology, economic restructuring and the urban-regional process. Oxford, England: Blackwell.

Deakin, N./Walsh, K. (1996) The Enabling State: The role of markets and contracts. *Public Administration, 74*, 33-48.

Decker, P. (2009) *Civil Society and Business: Crossing Boundaries and Keeping Distance.* Paper presented to the ISTR Latin American and Caribbean Regional Conference, Mexico City 1-3 July.

Earles, W. (1999) Institutional shape in an enterprise culture: What is it and why we should care. *Third Sector Review, 5(2),* 43-56.

Earles, Wendy (2009) *Nonprofit provider paradigms: excellence, sustainability, viability and identity.* Proceedings of the International Society for Third-Sector Research Eighth International Conference, 9-12 July, Barcelona, Spain.

Earles, W./Moon, J. (2000) Pathways to the enabling state: Changing modes of social provision in Western Australian Community Services. *Australian Journal of Public Administration, 59(4),* 11-24.

Edwards, B./Foley, M. (2001) Civil Society and Social Capital: A primer. In B. Edwards, M. Foley/M. Diani (Eds) *Beyond Tocqueville, Civil Society and the Social Capital Debate in Contemporary Perspective,* 1-14. Hanover, NH: University Press of New England.

Eikenberry, A./Kluver, J. (2004). 'The Marketization of the Nonprofit Sector: Civil Society at Risk?' *Public Administration Review,* 64(2): 132-140.

Evers, A. (2010) Observations on incivility. *Voluntary Sector Review*, 1(1), 113-117.

Gecan, M. (2002) *Going Public: An Organizer's Guide to Citizen Action*. New York: Anchor.

Giddens, A. (1998) *The Third Way: The Renewal of Social Democracy*. Cambridge: Polity Press

Herrmann, Peter, 2010: Unbalancing the Economy – Unbalancing the Social; in this volume (pp. 117 ff.)

Hustinx, L./Handy, F./Cnaan, R. (2010 forthcoming) Volunteering. In R. Taylor (Ed) *Third Sector Research*. Springer.

Kolm, A./La Piana, D. (2003) Strategic Restructuring for Nonprofit Organizations: Mergers, Integrations and Alliances. Westport, CT: Praeger Publishing.

Leat, D. (1998) Invention Research: The Development of Voluntary Studies in the UK, *Third Sector Review*, 4(2), 53-83.

Lyons, M. (1998) A History of Philanthropy and Nonprofits: A comment. *Third Sector Review*, 4 (2), 23-25.

MacDonald, C./Warburton, J. (2003) Stability and Change in Nonprofit Organisations: The Volunteer Contribution, *Voluntas*, 14(4), 381-399.

Otomo, A./Snyder, M. (2002) Considerations of Community: The Context and Process of Volunteerism. *American Behavioural Scientist*, 45(5), 431-441.

Ostrander, S./Langton, S (1987) *Shifting the Debate: Public/Private Sector Relations in the Modern Welfare State*. New Brunswick, NJ: Transaction Books.

Rawsthorne, M. (2005) Community development activities in the context of contracting.*Australian Journal of Social Issues,*40(2), 227-240.

Rees, S./Rodley, G. (Eds) (1995) *The Human Costs of Managerialism: Advocating for the Recovery of Humanity*. Leichhardt, N.S.W. : Pluto Press Australia.

Salamon, L./Anheier, H. (1996) *The Emerging Nonprofit Sector: An Overview*. John Hopkins NonProfit Sector Series.

Stewart-Weeks, M. (2001) Voice and the Third Sector: Why Social Entrepreneurs Matter. *Third Sector Review*, 7(2), 23-38.

Suhood, T. (2001) The Emerging Voice and Survival of Small Non-for-profit Organisations. *Third Sector Review*, 7(2), 123-138.

Van Til, J. (2009) A Paradigm Shift in Third Sector Theory and Practice: Refreshing the Wellsprings of Democratic Capacity. *American Behavioural Scientist*, 52(7), 1069-1081.

Wolch, J. (1999) Decentering America's Nonprofit Sector: Reflections on Salmon's Crises Analysis. *Voluntas: International Journal of Voluntary and Nonprofit Organizations*, 10(1), 25-35.

Zahra, G./Neubaum, S. (2009). A typology of social entrepreneurs. *Journal of Business Venturing*, 24 (5), 519–532.

Unbalancing the Economy – Unbalancing the Social

Peter Herrmann

Abstract

Precarity is commonly seen as 'social phenomenon', an injustice in an otherwise just world. At most it is suggested that this injustice is structurally conditioned, however the standards for assessment follows more norms, claims the need for ethical reconsideration and pleads to re-establish a system of just distribution. The principal question of the justice or injustice of the current system it its own terms is, however, not brought forward. Nor is investigated if and in case in which way we may face changes within the economic system that are structurally effecting the prism through which justice needs to be accessed. The present contribution will examine turns in the socio-economic system that re-define not just the question of work but more fundamentally the issue of the social.

Introduction

Though from a moral standpoint one may approach the capitalist economic system as unjust, it is actually in principal a 'just' system, following mechanisms of exchange that are not based on inequalities in pure power positions. Rather, capitalism is different to any tributary economy of the preceding societies, based on the economic distribution of resources according to strict rules.

> *The production of precapitalist social systems rests upon the stability of power (which is the basic concept defining the domain of the political) and of an ideology that endows it with legitimacy. In other words, politico-ideological authority (the 'superstructure') is dominant at this point. ...*
>
> *Capitalism inverts the order of the relationship between the realm of the economic and the politico-ideological superstructure. The newly developed economic life is no longer transparent, due to the generalization of the market: Not only does the near totality of the social product take the form of goods whose final destination escapes the control of the producer, but the labor force itself, in its predominant wage-earning for, becomes commodified. ... the content as well as the social function of power and ideology acquire, in this reproduction, new characteristics which are qualitatively different from those by which social power was defined in earlier societies. (Amin, 1989: 2 f.)*

If we accept this as starting point we have to consider looking for defining precarity as matter that occurs in a specific historical context that is marked by a fundamental shift of not only redefining economic relationships but that is characterised by a re-definition of (i) the social and (b) the emergence of a new mechanisms of governance structures reflect the emergence of a new mode of accumulation.

Some definitional pints of reference may be introduced here. First, the social is understood as

> *The Social Quality Approach understands the social as the outcome of the interaction between people (constituted as actors) and their constructed and natural environment. With this in mind its subject matter refers to people's productive and reproductive relationships. In other words*
>
> - *the constitutive interdependency between processes of self-realisation and processes of the formation of collective identities*
>
> - *is a condition for 'the social', realised by the interactions of*
>
>   ➢ *actors, being – with their self-referential capacity – competent to act*
>
>   ➢ *and their framing structure, which translates immediately into the context of human relationships.*[38]

Starting from the social quality approach, from which this definition is taken, we defined precarity

> *as a lack of people's ability to participate in the social-economic, cultural, juridical and political life of their communities under conditions which enhance their well-being and individual potentials for contributing to societal development as well.*
>
> *(Herrmann/van der Maesen, 2008: 13)*

Speaking of a new mode of accumulation we, have to go beyond the basic definition, which sees it as

> *a particular combination of production and consumption which can be reproduced over time despite conflictual tendencies*
>
> *(Jessop, 1990: 308).*

---

[38] The definition is taken from working papers by the European Foundation on Social Quality

This orientation is very much focused on the mode of production in the strict sense – proposing the shift from Fordism to Post-Fordism, however overlooking that we are not only facing a shift of the mode of production but also – and more fundamentally – a shift of the basis of the actual process of accumulation. The respective mode of regulation is then not only confronted with the need of searching for new mechanisms of regulating the system in an appropriate way. Instead, we are confronted with the necessity of considering of a system change, including changes of points of reference. Here it is proposed to focus on the following moments:

- the shift of the accumulation regime towards a different mode of production
- the redefinition of the point of reference of the social
- the change of the regulator
- the change of the regulandum changing meaning and position of work.

Crisis of Accumulation or Change of Capitalism?

Since the middle/end of 2008 we are facing a global crisis. And we may think of this in two ways – both equally justified: (i) it is just another event of capitalist development that continues a systematic pattern that is well known for decades, (ii) it is one of the most severe and global crisis, comparable with the developments at the end of the 1930s.

Economic theory – from different kinds – sees such irruptions as clearing mechanism. Basically they are answering two sets of factors. (i) The one has to be seen in the opening gap of supply and demand: overproduction simply means that the production of goods exceeds the effective demand. On the one hand this is simply a socio-economic mechanism which follows certain cycles of investment of accumulated capital in sectors that are productive in areas of marketable goods. On the other hand this follows cycles over longer periods which are based on the development of productivity rather than marketability. These are long cycles of economic conjuncture, characterised by socio-technological developments. These can be *considered as the disruption and the recovery of economic equilibrium over a long period. Their main cause has to do with the accumulation mechanism, whereby capital, sufficient to create new basic productive forces is accumulated and dispersed.*

(Kondratiev, 1926: 63)

(ii) The other feature of such crisis is the over-accumulation of capital going beyond the opening gap between production and effective demand power and is concerned with the more principal factor that the productive sector itself is loosing its basis. Accumulation needs to look not only for a different array in which it can be invested but for a way of shifting to a different mode of accumulation.

Looking at the developments over the recent decades we see this reflected in the following patterns:

- the long wave which is usually captured as shift from Fordism to Post-Fordism

- the temporarily stabilising effect of the WWII-period on the economy by the boost of war industries and the equally stabilising effect of the Vietnam War for the USA which had been at least one factor that allowed the development of a hegemonic role of the Americas in the confrontation of the two systems.[39]

- the temporarily stabilising effect of the years after the war especially for some countries that hugely profited from the European Recovery Program (ERP) – for instance the United Kingdom, France, Germany and Italy as the main beneficiaries (see Marshall Plan)

- and finally the asynchrony in the development of global cycles.

In a shorter time perspective, the development of the former socialist countries can be added as opening new markets – not only markets for consumables but also markets in terms of developing entire economies. All these are important factors, however by and large we are dealing with

---

[39] It is sufficient to note that this had been a political risky game with its own dynamics. On the one hand it undermined the hegemony in later years (the world-wide Anti-Vietnam movement which went far beyond the student movements) and on the other hand the same pattern of war mongering could be applied later again despite the critical voices that made themselves heard globally.

developments within a closely defined system of a productivist development.

Developments a field

Somewhat disguised though not hidden behind this development had been a more fundamental shift. What will be mentioned in the following is not an abrupt change but has to be seen as more or less swift development over decades and can even be seen as secular feature of capitalist economy.

A first u-turn can be seen in the ongoing division of labour. It is important to note that we are not dealing with the technical dimension but with instead with a social process that creates an increasing distance between what one is doing and what one can actually control. In this understanding it is a process that is relevant on both, the individual and the soci(et)al level. This development is first one by which had been characterised elsewhere as drifting apart of actual technical control and the property-based control function. However, although this division is still valid as basic pattern a further development consists of an increasing complexity: in tendency the actual controllability is distorted, shifting away from concrete practice to abstract systems. Behind such developments we can detect technological processes, the increasing globalisation as mutual and general interpretation (in detachment of the one-sided colonialist dependencies) and the process of individualist democratisation. As result we do not find the 'end of history' as claimed by Francis Fukuyama. Rather than such a well-ordered world on the basis of liberal democracy as one option for all, we find a system of apparent arbitrariness, taking power away from any kind of collective entities, opening the way for an age of uncertainty that is characterised

> *by the fact that contradictions of the system have come to the point where none of the mechanisms for restoring the normal functioning of the system can work effectively any longer.*

(Wallerstein, 1995: 268)

Coming from here we have to be careful with pointing on the notion of division of labour.[40] As valid as this is, we have to see as well that (i) the old lines of division of labour within the world system are overcome, (ii) at the same time new patterns are developed along the same old lines and

---

[40] The following borrows from Herrmann, a.

equally important is (iii) that the development is characterised by an increasing complexity of the world system. The old system can be seen as single centred system – though globally possibly hosting more than one centre, each being relatively independent from the other. Of course, this had been a rather complex, though assessable constellation as it is outlined in the following Figure 6.

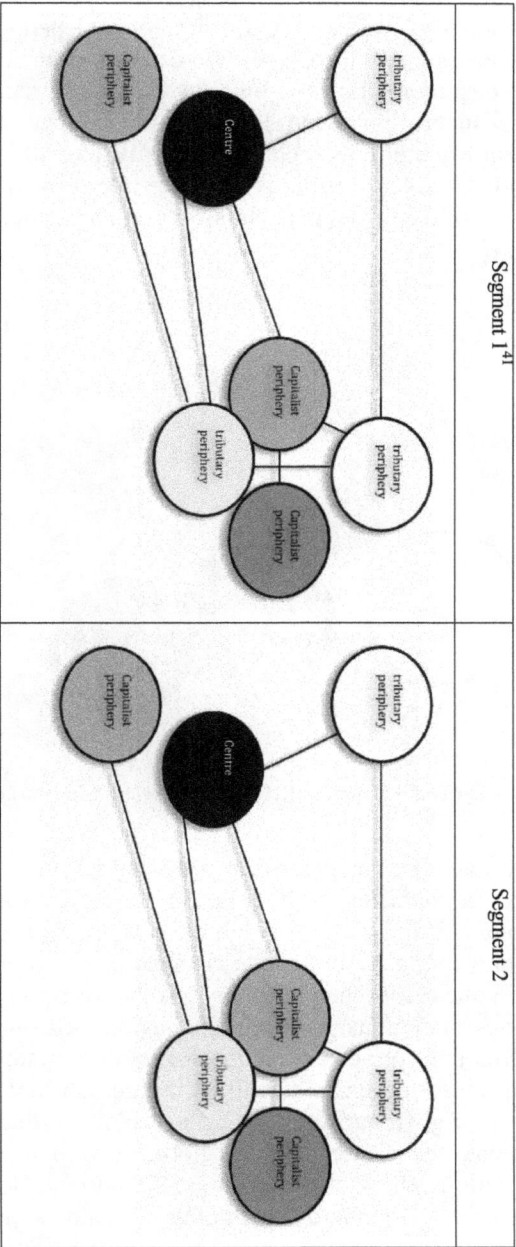

Figure 6: Traditional Centre-Periphery Relation

41 Though the figure suggests identical segments this should not be taken literally – they can be very different, although they are structurally the same.

The one option is that the two (or more) centres would stand independent of each other, with different strength and features but barely being in contact globally – we can see this more as independent side by side. The other option is a still looking at two or more centres. However, this time we have hegemonic power (-block) with its different smaller peripheries and being superordinate in relation to another centre which itself consists of its own hegemonic structure within this overall subordinated relation (it is not necessary to look here at the relationships between the peripheries of the different centres) – this is presented in Figure 7.

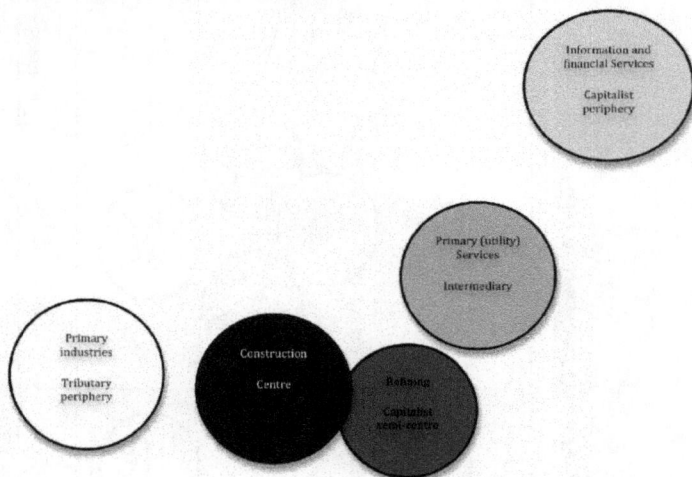

Figure 7: Centre-Periphery Relation in Developed Industrial Capitalism/Hyper-Capitalism

The new stage is characterised by a structure that is not necessarily more complex but characterised by a lack of straightforwardness. Borders and centres are shifting while it is not clear if this is a temporary movement or a lasting change. Nor are the changes themselves actually clear-cut – centres in one respect are periphery in other respects and the definition of a countries or regions position depends as well on other factors as the pure economic performance in the global system. Without further assessing these mechanisms and their true substance, the emergence of the notion of governance, claiming to replace traditional mechanisms of government, the existence of a global governance structure with the United Nations, the World Bank and IMF and the G-8/G20 play a role in setting different standards, including sometimes more confusing than clarifying social standards. All this has to be seen in the failure of modernist theories and practices in developing a rational world system in compliance with the claimed categorical imperatives of freedom, equality and fraternity (mind the sequence). However, rather than evoking a counter-enlightenment, the development went the way of a renaissance: following the shift of the development of a changing basis for accumulation (which will be looked at below), re-establishing mechanisms of politically dominant control. Paradoxically we see – in tendency – the increasing meaning of political power, independent of the nation states but also independent of the actual political class.

Subsequently, the current situation can be characterised by a whirl-pooling centre, a contest of different actors within this amalgamation as competing for hegemony within the system and equally for the maintenance of the overall system.

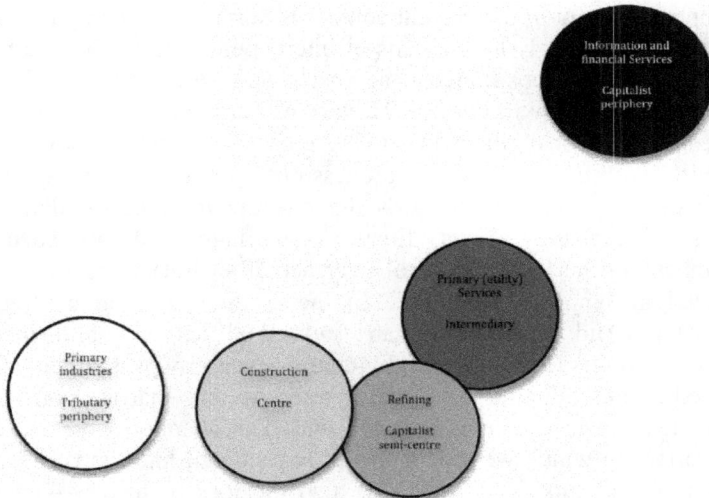

Figure 8: Centre-Periphery Relation in 'Casino-' or 'Finance Capitalism'

In the meantime China is despite its different outspoken political claim one of the main drivers for maintaining the global capitalist system. The meaning of other actors has to be mentioned as it throws a light on an important element characterising the shift we are facing – and this brings us to the second u-turn.

Karl Marx characterised production by four elementary forms, namely production (construction/manufacturing/fashioning), distribution, exchange, consumption (see Marx, 1957). We can translate this into a developmental perspective and outline the following dimensions for positioning accumulation:

- from orienting on utility value towards orienting on exchange value
- from productive processes towards 'communicative processes'[42]
- from production as all-encompassing social relationship towards the redefinition of social relationships as contractual link.

The reference to a contractual relationship has to be especially considered in its meaning not only as legally defined relation on grounds of reciprocity; moreover it is designed by contraction: an exchange process, ex ante exactly defined in terms of its scope.

The important point in the present context is that we are facing a paradox of socially increasingly long chains of interdependence on the one hand, however, counter-positioned against an increasingly limited understanding of how to control the various variables and possibility to intervene. A crucial moment for such increasing limitation, however, is the shift within the overall process of production: away from manufacturing goods and towards the enactment of accumulation on grounds of exchange. Thus, finance capitalism finds its soci(et)al complement in the loss of control over actual soci(et)al processes. The individual act appears as defined in the contractual (and contracted) relationship. And speaking of an 'individual act' is valid in two meanings: it refers to the act of individuals – even groups are then legally redefined as individual actors – and it refers to acts that are considered from a clearly defined beginning and end. The change in the mode of socialisation, to which we will return in more detail later, means for the now completely individualised actor also the loss of history – even of personal history. Speaking of biographical development as matter of patchwork-techniques validates how serious the actual changes are.

Having said this, it has to be emphasised that such limitation is at least to some extent politico-economically wanted: if we consider the cost and effort invested into decoding the human genome it is easy to imagine that similar investment would allow the decoding of the societal genome.

---

[42] The latter being concerned with administering and transport in the widest understanding

It had been said that these are general, secular features of the capitalist economy. The current crisis has to be seen not only in the culmination of these factors. Not less important is the synchronisation on a global scale. This led to the situation that both: the specific crisis which occurred with the crash on entirely overheated finance markets and the secular development of the emergence of a changed basis for accumulation fell together and persevered although the 'crash-situation' could be overcome relatively soon by some recovery measures. More important is, however, that (i) those countries that did exceptionally well before – as for instance Ireland or the United Arab Emirates – had been hit particularly hard and (ii) that all these recovery plans had been aiming on – indeed necessary – structural changes and (iii) failed doing so in a way that answering the causes of the crisis: artificial and short-ranging stimulation of demand and managerial control did not answer the principal imbalance nor could it make good for the lack for possibilities for temporary externalisation of costs.

New Patterns of the Social

Earlier it had been said that an investment in 'decoding the social genome' could well be possible, provided the necessary investment would be made. The discussion on this topic could well be extended: as much it is an issue of power and economic interest – investment of this kind in a high-risk area is not sufficiently profitable to accept the political risks – it is likely that another issue is involved: a fear of steering human behaviour, the ethical question being at least similarly challenging as the ethical questions for instance around stem cell research. And surely, the experiences from Germany's dark ages of the 1930s/1940s have to be seen as warning. However, despite the fear, we have to see another dimension in the fact that rational collective action would definitely undermine the existing power structures. It may be reasonably simple to define what a healthy human body may be,[43] but it is difficult to define a 'good society'.

Without underrating the problems, I want to put forward the thesis that the fundamental flaw is not the lack of generally accepted values, the lack of the ability of defining a 'general interest' – the latter is for

---

[43] Though mind the 'may be', as we are surely not moving on an uncontested field: as much as 'health' and inviolacy may be clear definitions, the problem comes if we pose the question the other way round and link to this the question of value of people in society or the value of their life.

instance frequently claimed by various political forces. In political discussions, this is not only the case when it comes to the question of services general interest where the term is explicitly used. It is the case as well in general views on the state as representative of some kind of 'general will' (e.g. volonté génerale or volnté du tout); and similarly the builders of the British Empire did not hesitate to look for a justification in a common wealth, again some kind of claimed general interest that can be explicitly taken back to the principle of competition as foundation of general wealth, outlined by Adam Smith. Actually with this we mention already the more important flaw: the fundamentally individualist approach towards the social.

Earlier it had been suggested that we face a development within the sphere of the overall production: a shift from 'manufacturing' over 'productive consumption' towards 'distribution' and 'exchange', all being and remaining to be part of the process of production. This shift is – so the present thesis – accompanied on the social side by a fundamental shift to individualism. 1) We may start with social processes sui generis: processes that are social as they are 'all-encompassing'; concerning the people who are acting together – and only concerning them. The division of labour may well exist and may even exist in an extensive way but it does not interfere with the homogeneity of the given society. Inequalities surely exist also but again they do not undermine the homogeneity of the given society.[44] 2) On a second stage we find the division of labour not only by way of technical processes but also – and primarily – developing as matter of division of power, linked to the development of property on the one hand and in distributional terms being established as tributary societies. The social – and we can apply the general definition as it had been suggested at the beginning of the article – had been divided: on the one hand we find it geared towards a claimed general interest, defined as the interest of the given society against others and thus including some expansionist notion.[45] On the other hand the definition of the social had been geared towards the self-sustenance of small units which we can describe as 'social units' in the understanding of Ferdinand Tönnies' 'Gemeinschaft'.

---

[44] A warning may be necessary: this is by no means the harmonious idyll as which it appears at first sight. Inequalities of the suggested kind would be mechanic (in the Durkheimian understanding); inequalities that go beyond such mechanic maintenance did not exist as exclusion had been absolute.

[45] We actually have to see this as contradiction in terms as the general interest is exclusionary.

Life of the Gemeinschaft is mutual possession and enjoyment and also possession and enjoyment and also possession of and enjoyment of common goods. The will of possession and enjoyment is the will of protection and defense: Common goods – common evils; common friends – common enemies. ... Possession is, in itself, will for preservation; it is enjoyment in the same sense of as satisfaction and realization of will are comparable to the inhalation of atmospheric air. This is true also for possession and interest which human beings have in each other. However, to the extent that enjoyment differs from possession through special acts of use, it can be by destruction, as, for instance, the killing of an animal for consumption.

(Tönnies, 1887/1912: 50 f.)

Reading Tönnies further it gets clear that – different to common perception – the Gemeinschaft had been first and foremost an economically defined frame of reference rather than the idyllic living together of like-minded people or any form of communitarian egalitarianism.

3) We find latest with the developed modern society, beginning with the Renaissance, a fundamental shift towards the individualisation of the social. To be clear: individualisation is not a recent development but has its fundamental roots in the Renaissance.

It had been an individuality that had been based in the fundamental separation between economic life, political control and individuality of civil life – a separation of which the consequence can be seen until today: as matter of analysing state, economy and civil society, as distinguishing social and civil dialogue as partnering towards the political system or as well as the separation that stands at the centre of this presentation's attention: as well the separation between science, social science and reality.

(Herrmann, c)

Furthermore, we speak of the individualisation of the social – this is distinct to the individualisation of persons.

We can now see two fundamental shifts – the meaning increasing on the one hand from the top to the bottom and on the other hand – to some extent in parallel – from the left to the right, pure individualism standing at the end of the development. But it means as well the emergence of a predominantly or even solely exchange-based economy.

manufacturing	consumption	distribution	exchange
Social	Social	Social	Social
Tributary	Tributary	Tributary	Tributary
Individual	Individual	Individual	Individual

Table 15: The Move to Individualised Economies

So far we can speak of the shift from the pre-capitalist society to the capitalist society as dualism: (i) the valuation is based on production of goods that have at least a utility value and with this on productivity and (ii) the commodification of these goods, consequently the commodification of work and the contractualisation of social relationships, entailing 'pure individualism' (see Herrmann/Dorrity, 2009).

However, there is another dimension to it, which is immediately linked to the appearance of the state which is highlighted by Giovanni Arrighi in his analysis of the early phase of the emergence of the modern capitalist system. He points on

> *[t]wo opposite elementary forms of capitalist organization. Venice came to constitute the prototype of all future forms of 'state (monopoly) capitalism,' whereas Genoa came to constitute the prototype of all future forms of 'cosmopolitan (finance) capitalism.' The ever changing combination and opposition of these two organizational forms, and above all, their ever-increasing scale and complexity associated with the 'internalization' of one social function after another, constitute the central aspect of the evolution of historical capitalism as a world system.*

(Arrighi, 1994/2002: 149)

The important aspect here is the internalisation-aspect. Taken together with the momentum of individualisation we can see the emergence of new governance as amalgamation in the form of 'individualist despotism': not necessarily authoritarianism in the crude form, but equally not at all immune to it.

Fading-Away of the Old Powers?

We can move the argument a step further and reach at a paradox result: as much as this process is originally based on valuation of productivity, it is also intermingled with the devaluation of this standard. To the extent to which the economic system destabilises towards individualism and exchange, this means that productivity looses its value (and standard for valuation). In actual fact, the permanent overproduction can only be discharged in the over-circulation of accumulated capital. In consequence a political shift is evoked:

- Whereas production in different sectors needs some coordination – and thus the state as ideal personification of the total national capital, capital is not only easily floating globally but it is also floating 'without sector'. There are surely in the detailed economic perspective differences between the different sectors of the finance market, and some relevant sectors are even still to a large degree nationally bound. However, as general rule we can state that finance capitalism is truly capitalism without borders.
This means as well that the state in its traditional understanding as nation state looses part of its rational.

This points on the principal contradiction which now comes to its climax. Philip Steinberg points out

that the territorial state emerged concurrent with the deterritorialization of political economy and geographical imagination

(Steinberg, 2009: 468)

The original dialectical tension between de-territorialisation of the economy and its re-territorialisation as political force seems to come to its end. Despite undeniable and in cases even increasing nationalism we see as well that the principle of territoriality and nationality is importantly undermined.

- Furthermore there is a lack of forces for sound economic development due to the lack of new products that could initialise an A-phase of a new Kondratieff cycle – this lack goes far beyond the usual B-phases as it is based on a structural shift away from actual production. Already the most recent innovation of this kind – the huge surge in information technology especially with the invention of easy to manageable – had not fully coming up to the expectations and had even some opposite effects. Investment had been only to some extent relevant for the sphere of 'social production'; to another extent this technological push had been contributing to a further shifting of the economy away from the productive sector towards the finance-sector.[46] Moreover, the

---

[46] One reason behind this shift can be seen in the low production costs: still

technological means facilitate the point that had been mentioned before: the borderless, global system.

- Taken together, this means that the standards for integration are not less undermined, loosing the foundation on which they had been built. The modern nation state had been resting on two important pillars: (i) capitalist economic growth based on production in the narrow sense (i.e. manufacturing/construction of commodities) which made distribution possible to an extent that allowed a sufficient degree of social integrity; (ii) territoriality as basis for defining membership, serving for the definition of citizenship. Michael Zürn and Stephan Leibfried – as quoted in the following – point on the 'rule of law' as characterising momentum of the modern state. We can go a step further and say that such rule of law is a core part of the standards that integrate society, law and the legislative system being an expression of the objective conditions of a given society and the normative transformation. If this is agreeable we have to state in the argumentum e contrario that the plunge of the underlying principles means as well the need for the search for new standards and their normative justification.[47] At this stage there are two option visible and already far developed. The one is an entirely individualised horizon of right; the other – and this can go well hand in hand – is the reliance on fundamentally moralised perspectives. For the rule of law remains only the space of formalised, but utterly mesningless formula.

We can take these points with the definition of the modern state given by Michael Zuern and Stephan Leibfried. They

> define the modern state in four, intersecting, dimensions. The resource dimension comprises the control of the use of force and revenues, and is associated with the consolidation of the modern territorial state from scattered feudal patterns. The law dimension includes jurisdiction, courts, and all the necessary elements of the rule of law, called 'Rechtsstaat' or constitutional state in German-speaking countries where it is most closely identified with the widely held concept of the state. Legitimacy or the acceptance of political rule came into full bloom with the rise of the democratic nation-state in the 19th century.

---

overpriced products and a permanently maintained race of a 'software-hardware bubble' are building up huge overcapacities which impend to collapse.

[47] Important candidates are surely the various post-modernist perspectives of seeming arbitrariness, the emphasis of individualisation and the different strands on – not least nostalgically glorified communitarianism.

And welfare, or the facilitation of economic growth and social equality, is the leitmotif of the intervention state, which acquired responsibility for the general well-being of the citizenry in the 20th century.

(Zuern/Leibfried, 2005: 2 f.)

And they summarise:

Territorial State, the state that secures the Rule of Law, the Democratic State, and the Intervention State, and which we connote with the acronym TRUDI.

(ibid.: 3)

Consequently it remains to ask at what stage we are now, if we can make out a fourth stage as it seems to be obvious that the traditional orientation is if not wrong so at least extremely inadequate?

The importance of the latter aspect is commonly underestimated. Widely acknowledged is the loss of national sovereignty asserted for instance by Giovanni Arrighi in the words:

The modern inter-state system has thus acquired its present global dimension through successive hegemonies of increasing comprehensiveness, which have correspondingly reduced the exclusiveness of the sovereignty rights actually enjoyed by its members. Were this process to continue, nothing short of a true world government, as envisaged by Roosevelt, would satisfy the condition that the next world hegemony be more comprehensive territorially and functionally than the preceding one. We are thus back ... to one of the questions raised in the Introduction. Has the West attained such a degree of world power under US leadership that it is on the verge of putting an end to capitalist history as embedded in the raise and expansion of the modern inter-state system?

(Arrighi, 1994/2002: 75 f.)

Frequently overlooked is the social dimension of these current changes, going beyond the effects of positioning people on an imagined scale of normality. It is frequently mentioned that the standard employment relationship does not exist anymore and people are drifting into new patterns of securing their existence. Also it had been occasionally highlighted that the systems of social security are under pressure: insurance systems are based on the assumption of 'full contribution' which cannot be guaranteed with standard employment relationship breaking away; equally tax-based systems rely on full employment, the latter being considered as the basis for a bulk of the public finances.[48] However, at least in the social policy debate we barely find consideration of the changes of the societal system and the relevant understanding of the shifts of the processes of value production. An easy answer can be given by stating a process of re-feudalisation. In actual fact we can see various parallels if we compare the situation today with the situation of the time when the foundations of modern capitalism had been laid, the Renaissance. We find during both periods the overwhelming power of finance capital – if recalculated on the bases of relevant weighing measures the financial power of the Medici or the Fugger is probably well comparable with the finance power of today's financial institutions. Moreover, then s today we find a close link between production, trade and finance: for instance the financial power of Medici had been very much based on sustaining the link, the textile industries of Flanders playing a pronounced role. His may well be comparable with today's situation for instance of many enterprises which seemingly operate in the productive sphere but for which have financial activities are more important than production and where the volume of activities on the financial markets exceeds the volume even of the volume of major banks. Another factor is that the over-accumulation reached such a volume that investment in arts, other cultural activities and also in non-cultural patronage reached a level that is comparable with that of the Renaissance. But more importantly, this goes beyond simple patronage: we are now concerned with a process where this kind of activity is in its own right a matter of special concern – this can be seen in two realms. (i) It is a matter of supporting the fine arts in as activity in its own rights, shifting investment into an unproductive area which is by any means comparable with the investment into other unproductive market segments, as the financial markets. Such development reflects very much the pattern as it had been described before. (ii) More important is probably the second factor, namely the change of the basis-superstructure relationship. In general terms, it surely has to be maintained that the basis determines the superstructure. Nevertheless we find a shift by which the basis-superstructure relationship is somewhat changed. As said previously, in economic terms it is important to fully recognise the shift from the core of production towards derived areas that are dependents of the actual capitalist cycle: the development of finance capitalism – a

---

[48] As long as this is the case, tax-based social security systems can hardly be seen as fundamentally distributional.

form of capitalism that has to be considered as misnomer. Consequently, we have to change the analytical perspective and detect the new mechanisms behind core categories, as for instance profit, surplus value, labour, cohesion, integrity and integration, exclusion and exclusivity, nation and territory.

But this shift challenges equally the mechanisms of political control. Though we may perceive a growing influence of non-economic forces and the extension of a political class: the power of celebrities including the celebritysation of politicians,[49] the technocratisation and managerialisation of politics, the ruling of committees and the introduction of governance etc., it is obvious that such development is disguising the fact that many of these patterns are only instruments of a direct and outspoken take-over of power-positions by economic actors. A clue for further consideration can be taken from Antonio Gramsci's notion of hegemony which allows the understanding of a ruling class as form of concentric circles around the 'prince' as core of the system of governance which includes the domestication of critical intellectuals, huge investments into an apparatus of mental control and the elaboration of the ancient strategy of *panem et circenses,* now on a global level and by employing the various means of sophisticated technology. – An important element of this is the close link to individualisation marking an important parallel and at the same time difference between today's situation and the era of the Renaissance. Nobert Bolz states in his essay on *Steering in the Era of web 2.0*

> *Johannes Gross once said that fortitude and courage are the only virtues that cannot be simulated. A new spirit requires a new charismatic leader that embodies it and an allegiance as partisans of the idea. Note well, it is about partisans, not about clerks. It is about charismatic leaders and not about managers. We are talking about charisma and not about bureaucracy. ... One can lead people only with ideas and passion.*
>
> *...*
>
> *The successful political leader is not simply 'professional politician' but see politics as vocation. His will to lead is getting obvious by his will to change, male a difference. ... For this one needs buoyancy to be able to react, ability to communicated to ne able to answer and*

---

[49] In the extreme the typical US-election campaigns as political showcasing, in which political discourse actually plays a minor role.

courage to take initiative. This vocation is only with somebody who believes in an idea and a community.

(Bolz: 58 f.; here: 59 – transl. PH)

We surely see in both cases an emphasis of the leader – and in both understandings we surely concerned with charismatic leaders – If one has a closer look at the history of the House of Medici, for instance, it had been very much the history of the exhibition of power *(see e.g. Hibbert, 1975)*. One could even dare saying that they had been initiators of a new ear in arts – not only by art patronage but also by the new powers they had been setting free in the areas of trade, optics, astronomy etc. – inventions allowing and requiring the development of entirely new perspectives, in part even allowing to qualify (though not at all to question) the role of the centrality of the church (and, of course, secular leadership which they easily overtook on grounds of their personal power and exceptional wealth). All in all, they created a new leadership, new princedoms by merging and welding together two distinct patterns: that of 'clinical governing' (the part of the financial systems of calculability) and that of exhibitionism – a matter of

self-legitimation in the form of the cultivation of a distinguished identity

(Barker, 2001: 4)

However, coming back to the statement Bolz puts forward, we stand today apparently at the opposite frontier: whereas – without denying the hugely problematic course this took – the earlier Renaissance had been oriented towards (re-)gaining ideas and virtue from an increasing rationalisation. This had been expressed especially by the increase of finance as matter of making production and trade manageable in terms of calculability and despite continuing to hold tight to irrational power structures. The current 'Renaissance', however, takes the opposite route: it rests on a detached mechanism of rationality – the 'financial market' – and rather than aiming on serving production it enters a circular mode, aiming on self-sustenance. With this we find on the socio-political side and the level of building a hegemonial power also a different pattern: not a façade of splendour, covering an – though only just emerging – productive foundation but a façade of splendour that obscures its short-term orientation of unjustified dissolution from the real world of productivity – and it may be added for further consideration elsewhere: unconnected also to the real problems of what had been presented as social quality elsewhere. Notwithstanding the at times brutal forms that the Medici applied to favour their splendour, today's 'new princes' apply not less brute forms – one of them being the severe ignorance when it comes to accepting the need of systematic and systemic approaches to answer the major challenges of our times as they had been outlined elsewhere in this volume *(see* Re-Feudalisation and Globalisation: Reaction or Savour, *pp. 52 ff. and* Outlook – Challenges Ahead, *pp. 70 ff.).*

An equally important feature is with this the return to an explicit moral guidance when it comes to policy developments – nearly unavoidably leading to eclecticism of proposed strategies. Even if we have on the one hand an ongoing claim of rational policy making, we find at the same time a strengthened meaning of religion: Not least the mounting fragmentation, as it is implied in technically lead policy-making, looks for a compensation in holistic approaches which are however, not looked for by elaborating new and complex rationalities. Instead, religious fundamentalism is approaching from the verge, and those who watched the Bush campaign launching the 'War against Evil' will know that the fundamentalism didn't come from outside of the centre of global powers but from the very midst of it: a fundamentalist crusade originating in the Unites States and perfectly linking into fundamentalism persisting in the periphery.

There is another dimension to this: War had been throughout history frequently employed means of 'anti-crisis policies'. And we can see that – with pretended good moral reasons – war and war-like intervention is increasingly again a means of politics not only on a very regional level but on the very global level and seeing not only warmongering by the United States but as well even by international institutions under the label of peace missions. It is a mission acting exactly in the borderline of internalisation and externalisation: external disasters are translated into internal profits; external conflicts are utilised to internal control. With this formulation we see as well that the meaning is not only – and perhaps not even primarily – a matter of immediate profitability but more a matter of maintaining at least temporarily and internally a quasi-equilibrium.

History doesn't repeat itself, but this shouldn't prevent us form looking back and contemplate on the current situation, asking ourselves if the current economic changes – as we face them as development over the last at least thirty to forty years – could actually mean a more fundamental shift in terms of governing: the emergence of a new state or the development of a stateless mechanism.

On the Way to a New State?

The following thought experiment might help us developing an understanding, first looking at developments of state-mechanisms. What we could prove up to here is a development of parallel developments of unfolding and contraction of power, shifting between the three fields of (i) economic capability of appropriation as matter of accumulation, (ii) control of social processes linked to economic expansion and social distribution and (iii) territoriality. The balance between these three fields can be grasped by three processes, namely (i) internal re-distribution, (ii) externalisation and (iii) internalisation. The fundamental mechanism is that the increase of accumulated power needs an immediate political organisation within a given territory. Linking accumulation and territoriality we witness the process of some form of state-building: beginning from the early oikos over the city states to the later modern states. These formations are characterised by an important contradiction. On the one hand we find the internalisation of social functions – the technical process of accumulating money and reinvesting the same into extended production had been emerging into an entirely social process of controlling processes of sociability. In tendency, the economic and political power are with this process falling into two distinct realms, being initially an unity. This does not mean a loss of control of political power by dominant economic forces. On the contrary, it does mean that the economically ruling class needed and could afford a distinct apparatus that could maintain its power. The need arose from the complexity of control tasks that emerged from the expansion of capitalist functions; and it emerged front the diversification of the ruling class itself as especially this diversification meant as well the intensification of power in the sense of what Giovanni Arrighi referred to as internalisation. However, in particular the city states of Northern Italy, but slightly later[50] as well the cities of the Hanseatic League showed that this territorialsation had been somewhat limited – as already quoted from Philip Steinberg

---

[50] actually for some time overlapping.

138

the territorial state emerged concurrent with the deterritorialization of
political economy and geographical imagination

(Steinberg, 2009: 468)

As much as this has to be seen as process of emerging and expanding economic forces, it merges into the general process of civilisation, which Norbert Elias describes not least by underlining a certain centrifugal tendency that dialectically makes possible the opposite development: centripetal developments. The pschychogenetic process of internalisation of certain norms allows and enforces individualisation – as well in form of increasing individuals' independence. However, it also meant that as long as these mechanisms of psychological control and steering could be translated into increased accumulation – be it in material or psychological form – it didn't play a major role: social structures and divisions could be retained. We can say: internalisation of control by psychological mechanisms of restraining behaviour had been complemented by internalisation of fields apt for accumulation. On a societal level this corresponds with the permanent expansion of control. Simplified one may say, the individual had been compensated for the loss of personal power by the gain of societal power. However, with the increasing limitation of possibilities to expand meant as well the limitation of such possibilities for compensation. – Let us look a little closer at the work of Norbert Elias. Sephen Mennell contends that

> [t]he dilemma throughout the period was that a central ruler's only means of securing services was to grant land to subordinates, yet giving away his own land only weakened his own power. This centrifugal tendency could be offset as long as kings and emperors were still conquering new land, still acquiring lands of their own … . But as conquest of land externally became more difficult, centrifugal forces gained dominance.

(Mennell, 1998, 64)

This extension of chains of (inter)action is dialectical in its structure – as much as it means the extension of reach (internalisation), this process means nevertheless also the limitation of reach as it is based on – partial and/or temporary – externalisation. Furthermore, this is a multilevel process as it is on the one hand concerned with processes on national levels or occurring within centres and also within peripheries of the global system; and it is on the other hand marking the development of the relationship between the centre(s) and periphery(/ies).

We find this in the form of three central patterns that can guide any further analysis, bringing together the analysis of sociogenetic processes with the economic analysis of developing and permanently shifting centre-periphery relationships and the thereupon based socio-economic formations and their crisis. These patterns are

- colonialism and imperialism and the centripetal force of globalisation
- changing accumulation regimes and the shift from construction/ manufacturing to the exchange side of the overall process of production and the permanent tendency of overstretching the pattern towards total finance-capitalism
- the move to total commodifation and the tendency of over-commodifation as total alienation.

Imperialism, Colonialisation and Changing Accumulation Regimes

This may be a simple matter of division of labour; it may be a matter of decisive cultural differences and transformation; or it may take the form of an elaborated system of power-imbalances. This moves immediately on to the other side: the expansion and deterritorialisation: it is not the nation state that secures power but now again the economic actors that are directly pushing forward with their 'foreign policies', pushing for free trade, pushing as well even for diverse mechanisms of social provision and security in other countries and regions, thus securing a workforce in accordance with the needs. For some time this can be maintained within the old framework – for some time meaning: as long as long as this is actually still a matter of 'foreign policies'.

Total Commodification

And 'for some time' means as well: as long as there is sufficient capital, securing this direct political control in form of private schools and healthcare institutions,[51] and even private armies. It is extremely important to acknowledge this social dimension of processes of privatisation for instance as part of the EU-debates on Services of General Interest or the General Agreement on Trade in Services (GATS): extension of economic power is one part only; a not less important focus is the gain of political control: the internalisation of various social

---

[51] in several cases being even based on donations.

functions now on a global level by way of a complete and more or less open total commodification – a process that is already depicted by Karl Marx.

New Governance

For the time being there is the political need of searching for a balance between 'new statehood' and self-regulation. For an interim phase we may expect a renaissance of tributary cultures. To the extent to which value is not depending on immediate production, the calculation of value changes as well its character: it is not depending on the calculation of the cost price but shifts towards a determination on the basis of tributes.

An example is given by the car manufacturer BMW and the confrontation with google. The homepage of BMW showed up on various searches though the links had been only very vaguely justifiable: BMW-London led to the homepage, BMW-Singapore lead to the homepage but as well 'used cars' led to the homepage even if not specified as used BMWs. Google intervened and blocked for some time the home page in general: it could not be found even by direct search, forcing in this way BMW to omit the manipulative practice.

Both examples underline that – for the good or for the bad – superpower managed to establish itself as 'benevolent', though surely applying the rule of law, not less surely leaving the rule of rights outside of this equation, pushing it on arbitrary grounds outside of economics.

In the long run, however, such patterns are unlikely to prevail. One feature of striving for new statehood is that it springs from two sources: (i) the need for a new, global mechanism of central regulation – this push is limited as it is only the need for coordinated action. As such it can and is well maintained by inter- and supranational organisations as IMF, UN, WB and the like; (ii) the need of looking for new statehood as refuge for the old socio-political elites, now looking for maintaining or translating their still given hegemonic positions into the newly emerging system. The EU is surely an example par excellence: striving with the new Lisbon Treaty and the establishment of a President of the Council further to some kind of statehood.

Giovanni Arrighi's question, namely

Has the West attained such a degree of world power under US leadership that it is on the verge of putting an end to capitalist history as embedded in the raise and expansion of the modern inter-state system?

(Arrighi, 1994/2002: 75 f.)

must probably be answered with scepticism. The hegemony is surely given and what appear to be new hegemons establish their positions actually very much on the basis of applying the screenplay of the old master. The sceptical pert of the answer is based on the shift of the definition of the centre. In strict economic terms, the centre is itself liquid: as production now plays a subordinated role and financial capitalism is dominating the entire cycle of accumulation, the centre itself is somewhat virtual. Though objective in existence, it is not tangible and vanishes easily behind a cloud of new mythologies of political celebrities, normative-motivated good doers and religious fundamentalists, processes of branding and … – the danger of strong and violent leaders, nationalist or not, in any case promising the return to old securities and also the emergence of new communitarian ideologies. – It may be worth to mention in a side remark that this is often a glue by which some movements with emancipative claims are easily caught as they misjudge the scope of historical changes and still maintain their formerly anti-imperialist ambitions without noting, however, that they slide themselves into simple nationalist or otherwise particularistic forces.

On the surface level we see managerialisation and technocratic elites gaining the mastery: an apparatus of complex, multitudinous interrelations, the 'legitimation by procedure' (Luhmann) and a seeming arbitrariness of choosing stakeholders as far as substantial criteria are concerned: it seems to be sufficient to register interest – and to avail of the resources to follow it up in the complex array of negotiations, hearings, debates and … defeats. This part of the development is caught in the tension of a 'power without subject', as Heide Gerstenberger (Gerstenberger, 1990/2006) denotes the emergence of the bourgeois state as specific institution of power in Germany; on the other hand it leaves however leeway for the emergence of a self-perpetuating power block that defines itself by its distance from the real life:

It is not so long ago that we still predominantly just made things. Economies were based on things we grew, or things we dug out of the ground, like iron ore, gold, or oil. We used materials to make things – general manufacture of things like tools or gates or carts, and later specialised high-tech sectors of things like cars or computers. Then the emphasis shifted towards services, like banking, or retail, or catering, with a focus on customer care.

(European Commission, DG for Education and Culture, 2009: 48).

From here development is perceived as one from 'things' to 'thinks', moving on to 'brings' and further to 'links', ultimately leading to 'non-thinks'

which covers aspects that depend on creativity or design, and that are appreciated not so much because they are functional but because they appeal or entertain.

Overall, it is a progress from the material, to the intellectual, and to the emotional.

(ibid.: 49)

The social, then, having been defined

as the outcome of the interaction between people (constituted as actors) and their constructed and natural environment.

is now not relying anymore on real processes of production but on virtual process of links. From here we can see that the labour market crisis and the emerging and rigidifying precarity is not (only) a crisis of the labour market and herewith related social security systems; rather we find at the core a crisis of (the understanding of) work itself: work as social relationship first faded away behind pure commodification; and it fades now increasingly away behind the meaningless of commodities.

Managerialisation – as specifically defining moment of the 'new social' is then not much more than the maintenance of links: a switchboard that actually does not guide where and why links are made but only secures that they can be made, answering the need of the minimalism of common denominators.

Social Policy as Managing Precarity – or: is there such thing as society?

Even if we cannot answer the question in detail, we can at least put forward some questions which social policy has to address in a more serious way.

The fact that we find on the one hand a direct link between or even representation by national governments and the majority of central supranational organisations (as the IMF, the World Bank or the EU) as one actor group and major business interests and on the other hand an increasing openness of governance mechanisms means not least that we have to look more closely at the meaning of citizenship. It would be too easy to speak of the defiance of these rights – though this is surely as well a relevant feature not least in so-called developed countries. More important for the present more principal considerations is to examine that citizenship had always been defined by reference to a clearly defined entity: the city, later emerging to the nation state. The question of a global citizenship is nowadays not simply a matter of answering migration. Rather, the crucial point is about finding a point of reference that reflects floating borders of the units that make decisions: on the one hand the nation state is breaking away as point of reference. On the other hand the institutional system, which secured at least theoretically the observance of relevant provisions of rights of citizens, is as well loosing its clearly defined structure: (i) the multilevel governance is one issue at stake; (ii) the multi-actor governance is another issue at stake, not allowing the clear determination to which instance one can turn. However, the citizen his/herself seems to have lost any intrinsic reference as human and social rights are now redefined as rights of individuals. The social itself is entirely moralised and thus open to contest and relativism (see as well: Herrmann, forthcoming b)

Global capitalism can be seen as a qualitative leap, not least as from here a new global culture emerges. It would be too simply to see current social policy trends simply as retrenchment,[52] workfare orientations and stigmatisation ('blaming the victims'). On another occasion I described this as

---

[52] Actually even empirically questionable as we see more a shifting of social spending rather than a straight decrease.

a fundamental shift of social policy making, namely the enforcement of an approach of 'contractualist social-policy', which goes far beyond any actual measures. What is more relevant is the shift that can be described in a secular perspective as being marked by roughly three steps:

- *social policy based on charity and mercy, being concerned with provision and control;*

- *social policy as rights-based system of provisions, though still performing as means of control, being different as much as control is in this case linked to clear conditions as employment status, some form of disability, age or as well the status of taking part in educational/training measures – typically though not exclusively defined by one of the systems presented as welfare regime (insurance based, solidarity based or citizenship based);*

- *social policy as matter of contractually defined relationship.*

(Herrmann, d)

We can go now a step further and say that we find actually a dual definition as with the orientation on 'social policy as matter of contractually defined relationship' we find simultaneously an orientation on charitable and good-will action. We can say that we find as supplement of contractualisation the ethicalisation as normative framework and moralisation and 'charitysation' as action framework. All this does not mean that the state looses its entire meaning: it continues acting as conglomeration of the economic class. However, at the same time it shifts towards an instrument following the very same logic as the capitalist enterprise: it is about stakeholders, management and corporate identity – and that corporate social responsibility plays a role there is as true as it is true that the princes of the early city states had been fostering the fine arts, holding up Christian values. But we should never forget that it had been them who also burned Girolamo Savonarola in front of the palace which had been build literally on the foundations of the poor who had been dislodged from the very same place which they inhabited before: Piazza della Signoria; and it had been them who burned Giordano Bruno at the stake on the Campo di' Fiori in Rome for using 'wicked words'.

Conclusion

We may then well hesitate to agree with Bob Jessop's confrontation of the Keynesian Welfare National State with the Schumpeterian Workfare Post-National Regime (see e.g. Jessop, 2000). As plausible as this is, the hesitation springs from the following considerations on the current situation. At least two aspects shall be contested here:

- While Jessop sees innovation and competitiveness, open economy and supply-side policies as crucial, the open economy is actually a borderless economy – he states himself the shift to a post-national regime. As well the mention of supply-side policies has to be qualified: In this contribution it is proposed that supply is actually seen as core of the economic process – directly supply or the process of distribution and making distribution possible, the sphere of circulation taking over.

- Furthermore, talking of the orientation on workfare as matter of subordinating social to economic policy, putting downward pressure on 'social wage' and attacking welfare rights tells only part of the truth. It overlooks the importance of the fact that social policy is not subordinated but suggested to be disjoined, which explains as well that social wages are actually not just under pressure but further and more in principal undermined: they are denied, re-defined in the perspective of individual contract law. The same holds true for welfare rights: the point at the core is not the pressure on the scope of these rights; importantly their individualisation is the centrally important development.

We arrive at a situation where circulation gains dominance over production and formal communication as matter of system maintenance is more prevalent than true exchange on a common ground.

References

Amin, Samir, 1989: Eurocentrism; New York: Monthly Review Press

Arrighi, Giovanni, 1994/2002: The Long Twentieth Century. Money, Power, and the Origins of Our Times; London/New York: Verso

Barker, Rodney S., 2001: Legitimating Identities. The Self-Presentations of Rulers and Subjects; Cambridge: Cambridge University Press:

Bolz, Norbert, 2009: Steuerung im Zeitalter von web 2.0; in: Change. Das magazin der Bertelsmann Stiftung. special edition 2009: Deutschland 2020 – Blick nach Vorne! Haltungen und Ideen für Wege aus der Krise; Ed. Verlag Bertelsmann Stiftung; Guetersloh: Verlag Bertelsmann Stiftung: 58 f.

European Commission, DG for Education and Culture: What Makes the Wealth of Nations? In: The Magazine. No 32; European Commission. DG Education and Culture; Luxembourg: Office for Official Publications of the European Communities, 2009

Gerstengerber, Heide, 1990/2006[2]: Die Subjektlose Gewalt. Theorie der Entstehung buergerlicher Staatsgewalt; Muenster: Westfaelisches Dampfboot

Herrmann, Peter, 2010 a: Globalisation revisited; in: Society and Economy; Budapest: Akadmiai Kiad, 32(2010)/2: 255-275

Herrmann, Peter, 2012 b: Human Rights: For Sale or Saviour in the Globalising Market Economy; in: Herrmann, Peter, 2012: God, Rights, Law and a Good Society. Overcoming Religion and Moral as Social Policy Approach in a Godless and Amoral Society; Bremen:Europaeischer Hochschulverlag: 132-148

Herrmann, Peter, 2012 c: Science – Social Science – Practice Or: Searching for Responsibility; in: Herrmann, Peter, 2012: God, Rights, Law and a Good Society. Overcoming Religion and Moral as Social Policy Approach in a Godless and Amoral Society; Bremen: Europaeischer Hochschulverlag: 2-69

Herrmann, Peter, 2010 d: Workfare – The Reinvention of the Social; in: Eyebiyi, Elieth / Sheen, Veronica / Herrmann, Peter (eds.), 2010: Global Crossroads in Social Welfare – Emergent Issues, Debates and Innovations across the Globe; Bremen: Europaeischer Hochschulverlag: 151-164

Herrmann, Peter/Dorrity, Claire, 2009: Critique of Pure Individualism; in: Dorrity, Claire/Herrmann, Peter [eds.]: Social Professional Activity: The Search for a Minimum Common Denominator in Difference; New York: Nova

Herrmann, Peter/van der Maesen, Laurent, 2008: Social Quality and Precarity: Approaching new Patterns of Societal (Dis-)Integration; MPRA Paper No. 10245, posted 31. August 2008/08:49; http://mpra.ub.uni-muenchen.de/10245/1/MPRA_paper_10245.pdf - 02/01/2010 11:02 a.m.

Hibbert, Christopher, 1975: The House of Medici: Its Rise and Fall; New York: Morrow; Hale, John Rigby, 2001: London: Phoenix

Jessop, Bob, 2000: From the KMNS to the SWPR; in: Lewis, Gail/Gewirtz, Sharon/Clarke, John (eds.); Rethinking Social Policy; London et altera: Sage: 171-184

Jessop, Bob: State Theory. Putting Capitalist States in their Place; Cambridge: Polity Press in association with Basil Blackwell, 1990: 308

Kondratiev, Nicolai D.: 1926; Long Cycles of Economic Conjuncture; in: Kondratiev, Nicolai D.: The Works of Nicolai D. Kondratiev. Volume 1: Economic Statics, Dynamics and Conjuncture; London: Pickering&Chatto, 1998: 25-63

Marshall Plan; on Wikipedia. The Free Encyclopaedia; http://en.wikipedia.org/wiki/Marshal_plan – 02/01/2010 11:13 a.m.

Marx, Karl, 1957: Introduction (to the Economic Manuscripts of 1857-1858 [First Version of Capital]); in: Karl Marx. Frederick Engels. Collected Works; Volume 28: Karl Marx: 1857-61; London: Lawrence & Wishart, 1986

Mennell, Stephen1989/1998: Nobert Elias. An Introduction; Dublin: University College Dublin Press

Steinberg, Philip E., 2009: Sovereignty, Territory, and the Mapping of Mobility: A View from the Outside; in: Annals of the Association of American Geographers; 99, 3, 467-495

Tönnies, Ferdinand, 1887/1912: Community and society/translated and edited by Charles P. Loomis. New York: Harper Torchbooks 1963

Wallestein, Immanuel, 1995: After Liberalism; New York: The New Press

Zuern, Michael/Leibfried, Stephan: A New Perspective on the State. Reconfiguring the National Constellation; in: European Review, Vol. 13, Supp. No. 1, 1–36 [2005]: 1-36

CSR – Corporate Social Responsibility versus Citizens Social Rights
Or: On Regaining Political Economy[53]

Peter Herrmann[54]

Abstract

The following wants to sketch some considerations on Corporate Social Responsibility in a ore philosophical perspective and the perspective of the principal positioning of the concept in regard of societal development. The concept is high on the agenda, suggesting a shift to a more comprehensive and 'holistic' understanding of entrepreneurial activities. However, in actual fact the concept can well be understood as step back, providing some selective changes, however principally shifting away from extending social rights.

The present contribution approaches the topic in a more fundamental way by looking at the economic shifts that are re-establishing looking for structural conditions in which the debate on Corporate Social Responsibility has to be located.

Setting the Framework

Corporate social responsibility is en vogue – roughly speaking it is especially since the middle of the 1990s an upcoming issue within the European Union. And here I am not speaking of the term in the strict sense. Rather, we can see at this time a shift marked by a fundamental tension:

1) On the one hand, neo-liberalism made its way. It had been the time not necessarily of massive neo-liberal action. More important is that we find the ideology of privatism and individualism striking firm roots.

---

[53] I am grateful for comments and inspiration from Grażyna O'Sullivan and Zsuzsa Ferge.

[54] In parts largely revised version of a draft version which had been published as William-Thompson Working Paper CSR – CSA – CSO: Responsibility, Accountability, Organisation or: On Regaining Political Economy; http://www.ucc.ie/en/socialpolicy/WilliamThompsonWorkingPapers/WT_WP-18_Herrmann_CSR.pdf - 03/01/2010 12:10 p.m.

2) On the other hand it had been the time of an ongoing crisis of the system. Exceptional conditions characterising the development after WWII, the early upswing of European integration and consolidation of the global hegemonic structure could not be maintained. In terms of Kondratjev-waves, we are now facing a phase B, i.e. a downturn. This includes the oil-crisis and a subsequent shift which manifested itself as energy and 'environmental' crisis. And it includes the depreciation of production through the rapid development of information technology. The move forward which had been established for some time by IT-industries could not be maintained as establishing a lasting u-turn towards an A-phase of the Kontradtjevian model. We can speak of hegemonic waves, the societal patterns that allow for at least some time socio-political reproduction despite existing contradictions. However, in this respect we are facing as well a downturn, to some extent directly linked, to some extent somewhat secular. The patterns of justification and legitimation are breaking away on the national and also the international level of world-orders.

We cannot further explore the complex developmental pattern. Importantly, this meant the emergence of a tension, urgently waiting for an answer. Again, only part of this can be presented here – proving to be important for the question of corporate social responsibility.

We can start with the crisis of the legitimacy of the European Union, especially noticeable at the end of the 1980. Leaving the discussion of the reasons aside, we can briefly point on two issues: the highly bureaucratic system of the EU couldn't have convincing results in terms of what became known as the Monnet-method of European integration: the idea that people would grow together from the bottom up, emerge as demos by close cooperation and developing mutual understanding. The reality had been a distant bureaucracy: 'Europe in Brussels', characterised by an inscrutable bureaucracy and represented by frequently Kafkaesque decisions. We can leave aside if and to which extent this picture reflects the reality – at least it defined the perception of many people who would soon gain formally the status of European citizens. And this perception had been underlined by a second feature – one that can surely be seen as reality: the process of European integration was and is led by a specific economic model. It claims a strong reference to the social market economy, is in actually fact however, dominated by a neoliberal approach. Though this does not foster monopolisation in the strict sense, it supports a reality that fosters a particular division of labour. SMEs play a major role in the entire economic process – from production to marketing; but at the same time two factors prevail: (i) the overall economy – as accumulation regime – is structurally based on large enterprises; (ii) on the micro level we find that the important role of SMEs is qualified by their subordinated position for instance as suppliers and subcontractors. It has also to be noted that this is not fundamentally changed by the shift from Fordist to post-Fordist (or post-Taylorist) restructuration of production.

It is also important to see this shift within the general framework of a globalising economy: though a large part production in the sense of construction/manufacturing had been relocated, being now based for instance in South American and Asian Countries, this did not change the image of Western industries towards 'socially clean industries'. On the contrary, issues arose around child labour and extreme exploitation, often widely publicised. An additional point had been what we may call a 'consolidated critique' of enterprises. This continued a critique of practice of some main enterprises and conglomerates during history – by and large these critiques have to be seen as part and parcel of the 'world-revolution from the 1960s', not least criticising the aggressiveness of many corporations during WWII and as well in connection with the Vietnam war and when it came to developing answers to the requests of the new movements.

In the longer run, this went hand in hand with developing consumer expectations or consumer consciousness in the vein of what Ronald Inglehart called the 'silent revolution', taking place after the noisy revolution of the 60s. A changing work ethos in respect of the 'meaning of work', protection of the environment, and the increasing awareness of 'poverty in the one world' – the emphasis laid on the need of poverty eradication but also on one world. Although to some extent being disputed, another factor had been a new push in secularisation: we find at least a remarkable push towards accepting and demanding taking responsibility for 'human action in this one world and on this one planet and its future generation'. In short, we find some kind of new awareness of time and space.

This sketches the background for steps taken by the EUropean institutions, some cornerstones being:

- the White Paper on Growth, Competitiveness, Employment: The Challenges and Ways Forward into the 21st Century (European Commission, 1993 (b)

- the White Paper on European Social Policy – A Way Forward for the Union – A White Paper (European Commission, 1994) and possibly more important the discussion on the preceding Green Paper – European Social Policy - Options for the Union (European Commission, 1993 (a)

- the debate on services of general interest and deregulation and finally privatisation of network industries (see for the official EU-positions:
http://ec.europa.eu/services_general_interest/index_en.htm - 29/11/2009 6:00 p.m.)

- finally the White Paper on European Governance (European Commission, 2001).

Important is the complex overall strategy rather than the individual steps and measures. If looking at the individual steps in such a wide perspective, we come across a shift away from the traditional and widely accepted rigid forms and borders. In political terms, the old pattern of democracy had been questioned in some way. The accepted division of power and more importantly the simple and sole principle of representative democracy had been seen in a new light as limited. It had been a question of extent but more importantly it had been seen as matter of a limited depth of traditional patterns. Governance rather than governing, the entire process from needs evaluation over decision-making to implementation has been seen as equal parts of the political process. With this a reconsideration of citizenship had also been required. And in economic terms, we find a seemingly highly paradoxical situation: on the one hand we see the orientation towards a strict application of market rules. It is important to note the politico-economic side of this shift, the 'social meaning'. Rather than assessing it as matter of simple economisation, the more important point had been the kind of economic model that had been fostered: a purely individualist model. On the other hand we see the call for a more comprehensive understanding of what economic activities are about: speaking pathetically, they had been seen as means to an end other than profit maximisation. (i) The economic actor has been seen as individual being responsible not (only) for generating profit but also for a wider field in which s/he had been acting; and (ii) it had been about seeing the economic acts as part of a wide socio-environmental setting.

This had been a paradox with respect to the question of individual and social responsibility: one could see all this as process of individualising the social. And it had been also a matter of voluntarising this process: the structural dimension had been left very much one of segmented decision making, the claim for socio-political orientation had been one of holistic orientation. However, it had not been a paradox insofar the reality of the need to reintegrate segregated realities had been more or less accurately reflected. The new individual – and also the new socio-economic model could only enhance productivity if it considered the internalisation of various – previously social – functions.

Determining the Actor Perspective

Individualisation had been defined as major overall determinant or even goal of the design of the current system. Individual development is in itself and for itself seen as means and end of development. The other way round, the economy is not considered as being condition of soci(et)al development nor is the development of individuals seen as condition and contribution to economic development. As such, individualisation appears to be a socio-economic process. However, hand in hand goes another – though parallel – view, namely the reinterpretation of the enterprise as economic actor not as individual but as corporation. Taking a standard definition of Wikipedia, we can refer to a corporation as

> *a legal entity separate from the shareholders and employees. In British tradition it is the term designating a body corporate, where it can be either a corporation sole (an office held by an individual natural person, which is a legal entity separate from that person) or a corporation aggregate (involving more persons). In American and, increasingly, international usage, the term denotes a body corporate formed to conduct business, and this meaning of corporation is discussed in the remaining part of this entry (the limited company in British usage).*

> *(Governance, 2009)*

It may be worthwhile noting that reference is made to the British tradition – we will come back to this at a later stage.

It is important to note an ambivalence of the argument that is arising from the perspective outlined above: It is the individual that is seen as independent and self-sustaining actor – this is the core of 'individualised society' (a contradiction in itself). Then individuality – in terms of sustenance, development and satisfaction – has as well a norm-setting role. This suggests that subsequently social norms are secondary and remaining external and abstract. One can go a step further and say that the social is bereaved from its actor perspective.

But – in contradiction – the social is constituted by 'immoral actors', i.e. actors that are in actual fact inhuman (mind: not inhumane). This follows in a way from the same pattern: It suggests that subsequently social norms are secondary and remaining external and abstract. Corporate social responsibility remains a logical impossibility, as a corporation cannot have any responsibility. Edward Coke a legal scientist rejects in 1612 corporations as they

> *cannot commit treason, nor be outlawed or excommunicated, for they have no souls.*
>
> *(quoted in: Guide, 2009)*

Its reference for responsibility is its own functioning, the maintenance of self-reference. In a perspective from systems theory, corporations as systems can include the environment only as reference for maintenance, and this means to include other systems in three ways:

- other systems may present a demand factor: they deliver their products to the environment without, however, allowing the environment to determine the character of the product;

- other systems may present a supply factor, i.e. the corporation depends on the conditions in which it can actually produce – the most important factor is surely the availability of factors of the productive process;

- finally, other systems may present a disruptive factor and source of irritation – reaching from being a background noise to appearing as acute intervention;

The interesting point is that it is indeed obvious that social factors are appearing within the corporation itself, i.e. the system, (i) as external factors that are (ii) defined in subjective forms. This external character may define and redefine to some extent the conditions for the functioning of the corporation. And it may also define and redefine to some extent as well the internal frame of reference.

However, it does not define or redefine the

> *[f]ive common characteristics of the modern corporation ... :*
>
> - *delegated management, in other words, control of the company placed in the hands of a board of directors*
>
> - *limited liability of the shareholders (so that when the company is insolvent, they only owe the money that they subscribed for in shares)*
>
> - *investor ownership, which Hansmann and Kraakman take to mean, ownership by shareholders. ...*
>
> - *separate legal personality of the corporation (the right to sue and be sued in its own name)*
>
> - *transferrable shares (usually on a listed exchange, such as the London Stock Exchange, New York Stock Exchange or Euronext in Paris)*
>
> *(Corporation, 2009; reference to Kraakman/Hansman et altera, 2004)*

And this supports again the interpretation of corporations as non-responsible actors – in this way even less than being irresponsible actors.

CSR – American versus European Dream?[55]

The American dream is defined by James Truslow Adam, 1931 as

> *that dream of a land in which life should be better and richer and fuller for everyone, with opportunity for each according to ability or achievement. It is a difficult dream for the European upper classes to interpret adequately, and too many of us ourselves have grown weary and mistrustful of it. It is not a dream of motor cars and high wages merely, but a dream of social order in which each man and each woman shall be able to attain to the fullest stature of which they are innately capable, and be recognized by others for what they are, regardless of the fortuitous circumstances of birth or position.*
>
> *(Adam, 1931)*

---

[55] Thanks for a comment by Brigitte Kratzwald on an earlier version. On that ground I made some changes, aiming on clarifying that there should not be any doubt on the meaning of CSR in different contexts. The concept can surely not be justified in the USA whereas it would be problematic in the European context. On the contrary, contextualising it in these two ways should allow an even more critical general assessment.

Milton Friedman stated in 1962

> *Few trends could so thoroughly undermine the very foundations of our free society as the acceptance by corporate officials of a social responsibility other than to make as much money for their stockholders as possible.*

> *(Friedman, 1962)*

At the end, all this points on fundamental questions concerned with two issues:

- the actors and
- the guiding values.

We may find a more or less fundamental difference between the American and the European dream, importantly starting from the definition of the actor perspective – though it may be disputed how far it actually is really a fundamental difference. In both cases we see a radical individualism – as had been shown, the social is somewhat externalised, confronting the individual as 'external entity'. However, on the one hand we see this as abstract set of values. It is not surprising that the American Declaration of Independence refers in some way to a theocracy. Then, the paradox of American individualism is actually an exceedingly strong emphasis of individual responsibility and on the other hand, however, it is responsibility towards God rather than the individual's responsibility towards him/herself or/and society as such. Does it not follow logically that the entire concept of individualism is subsequently undermined? At least it is striking that in America

> *as a nation dedicated to the free pursuit of private property ... the legal protection bestowed to contracts and the transaction they represent has been extended to the corporation. In many countries at many points in history corporate charters have been frivolously rescinded and companies nationalized or seriously manipulated by government to the detriment of many and the benefit of a selected elite. However, the Supreme Court case Santa Clara v. Southern Pacific Railroad Co. – where the court overturned a local tax law of significant cost to the railroad and of dubious justification – set the precedent that a corporation is entitled to the same legal protection as are private citizens, and it expanded American companies' freedom for general practice and from undue regulation*

> *(Olowski, without date: 5)*

156

On the other hand we see an however abstract 'social' – the 'good society' – derived from people living together: making reference to this 'social' as point of departure for determining origin and objectives of togetherness. We can see it in the fundamental values guiding the French revolution of the 18th century: Liberté, Egalité, Fraternité. But we can also see this when looking at various strands of conceptualising the state. The European understanding is strongly linked to individualism and the fostering of this individualism. It is also strongly based on the confirmation of the right 'to the free pursuit of private property' as it had been mentioned before with reference to the American dream – all major theories from Hobbes, over Locke to Rousseau, to name but a few of the main paradigms are arguing in this line. However, because of this even the enlightened understanding of European Christianity cannot easily be interpreted as the hatching a theocracy.

This is surely an idealtypical confrontation; and the European dream is equally individualist as the American dream (see on the fundamental individualism for instance Herrmann/Dorrity, 2009; Herrmann, forthcoming (c); Herrmann, forthcoming (a)). Nevertheless, pointing on such difference is of crucial importance when it comes to understanding the problematique of applying the concept of CSR in a European context. The concept is definitely a child of American thinking.

It finds its idea in the republican understanding of democracy, predominantly to be characterised as society based on civic virtues – born from the will to independence rather than taking the positive imagination of a 'free future' as point of reference. We can read this by looking at Thomas Paine's work on the Common Sense where we first read that

> [t]he cause of America is in a great measure the cause of all mankind. Many circumstances hath, and will arise, which are not local, but universal, and through which the principles of all Lovers of Mankind are affected, and in the Event of which, their Affections are interested. The laying a Country desolate with Fire and Sword, declaring War against the natural rights of all Mankind, and extirpating the Defenders thereof from the Face of the Earth, is the Concern of every Man to whom Nature hath given the Power of feeling; of which Class, regardless of Party Censure, is the AUTHOR.

(Paine, 1776)

Interestingly, it follows a clear distinction between and separation of society and government:

Some writers have so confounded society with government, as to leave little or no distinction between them; whereas they are not only different, but have different origins. Society is produced by our wants, and government by our wickedness; the former promotes our POSITIVELY by uniting our affections, the latter NEGATIVELY by restraining our vices. The one encourages intercourse, the other creates distinctions. The first a patron, the last a punisher. (ibid.)

Independence – and this is getting especially clear then when we look at Alexis de Tocqueville (de Tocqueville, Alexis, 1835/1840)– is thus not solely and perhaps not even solely concerned with the independence from the 'old homeland'. Rather, centre-stage is the independence of the people as collaborative, deliberative entity. From here, the absolutism of a French Louis XIV or the state as collective and responsible entity is neither thinkable nor desirable. – One may turn such statement into different directions, one is that such kind of Republicanism is easily the final triumph of pure individualism

This marks a quite different stance than the European approach that follows very much the orientation of enlightenment, leaning to a rational system, not least strongly engaged with the principle of separation of power and the rule of law rather than tending to rely on communitarian grounds for which Cass R. Sunstein claims the idea of the public forum and the ideal of deliberative democracy as decisive (see Sunstein, 2007: 23 f.).

Its application in Europe has to be seen in this context: marking limitations for its applicability is one notion of the argument; and another notion can be made by pointing on the extent and depth to which we actually find patterns of Americanisation already flooding over Europe.

But the actual point is a different one, namely the fact that the concept of CSR is falling short of dealing properly with borders of systems. Rather than fundamentally reconceptualising the actor-system, it is maintained as self-referential system. The only change is happening in the following regards.

(i) To a smaller extent we find a shift of borders, slightly moving the external border more to the outside. This is for instance reflected in the following definition.

CSR involves a business identifying its stakeholder groups and incorporating their needs and values within the strategic and day-to-day decision making process.

(Guide ..., op.cit: 1)

The existing structure, however, remains untouched. This is very much reflected for instance in the European Commission's Green Paper which

> *calls on the European business community to publicly demonstrate its commitment to sustainable development, economic growth and more and better jobs, and to step up its commitment to CSR, including cooperation with other stakeholders. More then ever Europe needs active entrepreneurs, positive attitudes towards entrepreneurship, and confidence and trust in business. Europe needs a public climate in which entrepreneurs are appreciated not just for making a good profit but also for making a fair contribution to addressing certain societal challenges.*

(European Commission, 2006: 2)

(ii) In a more fundamental perspective this means as well that the problem of defining and producing externalities remains very much the same – a generic and factual integration cannot be found.

As far as we follow this argument, the first hurdle to be overcome when dealing with CSR is how to deal with accountability, i.e. how do we actually calculate production. The traditional understanding only deals with issues on the level of exchange and to some minor extent with issues of distribution. And it possibly deals with issues from other areas by isolating them from the overall process of production. In other words, it tackles social questions of manufacturing, consumption, distribution or exchange in isolation.

All this actually fits well into the thesis of re-feudalisation of society – a thesis which should not be understood only as repetition of certain apparent patterns of execution of power but more fundamentally as shift in the foundation of power (see in this context already Herrmann, forthcoming (b); Herrmann, 2009 (a)). Importantly it is about the shift within the economy from a production-based system to an exchanged-based system. As such we see that the political economy changes itself to a somewhat voluntarist basis. Capital that does not or cannot return into the productive process may temporarily be invested in good-doing but remains outside of a process of building a new formational pattern.

So the wider perspective must actually searched for in another dimension: if we agree with the statement of a principle loss of the link between territoriality and accumulation (see as well: Herrmann, forthcoming e and the Prolegomena in this volume: 8 ff.), we have to look subsequently for three dimensions of a newly emerging system:

- the accumulation regime,

- the mode of regulation,
- the new dimension of territoriality.

The importance of the latter aspect is commonly underestimated. Widely acknowledged is the loss of national sovereignty asserted for instance by Giovanni Arrighi in the words:

> *The modern inter-state system has thus acquired its present global dimension through successive hegemonies of increasing comprehensiveness, which have correspondingly reduced the exclusiveness of the sovereignty rights actually enjoyed by its members.*

(Arrighi, 1994/2002: 75)

Then the question is what kind of new system will gain a comparable integrative force, being able to replace the old hegemonies. Examples as the Bertelsmann-Foundation, the Bill and Melinda Gates Foundation or the Soros Foundation Network clearly show that the claim of CSR is in actual fact something different: the endeavour to gain direct and explicit socio-political power and control – candidates for being member of the new hegemonic institutional system or even the 'new princes' (see in the following not least Bauer, 2007 (a) and (b)).

A palpable example is the Case Study on the German Telecom and 'Schools Online' (SaN)',i.e. a project on Connecting German Schools to the Internet – a study presented by the Bertelsmann Foundation (see Peters, without date).

The general gist for this working area as presented on the Bertelsmann-website says as follows:[56]

> *Finally it is the well-understood own interest of the enterprises to participate in the sustainable formation of societal development.*[57]
>
> *(Bertelsmann Stiftung, without date (a): CSR Einblick; translation P. H.)*

---

[56] I refer to my own translation from the German site on 'CSR Einblick' (Bertelsmann Stiftung, without date (a)) – the gist provided by the English website 'What is CSR' (Bertelsmann Stiftung, without date (b)) is actually rather different (thought it is presented as translation).

[57] German original: Letztlich ist es im wohlverstandenen Eigeninteresse der Unternehmen, sich an der nachhaltigen Gestaltung gesellschaftlicher Entwicklung zu beteiligen. Official English translation: Ultimately, the business community itself benefits when society develops in a responsible, sustainable manner.

The background is seen in the appraisal that

> *[c]ompanies can contribute by their competences and resources to address urgent societal problems – nationally and also in carrying out their international activities.*[58]

(ibid.)

Looking at the entire statement – and this is not a surprising factor as the topic follows through self-assessment of entrepreneurs from Owen over Rathenau to Mohn and Porst is, of course, frequently issued in economics – the debate is concerned with the wider issue of asking for the 'social role' of the entrepreneur and moreover the role and function of the economy in society and even the definition of economic activity itself. The point in question is, however, also and in practice primarily concerned with the generation of huge power machineries that are dealing with much more than responsible action in terms of shaping activities in 'circumspect ways', considering wider social and environmental effects and longer time frames. Centre-stage we find the question of utilising 'socio-economic circumspection' as means to corporate power.

Looking against this background at the Case Study mentioned before can be taken as an extreme example of merging different industrial interests (e.g. media, IT, service provision), governmental/state with some societal interests in order to enhance a very specific SPIRIT – understood as 'Superior value, Passion for the customer, Innovation, Respect, Integrity, Top Excellence'.[59]

If we return from here to the confrontation of the American and the European dream we can clearly see that it is not about any justification of CSR for the US whereas it would be suggested as problematic only for

---

[58] German original: Unternehmen können mit ihren Kompetenzen und Ressourcen einen Beitrag leisten, drängende gesellschaftliche Probleme zu adressieren – hier wie auch im Rahmen ihrer internationalen Aktivitäten. Official English translation: Given its expertise and resources, Germany's business community can play a key role in addressing pressing social issues both at home and abroad.

[59] The report states: "Deutsche Telekom uses the word 'SPIRIT' to describe its six corporate values. As an acronym the letters stands for: Superior value, Passion for the customer, Innovation, Respect, Integrity, Top Excellence. The corporate values were inaugurated in 2003; at the same time the sustainability strategy of Deutsche Telekom was launched." (Peters, op.cit.: 9)
and makes us points out that "'Schools online' is one of seven projects listed under 'Corporate Citizenship' on the Telekom Website." (ibid.)

Europe. The point in question is a different one. It is about a different understanding of democracy. To bring it to the point we may idealtypically point on the following differentiating lines:

	AMERICAN DREAM	EUROPEAN DREAM
RESPONSIBILITY	Individualised	Individualised
ACCOUNTABILITY	Private	Public
POWER	Corporate[60]	Corporatist[61]
SOCIO-ECONOMIC SECURITY	Abstract notion – although as matter of charity and sympathetic solidarity and general interest guidance/public goods	\concrete – also as matter of public services and general interest services
COHESION	Tolerating – as matter of trust and reciprocity	Compensating – as matter of solidarity and integrative support
INCLUSION	Harmonious	Rights-Based
EMPOWERMENT	Libertarian	Negotiational

Table 16: American and European Dream – The Individual between Public and Private

The terms used and references made in the bottom part of the table would surely need reasonably extensive discussion in their own terms which cannot be undertaken here. They are surely, to make at least two points again clear, (i) only 'idealtypical notions'; (ii) and equally sure is that they should by any means not be understood as assessments – instead, seeing them more as heuristic instruments is more appropriate. This is even more true if we consider that the terms are rather vague and can (and are) actually used in both different dreams and with – in many cases – different understandings.

It is important to look at the fundamental limitation of any CSR-perspective that remains in the traditional veins of thinking responsibility and accountability as self-reflexive manner. As much as it may show positive effects in individual cases, it remains very much on a symbolic

---

[60] The 'good society' based in the aggregation of individual contracts lead by the invisible hand as safeguard of 'fair negotiation'

[61] The reference to a general interest based on social contracts based in corporatist negotiation of different interests.

level – to the same extent as the focus of exchange remains outside of the actual economic process which can only be understood as process of production.[62] Symbolic power is set within this context and finds its objective reason in the shift of the economic system. Important is that this shift away from the actual productive process means not least that the power structures are as well undertaking an important shift – away from the systems that grew out of enlightenment.[63] Rather than maintaining and elaborating these systems we find a return of charismatic leaders and the increasing meaning of symbolic power. It is the completion of the original liberal idea of the free individual, only responsible to him/herself, without the existence of any society, and in its sociability solely depending on the good will: the moral sentiments (Adam Smith) and the generalised trust (Robert D. Putnam). However, such view does of course not acknowledge the social character of the formation of the habitus and moreover the meaning of social practice. In his discussion of Pierre Bourdieu's work, Martii Siisiäinen states:

> *Practices are the result of the co-influence of 'objective structures' as manifested in the forms of prevailing alternatives at a certain moment in history, and the 'subjective structures' inside the habitus, manifested as dispositions directing the choices of the actor toward alternatives that are homological with the structures that have produced the habitus (causalité du probable) (Bourdieu 1977; 1974). Bourdieu stresses that the habitus cannot be reduced to structures because it is born as practices. It is creative and thus the reproduction of social structures is never one-to-one reproduction but extended and creative reproduction by the habitus (Bourdieu 1977). Bourdieu does not deny the existence of 'objective' structures and their influence on the formation of habitus, which, for its part, becomes the structuring structure leading via practices to the development of new structures.*

(Siisiäinen, 2000: 15)

The reason for this lengthy quote is simple – though the matter itself is anything else than this: whereas CSR refers to abstract normative

---

[62] This is even the case in today's systems where some see it as justified to speak of service economies. Even these service economies are production dependent and related: on the one hand they are services directly related to productive processes (e.g. transporting produced goods); on the other hand they are productive though not producing tangible goods.

[63] The limitations of these enlightened systems of modern democracy and their link to the 'bourgeois state' have not to be discussed here. Some interesting insight is given not least by Boccara, 1973; Jessop/Sum 2006

systems of some kind of general character, the reference to Pierre Bourdieu makes obvious that we are dealing with a contradicting field of practice. If we emphasise, different to Bourdieu, structures as strong framing condition rather than seeing it as more or less vaguely defined set of fields, we can see the systemic limitations: any re-formation of habitus needs to secure the re-formation of these structures and can be only successful if it can actually build on such changed structures.

This means, of course, that governance has as well a double meaning: it is concerned with opening political systems for new actors and it also means the (re-)introduction of a system of charismatic and more or less uncontrolled and uncontrollable system of power that lacks a proper system of checks and balances. Consequently, assessing voluntary mechanisms – in the same vein as assessing voluntary sector organisations – needs to fully recognise the ambiguity of the respective patterns of limited participation and the limitation of participation (see in this context as well Herrmann, 2009 b).

However, this necessitates revisiting the entire structure of the political economy: Sure, CSR as voluntary action may occasionally lead to social improvements. However, as concept it is likely to undermine the systematic progress of welfare state developments. This is not primarily due to its voluntary character. More important is the fact that is anchored in a systematic turn of the economic system, systematically ignoring the need of a productive basis of the development of social quality.

Accountability – Economics and Economy

One of the fundamental problems of CSR is its individualist bias. This has been explored before in a very fundamental way. It had been said that individualisation is nowadays defined as major overall determinant or even goal of the design of the current system and that individual development is in itself and for itself seen as means and end of development. This is also reflected in the microeconomic toehold of the concept. It is important as well in terms of the voluntary and political character into which it is commonly linked. The actual problem, however, is that the basic reference is chosen wrongly. It sees economic processes and decisions – on the micro- and also the macro-level – as independent, neutral and leaving aside that they are fundamentally and genuinely socio-political in character. The question can now be turned around. The problem is not primarily about the responsibility within the system, and looking within this framework for the accountability of the individual actors or at the corporate responsibility. Rather, we have to look at the character of the economy itself, defining the accountability of the system itself. Then the question is far reaching and requires focusing (i) on what and in which way production takes place and (ii) in which way the integrity of the overall economic process is seen.

So it is advisable to look not only at the concept of CSR as such but also at the wider context in order to determine the character of the economic process itself.

It had been stated already that the debate on CSR can be traced back a long time, going much further than the debate that directly refers to this term itself. At this stage it is meaningful to remember not least the White Paper on Growth, Competitiveness, Employment: The Challenges and Ways Forward into the 21st Century. In this paper, the question of the social economy plaid a rather substantial role – and in the following years it had been fundamentally re-interpreted. Starting from an already limited understanding of the social economy as economic actors in niches, the reading shifted increasingly towards its instrumentalisation as employment providers – the keyword being Third System.

However, in terms of a sound conceptualisation we have to overcome such orientation. So far it looks very much at establishing new and somewhat different corporations, each of them having a wider scope, shifting the borders further, but maintaining the basic functional references of the system. Looking at the debate on the social economy, however, allows developing an understanding that reaches further. Recalling the words from Edward Coke which had been quoted above, we have to work against an understanding of corporations that

> *cannot commit treason, nor be outlawed or excommunicated, for they have no souls.*
>
> *(in: Guide ..., op.cit. 5)*

So, the starting point is to look for an economy that takes as part of departure not a purely functionalist approach as it is assumed by any orientation on corporate actors. The suggested focus for the further orientation is twofold.

(i) We should be concerned with economy as matter of people working together and producing in this vein their own life and also the respective conditions.

(ii) We are concerned with a perspective on the economic system as such. However, rather than seeing this as a structural entity, guided by functional, value-neutral interests, it is understood as entity structured by different interests, and thus not least power questions and conflicts.

> *Corporatism is a system of economic, political, and social organization where corporate groups such as business, ethnic, farmer, labour, military, patronage, or religious groups are joined together into a single governing body in which the different groups are mandated to negotiate with each other to establish policies in the interest of the multiple groups within the body.[1] Corporatism views society as being alike to an organic body in which each corporate group is viewed as a necessary organ for society to function properly.[2] Corporatism is based on the sociological concept of functionalism.[3] Countries that have corporatist systems typically utilize strong state intervention to direct corporatist policies and to prevent conflict between the groups.[4]*

> *The word 'corporatism' is derived from the Latin word for body, corpus. This meaning was not connected with the specific notion of a business corporation, but rather a general reference to anything collected as a body.*

> *Corporatism has been supported from various proponents, including: absolutists, capitalists, conservatives, fascists, progressives, reactionaries and theologians.[5]*

> *(Corporatism, 2009)*

The same is actually true within the corporation. If they are seen as 'body', as the etymology suggests, they are entities in which different interests come together and have to find a balance. As much as any body is an entity, it is concerned with its own maintenance. And equally it is limited to a functional equilibrium that exists only in a temporary limited span. The environment only functions as background noise, as externality. As such it is not genuine part of coporate considerations.

On one level, questions around the economic system are surely concerned with values. However, these values are not primarily a matter of subjective valuation but of relation. In this light we have to look at responsibility as matter of responding to reality – and this is not least a matter of acknowledging the changed and permanently changing reality: the existing opportunities as matter of technical and technological development and also the recognition of rights – their 'qualitative extension' and also the acknowledgement of their universality (see in this context as well Herrmann, forthcoming (d)). It is important to note this against the background of the voluntary character of CSR in relevant documents: CSR is suggested as set of additional and voluntary measures. Such interpretation, however, contradicts fundamentally such view that responsibility is about answering an objective reality.

We actually have to move on to a different perspective on economy and the economic system as such. Veli-Matti Poutanen mentions four aspects that are frequently referred to in European debates on the social economy which are as well relevant for our context. (Activities by) Enterprises of the social economy are characterised by: (i) the economic and social 'usefulness', (ii) the orientation on well-being within and outside of working life; (iii) the requirement to structure the economic process to support democracy and the full participation of the various actors; (iv) a certain independence of the operation of the economic entity in order to enable the fulfilment of their genuinely own goals (see Poutanen, 2009: 11). He concludes his further discussion by underlining the definition brought forward by Niina Immonen:

> The social economy is the economic operation carried on by co-operatives carried on by co-operatives, mutual companies, associations and foundations, the objectives of which is to promote [.] the democratic co-operation and economically and socially lasting welfare of the surrounding community.

> (Immonen, 2006: 12)

Although this seems to be a different debate, namely that on social economy, it marks the need for reformulating the reference point not of responsibility but of accountability: it is about accounting the overall internal and external setting. As such it is actually not about the reduction of externalising costs but it is about the reduction of externalities. And this is a process that has to redefine fundamentally the borders of the enterprise but moreover it has to redefine the understanding of the economic process itself by emphasising the fact that the economy is a socio-processual relationship not as matter of a different interpretation but by its different organisation. Coming back to the etymological reference that looks at corporations as bodies, the challenge is to redefine these bodies rather than redefining the way of how an existing body acts.

An interesting perspective is then opened by looking at (enterprises of) the social economy. They provide probably the closest realisation of the claim of understanding the social economy as socio-organisational structure that applies a wide understanding of what profitability is, going beyond any restricted understanding of monetary measurement and also aiming on integrating the different elements of the productive process, i.e. 'manufacturing'/'constructing, consumption, distribution and exchange. Rather than discussing this in depth, the following quote provides an interesting inside of the actual meaning of such orientation. It refers to the performance of cooperatives during the crisis and comes from a study from CICOPA, the International Organisation of Industrial, Artisanal and Service Producers' Cooperatives.

> *CECOP members do not indicate any closing down among their affiliated cooperatives so far. We can consider this good performance of cooperatives as a result of their capacity to combine security and flexibility while pursuing their mission of creating sustainable jobs. In particular cooperatives are characterized by the capacity to modernize their products, services or production processes while at the same time they show their ability to substantially modify their production line or services which are crucial skills especially under the threat of the current global financial crisis.*

> *(CICOPA, 2009: 2)*

We can now come back on the question of the voluntary character of CSR as it is usually suggested for instance in the statements of the European Commission as one major driver of this concept in the EU. In the perspective taken here, the common concepts fall short in answering the fundamental character of the challenge. In many cases they are not much else than (i) means of 'social sponsoring' (though in a wider sense) and (ii) the reduction of costs arising from a temporary externalisation (production of externalities and their later return into the company). The need for the actual reorientation of the economic process and within this: of 'production' itself, does not play a role. The concept easily depraves to a vehicle for meals: the famous and surely in instances useful meals on wheels rather than providing a means that fosters the orientation of the economic process as matter that has to be linked to citizens' social rights. The other way round the point gets clearer: it is about establishing a new rulership that is based on political power rather than economic power in the strict sense. The economic power itself is derived from gaining hegemony over distributional processes rather than the production of values. The vision of the new princedoms of Microsoft, Wal-Mart, Bertelsmann, Tata and not least google, apparent as 'non-enterprise', indexing and mapping the world, new princedoms united with the world leaders in negotiations of the G8, G20, IMF and World Bank, and showing responsibility by gracious gestures of following Bono's plea to fight poverty by donation (http://www.live8live.com - 03/01/2010 12:08 p.m.).

Responsibility versus Organisation?

From what had been said, it should be clear that on the other level, i.e. when it comes to going beyond value dimensions, questions around the economic system are surely concerned with factors that go far beyond including normative factors into the balance sheet. We need to redefine the understanding of the economy and the respective actors themselves; and with this we have to overcome the individualist orientation of the interpretation of society. Now we can take up the reference which had been made to the social economy and go a step further by emphasising the concept's strong connection to the economy of the social in terms of widening the understanding of social policy. Veli-Matti Poutanen highlights with Ari Nieminen as four

> *main sectors of the economic sociology ... 1) social and cultural preconditions for the economy 2) consequences of the economy, 3) ... the economy as such 4) and study of the interaction of different institutions*
>
> *(Poutanen, 2009: 16 f.; with reference to Nieminen, 1996: 104)*

However, we have to move a step further, highlighting the need to develop the integrity of such a perspective. Corporate Social Responsibility will fail as long as it is not concerned with a fundamental change of the corporation and its external borders. And the latter requires as well a fundamental reorganisation of the accountability of the economic system itself.

Before reference to the Anglo-Saxon tradition had been en passent noted and we can come back to this by way of conclusion. The Anglo-Saxon tradition is not least characterised by its utilitarian shift in the interpretation of enlightenment. It is in this way as well that CSR, as it is mainly understood in a limiting individualist vein, actually opposes the claims of the European Model.

From Where We Come – To Where We Go?

In conclusion some points may be highlighted as pointing on some major issues in the understanding the concept and also in terms of developing a perspective. These are put forward in two groups, namely 1) locating the concept in the historical and socio-economic setting and 2) looking at the current conceptual difficulties in practice an application.

Locating the Concept

The following four points are decisive to locate the concept in order to avoid a structurally limited understanding of CSR. (i) Capitalism, though of course a social formation, is genuinely oriented along the lines of individualism. It defines itself as geared towards the development of individuals as sole decision maker, competition as driving force of social relationships. In this way it establishes its formative tension as aiming on denying a genuine sociability. Social responsibility, one may say, is structurally ruled out.

Subsequently, the loss of the commons as guiding the moral standard appears as having a much more central role as the frequently deplored loss of communitarian spirit.

The offered solution: the ex-post internalisation of morals – completely following the tradition outlined by classical economics, must remain misleading. Adam Smith, for instance, can be said to have reinterpreted the economy as management of the household by transforming it from a social into a technical process. Rather than leaving the definition of the 'good life' inside the household-economy we find it now outside, coming into play as invisible hand that lost its own steering capacity and is – occasionally forced to fall back on moral sentiments.

Taking this as background, the answer on the question of corporate social responsibility versus citizens' social rights has to ask not least the very generic question of the societal structure. Put differently, are we looking for a better capitalism or for a better society? A strict corporatist view suggests that there is no such thing as society, the alternative R. Edward Freeman and Jeanne Liedtka put forward, appears to be a logical fallacy. They state:

> However, after examining the 'good society' that capitalism has created – the damage to the environment, the hunger and homelessness that exist even in wealthy areas of the world - can anyone today (even Milton Friedman) really believe that the pursuit of self interest has culminated in the common good? The alternative to capitalism as we know it is not socialism, but a better form of capitalism – one that recognizes the existence of the commons and acts to prevent the single-minded individualism capable of destroying it.

(Freeman/Liedtka, 1991: 93)

170

If society is reduced on competing individual actors and if corporations are in this context defined as 'a legal entity separate from the shareholders and employees' (see above), we have to emphasise again that the actual concern is the reflexive and circular character of corporate action. In turn, this indisputably limits as well the application of surely in many cases well-meant measures under this heading.

Assessing Its Application

In many cases the concept is not more than changing the wrapping for measures that are nothing else than 'advertisement' or a simple matter of labelling basic rules of human behaviour. (Social) Sponsoring and advertisement and (reasonably) good manners apparently deserve in the meantime in the eyes of some this new label.

A second trend is that the label of corporate social responsibility is now (ab)used when certain kinds of investment are discussed and investment aiming on increasing productivity is considered as led by the interest of the employees rather than acknowledging the fact that the 'social character' is merely more than a possible positive side-effect.

The problem becomes obvious when we reach the point of possible relative disadvantage due to costs incurred by relevant measures. Answering this challenge depends on a redefinition of responsibility in the said context – and thus it requires the redefinition of the point of reference. Rather than referring to reproduction of the self-reflexive system of the corporation,[64] we are now urged to refer to the rights of citizens. The question of covering costs gets now surely as well profoundly a matter of (re-)distribution. And doing good stands now against the extension and defence of social rights which have to be secured by a new organisation of economic processes and economic actors.

– Altruism in the name of corporate maintenance cannot be a tool against accountability for social progress.

---

[64] Though such reproduction may mean extended reproduction.

References

Adam, James Truslow, 1931:
http://memory.loc.gov/learn/lessons/97/dream/thedream.html - 24/11/2009 7:17 a.m.

Arrighi, Giovanni, 1994/2002: The Long Twentieth Century; London/New York, Verso: 75

Boccara, Paul, 1973: Études sur le capitalisme monopoliste d'État, sa crise et son issue, Paris: Éditions sociales

Bourdieu, Pierre, 1974: Avenir de Classe et Causalité du Probable; in: Revue Française de Sociologie, 15, 3: 3-42

Bourdieu, Pierre, 1977: Outline of a Theory of Practice; New York: University of Cambridge Press

CICOPA: The impact of the crisis on worker and social cooperatives; Brussels, July 2009: 2 - http://www.cecop.coop/public_docs/RaportCriseEN.pdf; 08/12/2009 7:15 a.m.

Corporation, 2009: http://en.wikipedia.org/wiki/Corporation - 20/11/2009 7:25 a.m.

Corporatism, 2009: http://en.wikipedia.org/wiki/Corporatism - 20/11/2009 7:30 a.m.

European Commission, 1993 (a): Green Paper – European Social Policy - Options for the Union; Brussels, November; (COM[93] 551)

European Commission, 1993 (b): White Paper on Growth, Competitiveness, Employment: The Challenges and Ways Forward into the 21st Century; Brussels December (COM[93] 700)

European Commission, 1994: White Paper on European Social Policy – A Way Forward for the Union - A White Paper; (COM[94] 333, July)

European Commission, 2001: White Paper on European Governance; Brussels: July; (COM[2001] 428, July).

European Commission, 2006: Communication Implementing the Partnership for Growth and Jobs: Making Europe a Pole of Excellence on Corporate Social Responsibility; Brussels 22.3.2006; (COM[2006] 136 fin.)

European Commission: services of general interest and deregulation and finally privatisation of network industries (see for the official EU-positions: http://ec.europa.eu/services_general_interest/index_en.htm - 29/11/2009 6:00 p.m.)

Freeman, R. Edward/Liedtka, Jeanne, 1991: Corporate social responsibility: a critical approach – corporate social responsibility no longer a useful concept. In: Business Horizons, July-August

Friedman, Milton, 1962: Capitalism and Freedom; Chicago: University of Chicago Press

Governance, 2009: http://en.wikipedia.org/wiki/Corporation - 20/11/2009 7:25 a.m.

Guide, 2009: A guide to corporate Social Sustainability: 5; www6.miami.edu/ethics/pdf_files/csr_guide.pdf - 29/11/2009 6:03 p.m.

Herrmann, Peter, 2009 (a): Godless Laws or Lawless Gods – Islam, Fundamentalism and the Economic Crisis; William Thompson Working Papers, 14; Cork/Aghabullogue - http://www.ucc.ie/en/socialpolicy/WilliamThompsonWorkingPapers/DocumentF ile,67425,en.pdf; 29/11/2009 8:31 p.m.

Herrmann, Peter, 2009 (b): Multilevel Governance – Participatory Democracy and Civil Society's Role in Governance in the Perspective of the Lisbon Treaty; in: Current Politics and Economics of Europe; New York: Nova

Herrmann, Peter, 2012 (a): God, Rights, Law and a Good Society. Overcoming Religion and Moral as Social Policy Approach in a Godless and Amoral Society; Bremen: Europaeischer Hochschulverlag

Herrmann, Peter, 2012 (b): Human Rights: For Sale or Saviour in the Globalising Market Economy; in: Herrmann, Peter, forthcoming: God, Rights, Law and a Good Society. Overcoming Religion and Moral as Social Policy Approach in a Godless and Amoral Society; Bremen:Europaeischer Hochschulverlag: 132-148

Herrmann, Peter, forthcoming (c): Searching for Global Social Policy – Economy, Economics and Governance (working title)

Herrmann, Peter, 2012 (d): Science – Social Science – Practice or: Searching for Responsibility; in: Herrmann, Peter, 2012 (a): God, Rights, Law and a Good Society. Overcoming Religion and Moral as Social Policy Approach in a Godless and Amoral Society; Bremen: Europaeischer Hochschulverlag: 2-69

Herrmann, Peter, forthcoming (e): Unbalancing the Economy – Unbalancing the Social; in: Hepp, Rolf [ed.]: Precarity and Flexibility [working title]

Herrmann/Dorrity, 2009: Critique of Pure Individualism; in: Dorrity, Claire/ Herrmann, Peter [eds.]: Social Professional Activity – The Search for a Minimum Common Denominator in Difference; New York: Nova Science

Immonen, Niina, 2006: Yhteisötalous Suomessa. Sisäpiirin slangia vai uutta yhteistyön taloutta. Tampereen Seudun Osuustoiminnan Kehittämisyhdistys ry.: Tampere

Jessop, Bob/Sum, Ngai-Ling, 2006: Beyond the Regulation Approach Putting Capitalist Economies in their Place. Cheltenham: Edward Elgar

Kraakman, Reinier H./Hansman, Henry et altera, 2004: The anatomy of corporate law: a comparative and functional approach; Oxford: Oxford University Press

Nieminen, Ari, 1996: Miten analysoida talouden ja yhteiskunnan muutosta. Teoksessa heikki Niemelä, Juho Saari ja Kari Salminen (toim.) Sosiaalipolitiikan teoreettisia lähtökohtia. Sosiaalitaloudellinen näkökulma. Kansaneläkelaitos. Sosiaali- ja terveysturvan katsauksia 18. Kelan omatarvepaino: Helsinki, sivut 95–130

Olowski, Lew Jan, without date: Corporate Social Responsibility: Its history, Ethical Justification and Abuses in the Business World; http://www.rockhurst.edu/news/events/images/projecti/olowski.pdf -30/11/2009 11:52 a.m.

Paine, Thomas, 1776: Common Sense; Editor Foner, Philip S.; The Complete Writings of Thomas Paine, Vol. I; http://www.thomaspaine.org/Archives/commonsense.html - 27/06/2010 6:41 a.m.

Poutanen, Veli-Matti, 2009: From Social Economy to Social Economics. Diverse Discussion on Social Economy in Finland; Presentation in 2nd International CIRIEC Research Conference on the Social Economy; October 1 - 2 2009, Östersund, Sweden; Manuscript

Putnam, Robert, 2000: Bowling Alone; New York: Simon&Schuster

Siisiäinen, Martii, 2000: Two Concepts of Social Capital: Bourdieu vs. Putnam. Paper presented at the ISTR Fourth International Conference 'The Third Sector: For What and for Whom?' Trinity College Dublin, Ireland, July 5-8, 2000 – http://www.istr.org/conferences/dublin/workingpapers/siisiainen.pdf - 30/11/2009 2:02 p.m.

Sunstein, Cass R., 2007: Republic. Comm. 2.0; Princeton: Princeton University Press

Tocqueville, Alexis de, 1835/1840: Democracy in America; translated by Henry Reeve; edited with an introduction by Henry Steele Commager; London: Oxford University Press, 1946

Precarity and Responsibility – Techniques of Governing the Neoliberal 'Consumer-Subject'?

Brigitte Kratzwald

Abstract

During the last 30 years we have been facing shifts in the global economic system, often referred to as 'neoliberal globalisation'. This process can be characterised as a shift from production to circulation and exchange as the main sphere of capital accumulation (cf. Herrmann à p.6) that comes along with shifts in the mode of production as well as in the mode of regulation and the role of states and governments. In the last decade not only intensification but also new specifications and new lines of conflicts and ruptures can be observed as part of this process. Some authors like Biebricher (2008: 318) or Brand/Sekler (2009) speak of 'Post-neoliberalism' to refer to these 'social, political and/or economic transformations of shifting terrains of social struggles and compromises' (Brand/Sekler 2009a: 6). Though one might question if neoliberalism is really coming to an end, one can hardly deny that, in the last decade, neoliberal policies were fiercely challenged by the 'five crises of neoliberal financial market capitalism': an over-accumulation crisis, crises of ecological and social reproduction, a crisis of social integration, a crisis of democratic legitimation and a security crises (cf. Brie 2009: 20-22). The agents of neoliberalism are confronted with increasing critique and resistance from social movements, NGOs and scientists and in search for regaining their legitimation often co-opt arguments of their critics to enhance their credibility.

Some features observed in this context are an increasing precarisation of living conditions for an increasing number of people, a degradation of social rights and as a consequence the growing dependency on individual good will, the reliance on individual moral behaviour instead of binding laws and a weakening of democratic structures of the national state in favour of – often supranational – governance processes with more arbitrary modes of participation, all together showing signs of a kind of 're-feudalisation' of society (cf. Herrmann, in this volume: 134).

Against this background this text takes a Foucauldian perspective of governmentality, considering that shifts in the mode of production and mode of regulation and especially the mentioned 're-feudalisation' are very likely to go along with a new rationality of governing. From this

175

point of view precarity, the responsibilisation of individuals, new modes of participation in governance processes, etc. appear as changes in governmental techniques aiming on governmental techniques aiming on governing individuals from the distance (cf. Rose 1996: 43). The hypothesis of this text is that within the last decade – and enforced by the crises of the last years – a new mode of governmentality has developed in western Europe, turning from the main discourses of competition and human capital to a strong discourse of individual moral responsibility. Thus the 'responsible consumer' emerges as the new mode of subjectivation, substituting - or at least modifying - the 'enterprising self' of the first period of Neoliberalism. Referring to autonomist Marxism these transformations of governmentality can be understood as results of social struggles (cf. de Angelis 2007: 3). This perspective eventually opens the possibility to discuss the meaning of current shifts in governmentality for further political action.

Introduction

The implementation of Neoliberalism since the 70s of the 20th century usually is seen as a shift of the economic paradigm, away from Keynesianism leading to a withdrawal of the state and a loss of state power against an increasing power of economic actors, especially international organisations and transnational corporations. Brand, however, emphasises that we are not facing a loss of power or a withdrawal of the state but an 'internationalisation of the state' and the development of 'transnational state apparatuses' (cf. Brand 2007: 12f.) to manage global conflicts and problems. This does not mean that some kind of global empire is emerging, but rather, that national states on the one hand get involved in international competition for power and influence in those international organisations and on the other hand national politics are deeply influenced by these global power struggles and relations and thus national states themselves and their institutions are transformed into 'National Competition States' (Hirsch 2002: 110). In this position 'the nation state has been instrumental in creating global market discipline' (de Angelis 2007: 113). National power relations and the modes of socio-economic reproduction on national level get closely linked to global economic processes.

> *It is not only that, in particular, the capital itself is transnational, but also that the requirements which are mediated by the world market, as well as the related interests and relations of forces, are interiorized into specific local and national constellations. This becomes clear*

> *when the trade unions are called to accept cuts in wages in order to*
> *guarantee the competitiveness of a production site (Brand 2007: 17).*

Similarly Araghi states, that Neoliberalism did not put an end to Keynesianism concerning the role of state intervention in the economic sphere, but he poses

> *'neoliberalism' as a moment within Keynesianism and show[s] that*
> *from being an antithesis to it, neoliberalism was the Keynesian*
> *response to its own contradictions. Reacting to wage inflation and*
> *stagflation at home and unruly developmentalism abroad [...] it used*
> *the state (and supra state) intervention to shift the basis of demand*
> *management from wage contracts and the 'development compromise'*
> *to micro and macro credit and debt-based globalisation. (Araghi*
> *2010: 40)*

These diagnoses of the changing role of the state within different economic and political formations encourages a Foucauldian point of view, seeing the state not as entity with given functions and characteristics existing independently from social and political interactions, nor as the centre of power, but rather as a 'function of changes in practices of government' (Gordon 1991: 4) with the purpose of preserving the power of the ruling classes. Hence, the object of research cannot be the state, but the processes of governing populations within particular power relations and orders of knowledge at a certain historical moment (cf. ibid.). According to different political rationalities different duties and functions are assigned to the state, so that we cannot speak of 'the state' but of different 'state projects' in which different and changing technologies and rationalities of government are deployed.

These rationalities of government, together with a set of respective techniques, instruments and institutions, used for governing the population, Faucault called 'governmentality' and linked it with the development of the capitalist system of reproduction. With governmentality Foucault means

> *[t]he ensemble formed by the institutions, procedures, analyses and*
> *reflections, the calculations and tactics that allow the exercise of this*
> *very specific albeit complex form of power, which has at its target*
> *population, as its principal form of knowledge political economy, and*
> *as its essential technical means apparatuses of security (Foucault*
> *1991: 102).*

With the concept of governmentality, by referring to the term 'governing', Foucault connected the development of modern states with the emergence of modern ways of subject formation, as governmental techniques intervene with the processes by which individuals shape themselves and construct their identity (cf. Lemke 1997, preface). Modes of governmentality change over time including criticism and resistance in new governmental programs, so, in a 'strategic reversibility of power relations', governmental practice may be influenced by resistance and, on the other hand, can be turned into a means of resistance again (cf. Gordon 1991: 5). Thus governmentality is a mutual process of self-conduct and conduct of others in which the gain of autonomy and subjection to social norms coincide. The perspective of autonomist Marxism contributes an important aspect to this concept by stating that the transformations of governmentality are neither arbitrary or contingent solutions for somehow emerging societal problems, nor simply following some 'natural' rules of economic development, but are the results of social struggles.

> An apprehension of the process constituting capitalism must understand how struggles, conflict, subjects or, to put it more generally, in the aseptic terms loved by social theorists, 'agency' is a constituent element of the social processes we call capitalism' (de Angelis 2007: 7).

Autonomist Marxism uses a broad concept of working class, sometimes also called the 'social forces other than capital', including all social groups that are in some way exploited by capitalist modes of reproduction (cf. Cleaver 1979: 18): not only waged labour, but also the unemployed, housewives, students, peasants, slaves and, very important in the current situation, the thousands of illegalised migrant workers. Thus also the movements of women, students or indigenous people are peceived as part of the struggles against the capitalist system of reproduction. The resistive and troublesome behaviour of the subordinate classes force the ruling class to search for ever changing modes of governing and techniques of power to prevent social uprising and loss of domination. In this perspective also the shifts of the last decade can be seen as results of activities of the social movements in different social struggles all over the world, as the attempt to find answers to the multiple crises that threaten the power of the ruling class.

> The neoliberal set of strategies introduced by capital from the late 1970s, was able to ride the antiauthoritarian elements of this explosion of subjectivities and to a certain extent reabsorb it into mechanism of planetary capitalist accumulation. It rode these movements while at the same time repressing and criminalising some of its expressions, as well

as re-articulating their demands and desires into the mechanisms of global markets and accumulation and through cultural changes in the forms of governance. In other words, the objective was to forcefully couple the antiauthoritarian anarchy expressed by these struggles to the 'anarchy of the market' (or at least this was the intention) that is to newly emerging and intensifying market processes pervading new and new spheres of lives. (de Angelis, 2008a: 2)

Transformations of governmentality

A short historical review on the development and transformations of governmentality opens the way for an analysis of the ongoing processes mentioned above. Foucault states that governmentality first appeared at the turn from the 18th to the 19th century together with the emergence of liberal theories, building on the basic assumption of men as free individuals able to make their own rational decisions to their benefit. This notion fundamentally questioned the sovereignty of absolute rulers, the prevailing rationality of governing in the time of Feudalism, and finally the necessity of government at all, and led to this new rationality for the 'government of free individuals' which Foucault called governmentality. However, the older methods of governing, sovereignty and discipline, were not abrogated. On the contrary, Foucault states that a triangle of sovereignty, discipline and governmental strategy forms the basis for this new mode of governing the population (cf. Foucault 1991: 102), the relations between these elements being subject to changes over time.

Liberal government, as the conduct of free individuals, however, had to meet the challenge to produce individuals amenable to this method of governing, individuals '... who do not need to be governed by others, but will govern themselves, master themselves, care for themselves' (Rose 1996: 45). It was on this basis of liberal governmentality that industrial capitalism could be established and spread all over Europe, drawing on the concept of the homo oeconomicus and at the same time producing this type of subjects. By the end of the 19th century its disastrous consequences on the population became highly visible and caused a crises of liberal governmentality. Due to the increasing power of the workers' movement, which threatened state power, and the need to secure the reproduction of labour power, the state had to compensate the failures of the capitalist mode of production. Class compromises as labour laws and first forms of social insurance systems and, later on, the development of welfare states led to a new mode of governmentality. Government in welfare states meant 'governing the social' and governing

179

things and persons 'through society' (cf. ibid.: 39). The individual in welfare state governmentality was constituted as '... a subject of needs, attitudes and relationships, a subject who was to be embraced within, and governed through, a nexus of collective solidarities and dependencies' (ibid.: 40). In the special situation of the post WWII period this system allowed a thriving economy and an enormous increase of wealth also for the working class, but only by devastating exploitation of the population of developing countries and natural resources.

At the end of the 70s of the last century the welfare state was subject to critique that finally led to a crisis of welfare state governmentality. The arguments were twofold: on the one hand welfare states were supposed to be economically inefficient and unaffordable because of increasing costs, on the other hand they were accused of incapacitating people and suppressing their activities. The neoliberal paradigm claimed to provide a solution for both problems by linking market success to individual self-realization and thus functionalising the emancipatory claim for autonomy for market goals. The main task of neoliberal governmentality is the permanent re-establishment of competition between states as well as between individuals. Subjects are supposed to perform as 'enterprising selves' (cf. ibid.: 57). The prefix 'self' became the predominant characteristic for the description of this new form of workers, finally pervading their whole lifestyle: self-management, self-reliance, self-determination, self-marketing including individual responsibility, competitiveness and the continuous strive for increasing one's human capital are the requests to the enterprising self (cf. Gorz 1991: 27).

The development of neoliberal governmentality was not restricted to the national level but reflected the enormous restructuring of the economy on a global level that is usually referred to as neoliberal globalisation. The main characteristics were the opening of the borders for commodities, services and capital, establishing global chains of production and an international division of labour and the growing influence of the financial markets on the production sphere. These economic processes went parallel with the growing importance of international organisations as the WTO, IWF and World Bank, in the sense of the above-mentioned internalisation of national states. In the last 30 years neoliberal policies have spread over almost all countries of the world, even though in different specific configurations depending on the political system and the state of economic development. Neoliberalism occurred in various political and social practices but, nevertheless, showed some common denominators: the strong emphasis on competition and human capital with the respective practises to interfere with people's everyday lives, thus developing a kind of 'global hegemony' and 'global governmentality' (cf. Brand, 2007: 17).

After the end of soviet socialism the victory of capitalism seemed to promise a glorious future with ongoing growth and wealth for all, the few warning voices were ignored. But soon these promises were disguised as fallacies. Instead of the expected benefits unleashed capitalism caused various problems that culminated in the current multiple crisis. Growing social resistance movements and uprising social struggles on many different places forced the ruling class to new modifications of power techniques and on the other hand led to growing repression.

To summarize shortly, we can say that on a global level a shift in the regime of accumulation from production to exchange (see Herrmann, forthcoming: Searching for Global Social Policy – Economy, Economics and Governance) was accompanied by an internationalisation of the state as the respective mode of regulation leading to a 'global govern-mentality' arranged around 'a global culture of competitiveness' (cf. Sum 2009: 158). While these processes appear across the globe, the national patterns differ, especially between the affluent societies of the West and North and the developing countries or emerging markets in the East and South.

It is against this background that we have to question, whether the model of neoliberal governmentality with the 'enterprising self' as its main pillar, as described by Foucault and his students some ten years ago has to be revised and – given the international dimension of these processes – governmentality as an instrument of analysis can be extended beyond the level of the policies of nation states. Given the above-mentioned 're-feudalisation' we should also ask, whether this is connected with a re-emergence of discipline in governmental rationality. Due to the assumption of individuals as 'creatures of freedom, liberty and autonomy', however, we may assume that discipline has to be imposed by 'means by which individuals may be made responsible through their individual choices for themselves and those to whom they owe allegiance' (Rose 1996: 57).

In the following I propose that in the last decade the modifications of neoliberal governmentality followed the shift of the accumulation regime. As profits are made from exchange rather than from production seems reasonable that the market, as the place of exchange, becomes a target for governmental techniques. In this context it can be observed that the shift from production to exchange on the level of accumulation corresponds to a shift from labour to consumption – the latter usually equated with the activity of buying and hence also refering to an exchange process – on the level of everyday lives and practices of individuals and thus also of governmental practices. Discipline is deployed increasingly through and for these exchange processes. I want to show the interplay between these structural global changes, political programs and social practices and the activities of individuals when coping with them in their every day lives, building their identities on them, individually or collectively, but at the same time appropriating and modifying them and making them to starting points for criticism and resistance. These connections cannot be seen as causal relations but are intertwined, either enforcing or constraining each other, building complex patterns of discourses and practises that can deploy coercion and domination, but may also turn into means of resistance and promote social struggles and shifts in power relations. In this context I will also show that EU legislation plays an important role in constituting individuals as consumers – or rather as customers - through weakening labour rights while at the same time enforcing legislation on security and consumer protection.

In the next two chapters two main and interdependent aspects of this shift in governmentality are described in detail: precarity and the shift from labour to consumption coming along with a strong claim for individual responsibility. There is no doubt that these processes are embedded in a set of different, sometimes contradicting, discourses and practices and not always appear in this clear-cut version. But, nevertheless, it is necessary to be aware of them as, in my opinion, they are crucial in the current phase of restructuring the global economy, global power relations and the ongoing social and political struggles. In this context it is remarkable that this shift appears not only in hegemonic discourse but also within the slogans and demands of the social movements, an issue that will be dealt with in the last chapter.

From autonomy to precarity – co-opting emancipatory ideas for capitals goals

The assumption that the neoliberal paradigm appropriated originally critical and emancipatory claims deriving from welfare state criticism is confirmed by the changes in labour relations and enterprise structures. Furthermore this is an outstanding example for the coincidence of more freedom and more control Foucault named as characteristic of neoliberal governmentality. The critique of Fordist working conditions, the monotonous work subordinating workers to machines, provoked the desire to escape from this realm of alienated labour and finally the claim for workplace autonomy. Various experiments of self-organised labour in the 70s and 80s, collectively and individualist, first led to the development of new kinds of labour contracts for 'self-employed' workers that opened up unknown liberties and leeways of self-management at least for a short time and a relatively small elitist group, by Horx described as the 'development of an innovative, 'entrepreneurial' class' (Horx 1985, quoted from Neumann 2008: 64, translation B.K.). The call for workplace autonomy, however, was co-opted by new management programs restructuring enterprises with the goal to dissolve hierarchies and handing more responsibility over to the workers. What seemed to be a real success and improvement of the quality of work in the beginning turned soon out to be a more efficient instrument of control. The seemingly autonomous workers internalized the coercion of efficiency and profit maximisation and self-exploitation largely exceeded the degree of accepted exploitation by employers. 'Within only few decades autonomy, from its revolutionary starting point, has turned to a means of exploitation' (Neumann 2008: 78, translation B.K.). Autonomy was only required and allowed as long as it increased the profit of the employer, the pressure of market competition was handed down to every single worker. In the words of André Gorz:

> *Die Person muss für sich selbst zum Unternehmer werden, sie muss sich selbst, als Arbeitskraft, als fixes Kapital betrachten, das seine ständige Reproduktion, Modernisierung, Erweiterung und Verwertung erfordert. Sie darf keinem äußeren Zwang unterworfen sein, sie muss vielmehr ihr eigener Hersteller, Arbeitgeber und Verkäufer werden und genötigt sein, sich die Zwänge aufzuerlegen, die zur Lebens- und Wettbewerbsfähigkeit des Unternehmens, das sie ist, erforderlich sind.'*
> *(Gorz, 2004: 25)[65]*

Spread by media and implemented in education programs from early years, the notion that everybody has to take responsibility for his own life, that dependency means weakness and that our whole life is a competition we have to successfully pass, became the prevailing and

---

[65] The individual has to become an entrepreneur for itself, it has to perceive itself, its labour power, as fixed capital that requires continuous reproduction, modernisation, extension and utilisation. It must not be subject to external coercion, but has to become its own producer, employer and vendor and is compelled to enforce to itself the restraints, necessary for the viability and competitiveness of the enterprise it represents. (Translation B.K.)

broadly accepted attitude in large parts of society and made the performance as an 'enterprising self' a common objective, to be found in all social groups and classes.

These developments at organisational and national level coincided with the globalisation of the markets and capital, with the transfer of production to low wage regions, thus implementing an new kind of international division of labour imposing enormous pressure on national labour markets and wages by setting the different world regions 'against each other in a competitive race to lower the labour time necessary for their *reproduction*' (de Angelis 2007: 72, emphasis in original). With the closure of large parts of the industry in the North a huge amount of workers was set free and forced into a broad range of different working contracts and modes of employment. The working class was highly individualised, trade unions were not able to follow this development and lost even more influence – on politics as well as among their members.

Government programs – on national and on European level – in their reaction, took up the human capital discourse and combined it with the requirements of state competition, the outstanding example being the Lisbon goals of the European Council from 2000, proposing that Europe should become 'the most competitive and dynamic knowledge-based economy in the world capable of sustainable economic growth with more and better jobs and greater social cohesion' (European Council 2000). According to this goal the European Social Fonds set up 'Entrepreneurship for All' activities, aimed at 'removing the key barriers or obstacles that prevent disadvantaged groups and deprived areas from being able to set up viable businesses',[66] thus praising self-employment as the key for the solution of labour market problems. Under the catchword of 'flexicurity' the improvement of the flexibilty of labour force was the second pillar of EU programs, flexibilisation meaning the weakening of labour rights, longer working hours, less protection against illness and dismission and an increase of 'atypical' labour contracts. This was the source of growing socio-economic insecurity for a large part of the population, the restraints reaching far into the middle classes. Even graduates could no longer be sure to get an adequate job, whereas many young people did not see even an opportunity for a decent and valuable life. This combination of long term unemployment, short term labour-contracts, unpaid work placements, low wage jobs and finally increasing poverty even in rich countries due to 'atypical' modes of employment led

---

[66] http://ec.europa.eu/employment_social/equal/activities/etg2_en.cfm

184

to the emergence of a concept which unfolded unpredictable effects: precarity.

We have to be aware that this situation of widespread uncertainty, the impossibility of planning one's life and the growing social polarisation, frequently present in many places of the world, occurred under special historical conditions. Only after a long period of growth and wealth, technological and medical progress and the institutions of the welfare state had consolidated the feeling that our life is predictable, and therefore we are able to manage it and everyone can forge his own destiny, people could willingly accept the requirement of self-reliance imposed on them, because it promised independence and the opportunity for self-realisation. And exactly this certainty and the confidence in the economic and political structures, in scientific and technical progress guaranteeing these possibilities forever were violently shaken by the experience of precarity. The promises turned out to be fallacies, autonomy and self-realisation developed into traps that nobody could easily escape. Only against this background the emotional reactions – from outrage over disappointment to frustration and despair – can be understood. People seem permanently involved in struggles for every day life, societal and political engagement often is laid off, even personal and family relations are affected. Everybody has to fear to loose his/her job and therefore to accept the worsening working conditions, conflicts deepened between different groups of workers and between workers and the unemployed. Individuals are more isolated, especially in the moment when they would need social networks and support. Precarity seemed to be the ultimate instrument of discipline for independent, autonomous 'enterprising selves' by 'reproducing scarcity in the midst of plenty' (de Angelis 2008b: 14). Instead of external coercion, self-coercion and self-exploitation was enforced by means of the threat of social exclusion of those who were not able or not willing to fulfil these requirements.

But, while capital seemed to have increased its power and trade unions had been pushed back to a defensive position, reducing their activities on mitigating the effects of global flexibilisation and wage competition and the reduction of labour rights for those, who still had fulltime employment, and did not feel responsible for the marginalised groups, something unexpected happened. Precarity was the shared experience of a whole generation all over Europe. And it was exactly this concept that gained revolutionary power and became the synonym for a new wave of social struggles. This very heterogeneous group re-united to a social movement of 'global precariat'. The 21st century started with labour struggles all over the world also in countries where class struggles seemed to be only an occurrence in history or had been for a long time suppressed by absolutist governments. And it had not been the unions but those who did not expect to have any opportunities on the labour market and felt condemned to a life without dignity, who were the subjects of the struggles, sometimes not only against the governments but also against the unions, sometimes forcing them to take a clear position. In Europe there were youth revolts from France to Greece, self-organisation of unemployed embodied for example in the 'Euromarches' or the movement of the illegalised migrants under the catchword of 'sans papiers' and, most recently, student protests all over Europe. But struggles rose as well in Latin America, the most famous proponents being the Zapatista movement and the Landless Workers' Movement MST in Brasilia, strikes of the oil-workers in Iraq or the struggles against oil-companies in Nigeria, only to mention some examples, representing a much larger number of incidences.

And while trade unions still were bargaining for wage increases – or at this stage rather trying to prevent wage reductions – and trying to prevent extension of labour time, these groups turned their backs to the bad and humiliating jobs they could expect and focused their demands not on jobs or wages, but on dignity, human rights and the possibility of a 'good life' to be guaranteed independent of waged labour. One of their most important claims is that for a basic income, still following the rationality of a consumer society that a good life is a question of money, a question of being able to buy, what one needs. Though not questioning the capitalist mode of reproduction, these demands, however, signify a turn away from labour to exchange/consumption as the field of social struggles. Although the struggles were answered with more or less repressive methods, parts of capital also followed this turn, withdrawing from the field of the newly emerging labour-conflicts and trying to co-opt these demands for new ways of achieving control and discipline.

The responsible consumer – a solution for a capitalist dilemma?

The demand for ethical consumption as an instrument of resistance and political action had been primarily an answer given by civil society, engaging with the destructive effects of the mode of production in Western industrial countries. When in the 70s and 80s of the last century it became broadly known that water and air pollution, as well as famines in Africa, were consequences of the increasing wealth in industrial welfare states, this was a shocking experience for many people, who did

186

not want their well-being to be on the cost of other peoples' poverty or the destruction of natural resources. The original idea of 'conscious consumption' stood for using consumers' power on enterprises claiming for organic agriculture, commitment to labour right standards, fighting child labour and pleading for an improvement of living conditions, including health and education for the developing countries, so that at last they should achieve European standards. Consumer education, exposing exploitative methods of production and boycott against the concerned companies were their instruments of political action and finally forced enterprises to react. Driven by media campaigns and the refusal to buy from some companies, these showed willingness to more transparency and concern about environmental and human rights problems, even if many of these attempts remained on a marginal, often only rhetoric level. From here the conception of the responsible entrepreneur, under the label of 'Corporate Social Responsibility' (CSR) as well as the conception of the 'conscious consumer' could gain societal and media relevance. We have to understand that the two concepts depend on each other. Only if companies react, conscious consumption can achieve its goals, only if consumers appreciate sustainable modes of production, CSR can work as a means of marketing and economic benefit. And only this connection makes it possible to turn the field of consumption into a field of control, discipline and moral appeals because capital benefits from 'correct' behaviour in the supermarket.

We can suppose that the outsourcing of 'dirty' and labour-intensive industries to low wage countries with also low environmental standards and the implementation of 'clean' technologies and innovative industries in the West were – though provoked by problems of overaccumulation – also influenced by these rising social conflicts in Western Europe. The concerns of NGOs and social movements were answered with market-based solutions, claiming 'development by trade' and offering technical solutions to environmental problems.

This dislocation of industries, however, marked also the end of the industrial labour relations of the Fordist period in the developed countries. The terms of 'services society' and later on 'knowledge society' reflect the move towards new sectors in the search for profit. The marketisation of former public services in the health, education and social sector paved the way for the growing importance of the field of circulation and exchange for capital accumulation. Employment in the service sector increased, especially in those sectors that represent 'apparatuses that shape and manage individual and collective conduct in relations to norms and objectives' (Rose 1996: 38), i.e. the broad field of counselling, coaching, therapy, public relations, advertising and human resources management. The boom of these institutions on the one hand signifies the emergence of new requirements for self-conduct and the management of human capital, on the other hand, however, they only provide precarious working conditions for those – often self-employed – offering these services. This shows that these sectors fall short of reproducing themselves and still depend on the production sphere for their maintenance. To circumvent this problem, even aggravated by a long lasting crisis of overproduction, it seemed reasonable to turn to the financial sector for acquiring profit. The growing importance of intellectual property rights in international trade agreements, turning knowledge into a commodity, or the attempt to reduce CO_2 output by means of emission certificates are expressions of this shift.

The turn from demand-oriented state intervention to micro and macro credit and debt-based globalisation pointed out by Araghi (see above: 177) is another aspect of this process, showing different effects in different regions of the world.

> In the countries of the global North, this regime, accompanied by relatively liberal bank regulations for credit, leads to increased personal indebtedness necessary for countering the erosion of wages and other entitlements. On the other hand, in the global South, cuts in entitlements and enclosures are imposed over the social body through the management of the debt crisis and structural adjustment policies (de Angelis 2007: 72).

As we can see during the current crises this practice is applied also in European economies, Greece, Spain and Portugal being the most recent examples. States not only have to compete to attract capital to their territory but also for their trustworthiness as debtors, to get high rankings on the financial markets. These efforts interfere massively with people's every day lives due to cuts in public spending. Reproduction work is handed back to the private sphere, while, to prevent economic downturn, private consumption is supposed to compensate for the decline of public demand.

It were three critical factors that led to the final turn of governmental rationality to individual responsibilisation on the field of consumption drawing on the demands of the social movements and turning them into power instruments.

Changing lines of conflict

The first factor can be seen in the shifts in the field of labour and the raise of new labour conflicts as described in the previous section of this contribution, showing the interdependence of both topics. It is important to mention that addressing people as consumers instead as workers or self-entrepreneurs does not mean that working is no longer necessary for earning a livelihood and that labour is no longer an instrument of control in current societies. Instead I want to suggest that the arguments to bring people to work changed and so did the field and the lines of conflict and the instruments of power and discipline.

To understand this shift we have to consider that there are two important tasks for the implementation and maintenance of the capitalist system, the need to capital accumulation and the need to maintain control over individuals. Bringing people to work for a long time met both of them and was achieved either by coercion or by promising some reward, mostly by a combination of both. In its early stage capitalism could draw on religious attitudes. In misinterpretation of the Christian faith, working hard and living modestly was supposed fulfilment of the will of god and should lead to final salvation, at the same time allowing the beginning of accumulation of labour-power and capital. In the period of Fordism the ascetic aspect was abandoned. On the contrary, the enormous increase of productivity made it reasonable to stimulate needs and encourage people to buy more. Thus already Fordism recognized the importance of consumption for economic growth, making people to consumers by increasing wages to raise economic demand, but keeping people able to buy was not an end in itself. Still the field of accumulation as well as of discipline and control was the field of production, first of all the factory. Surplus production required that people had to be brought to work. The possibility to participate in the growing wealth through consumption was the reward for the acceptance of a loss of dignity and control in their jobs as well as a means of accelerating economic growth. Individuals were first and foremost addressed as workers entitled to social rights and services through their participation in the labour process.

The new development tended in another direction. For a short time, in Post-Fordism, coercion was replaced by self-coercion, the time-punch machine was implanted into the heads of the workers. Due to the growing productivity that made it increasingly difficult to provide jobs for all, the following social conflicts and finally a long lasting crisis of overproduction and over-accumulation, labour was more and more reduced to a means of control and not longer seen as a means of production of surplus value. As the field of production and labour had become highly conflicting, partly because its inherent environmental problems, partly because of precarious working conditions and growing unemployment, the promise of full employment being further away then ever, capital and governments left the field of conflict and focussed, instead on the reproduction of labour power, on at least maintaining the purchasing power of the population. Given that flexibility and creativity had become the main requirements on the work place it seems difficult to deploy at the same place disciplining measures. Hence the shift from the 'labour market' to the 'supermarket' as field of discipline appears quite obvious and is enhanced by the other two factors.

The second one can be described by the catchwords of climate change and peak oil[67]. Environmental problems, the limitedness of natural resources and the arising conflicts in the countries of the South could not be ignored anymore. Before the financial crises climate change was the major topic in international politics and media and measures to reduce the CO_2 emission were fiercely required by NGOs and social movements and forced governments to act. The limitedness of oil resources was another strong incentive to turn to renewable energy. Regions, cities and national governments, as well as international organisations, started programs and campaigns but, as governments could not agree on international common action and corporations and enterprises were concerned about their competitiveness, these programs, targeting the fields of production and use of resources, could not exceed the rhetoric level. Hence governments focussed on individual responsibility on the side of enterprises as well as on the side of consumption. The concept of CSR was revived and supported and promoted on national and European level, also becoming an object of competition, e.g. in the European Commission's communication on 'Implementing the partnership for growth and jobs: making Europe a pole of excellence on Corporate Social Responsibility' (European Commission 2006). The other pillar of these programs, as outlined above, had to be encouraging citizens to involve in different activities of responsible and sustainable consumption drawing on the arguments of environmental and development movements and often supported by them.

---

[67] Peak oil is the point in time when the maximum rate of global petroleum extraction is reached, after which the rate of production enters terminal decline. http://en.wikipedia.org/wiki/Peak_oil - 05/05/2010

The third and last occasion was the financial crises that shook the very foundations of the neoliberal system. To regain legitimacy and acceptance mistakes had to be admitted and serious changes had to be promised. But the search for culprits again ended up in blaming individuals. To avoid the conclusion that the system itself is deficient, individuals had to be blamed for the financial crises. Greed, egoism, wrong decisions and lacking responsibility presumably had caused the disastrous effects. Politicians and economic experts agreed that there had to be some changes of the system in order to prevent that such development would recur. But, according to the suggested reasons for the crises, the proposed changes and 'social innovations' again were reduced to personal traits and moral values. Managers, entrepreneurs, actors on the financial markets had to act responsibly instead of egoistically and execessively risk-taking. And again it is the consumers who have to appreciate these attitudes in their behaviour on the market.

It was through these processes that the concept of the 'responsible consumer' could be established and promised a solution for all of the problems: it avoids the conflictual field of labour, turns to the field of responsible consumption that is highly appreciated by citizens and NGOs, remains at an individual level, thus not challenging the capitalist system itself and, by suggesting to buy less but spend more, allows to combine a reduction of the use of resources with continuing opportunities for profit generation. The concept, however, falls short to fulfil the hopes pinned on it because of a reduced understanding of consumption and an overestimation of the role of the consumer.

It builds on the – in principle correct – assumption that the developed countries have to reduce their consumption of natural resources. The concept of responsible consumption as frequently used, however, fails to meet the correct goal, namely the process of production where most of the resources are consumed. Instead, it focuses on the acts of buying, thus reducing consumption to the act of purchasing. Then, consumers are reduced to the role of 'pure customers'. Individuals are reduced to the function of buying, constraining at the same time their space to act and to get involved in decisions about what and how is produced. Even if customers on the market decide to buy commodities produced in a sustainable way, proposing such solution starts from a wrong angle: it requires decisions to be made at a time when the activities these decisions aim on have already been completed. It is evident that individual lifestyle can only influence to a small degree the actual sustainability of production. The idea that conscious 'consumption'[68] can solve the problems of climate change and is a sufficient strategy to energy change, largely overestimates the power and the possibilities of 'consumers' seen as customers in the (super)market.

Hence it assigns tasks to individuals which they can never fulfil, which is a main characteristic of governmental strategies. Neither the 'enterprising self' nor the 'responsible consumer' can be understood as 'ideal types' in the sense of Max Weber, they are not to be used as 'a tool for describing reality, but a device to its change' (Bröckling 2007: 48, translation B.K.). Their traits are not empirically observable, but are objectives to which individuals have to adhere without being able to meet completely. Individuals are supposed to strive continuously to these goals and – due to the impossibility to reach them – perceive themselves as deficient and permanently feel a sense of guilt. But on the other hand, it is exactly this gap between the idealised goal and the impossibility of realisation, that opens the way for appropriation and resistance (cf. Rose 1996: 61).

Promoted by politicians and media, the idea of consumer power was broadly accepted, establishing the notion that people are morally obliged to buy, to spend money either to help the economy to grow or to foster social or environmental goals. Working then is the precondition to fulfil these duties as a responsible citizen. The need to buy is enforced by measures that make it more difficult to get the things people need for their living beyond the market or even criminalises those attempts. Thus coercion to work is enforced without getting involved in labour struggles. The argument is not longer 'You have to work, then you can buy', but 'You have to buy, therefore look to find a job, how bad ever. And of course in this difficult situation we cannot offer you good jobs, but if we all do our best, times will change and all of us will be better off.' Hence the market becomes the target of disciplinary instruments, which allow to control labour-relations from the distance, including further cuts of labour rights and social entitlements through ongoing precarisation and flexibilisation.[69]

---

[68] In the following I use the terms 'consumer' and 'consumption' with quotation marks if they are used – according to the common practice – in the sense of 'customer' and 'buying'.

[69] While discipline is deployed directly on every single individual within distinct institutions, control means that disciplinary mechanisms extend outside the institutions to the social field, dealing with '… circulations of decoded flows (of money, of people, of signs, of culture)' (de Angelis 2007: 122). But discipline and control depend on each other: 'If we take 'discipline' a factory of ethic, as

This, of course, could only be achieved because critical NGOs and media had paved the way and by the use of governmental techniques comprising a set of institutions and practices developed to constitute individuals as customers.

Putting customers on a pedestal

If we speak about a new mode of governmentality, according to Foucault, it includes discourses, but cannot be reduced to them. Instead, it is realised through different institutions, laws and social practises, supporting and reproducing these discourses and in addition shaping the way individuals perceive themselves and construct their identities. Governmentality is thus not only a set of moral appeals, but provides knowledge and instruments to (re)produce what it proposes to be social reality. Governmentalities are 'practices for the formulation and justification of idealized schemata for representing reality, analysing it and rectifying it' (Rose 1996: 42). As a consequence this, though contingent, conception of reality becomes part of the everyday knowledge of individuals of all social strata and is perceived as something 'natural' or 'universal', delegitimising contradicting knowledge.

The perspective of governmentality does not aim on describing or criticising this special social 'reality', instead it aims on 'problematising' what is broadly perceived as reality, as something that seems to be natural and cannot be questioned. It does so in demonstrating how this notion of reality had been constructed through practices of discourse and power and that thus it is only a contingent view of reality. Problematising reality means to show the contradictions it includes and the power effects it deploys. It shows how a hegemonic order of knowledge is enforced, while other kinds of knowledge are suppressed.

Starting from the question how the concept of the 'responsible consumer' could become such broadly accepted knowledge, we can figure out a set of discourses, practices and institutions contributing to this task. That does not mean that these have been originally intended to this goal, nor that they show only this effect, but rather, that in a strategic arrangement, these elements altogether produce, willingly or not, this outcome. From

---

Foucault would put it, that is, the mechanism of reward and punishment that creates norms, then control mechanisms are those that use these norms to regulate flows' (ibid.: 123)

this point of view I want to give a short overview over what, in my opinion, are essential discourses, practices and institutions to bring forward an order of knowledge that fosters the mode of subjectivation as 'responsible consumer'.

For the constitution of individuals as 'consumers' we can find three lines of discourse: first addressing individuals as 'consumers' in nearly all situations of everyday life, connecting the concept with positive connotation and thus making 'being consumer' part of their identity. Secondly, the notion that 'consumption' generally is inevitable for economic prosperity and thus individuals, as responsible citizens, are committed to buy. Thirdly, environmental problems enhance the claim for 'conscious consumption', meaning to buy less, but the right things and spending more money for ethically correct products. With these different lines of argumentation and the respective practices the responsibility for his/her behaviour as 'consumer' could be extended to almost everybody, also to those groups, the discourse of 'conscious consumption' as brought forward by civil society organisations – to a high degree remaining an elitist project – was not able to reach.

One starting point certainly was, that people were more often addressed as customers by administration and governments instead of being seen as users of services, or as citizens entitled to these services as it had been previously the case – the marketisation of this services enforced such changed notion. The patients in the hospital, parents in child care facilities, clients of labour agencies and students at universities were constituted as customers buying a service, even if they did not 'buy' these services voluntarily and if they did not pay themselves but via public transfers or insurance payment. The role of a customer, however, was announced as a higher appreciation and valuation of individuals, as the wishes of the customer were promised to be the criteria for the services.

The next step had been marked by the efforts of governments to support peoples' ability to buy, a very significant example being the US policies of democratizing credits. The idea was, if it only was possible to keep people buying, constantly growing profit even without growing production seemed within reach. For years, US media and financial experts have constructed the myth of the American 'consumer' being the driving force of economic growth and an indicator of the economic climate. Few days after 9/11, President Bush adjured the Americans to 'go shopping' to prevent economic throwback as a result of the shocking terrorist raid (cf. Frank 2009: 39). For years the President of the US central bank, Norman Greenspan, promoted subprime credits as valuable instrument to foster 'consumption' and thus enabling the USA to remain the leading economic power (cf. ibid.: 42). The idea to provide credits to more people and thus stimulate the real estate market and construction industry and turning subprime credits into lucrative investment products seemed to be a solution for both problems, the lack of demand and the lack of investment possibilities.

> *The mandarins of finance have thought it out well: how to provide homes for the needy while at the same time reducing the investors' risk? The answer is the same as to every capitalist conundrum: turn 'risk' into a commodity and pass it along (de Angelis 2008b: 4).*

For some years it had been possible to conceal the weakness of this construct by always new financial instruments with increasing risks and, on the other side, increasing revenues. As a consequence outstanding profits occurred together with growing social polarisation.

European policies follow the same rationality: the EU Commission in its working document for the consultation of the Future 'EU 2020' Strategy (European Commission 2009) assumes that 'citizens must be empowered to play a full part in the single market. This requires strengthening their ability and confidence to buy goods and services cross-border'. To overcome the financial and economic crisis once more the enormous importance of 'consumption' was stressed by politicians.

This glorification of the 'consumer' is also apparent in the EU legislation that declares the 'consumer' to be an object that is worth protecting, which on the one hand contributes to the reproduction of the view of citizens as 'consumers', but on the other hand, already draws on this notion and the fact that individuals increasingly identify themselves as 'consumers'. Only under this condition 'consumer' protection could become one of the best accepted fields of European policies and help the EU to regain legitimation, in a time when trust and acceptance of the EU had declined and citizens claimed that their interests were not represented by the bureaucrats in Brussels. But again the concept of 'consumer'-protection actually refers only to the role of citizens as customers and thus rather should be called 'customer-protection'. This implies some more problems and contradictions to which I will return later in this text.

Finally, the challenges of climate change and the turn to renewable energies again were delegated to individual responsibility. Moral discourses on corporate social responsibility, as well as ethical 'consumption', and the need to restrict one's individual claims in favour of the saving of the economy and the planet at the same time, once more were based on the assumption of an unlimited 'consumer' power. Programs of 'consumer' education and projects for sustainable 'consumption', by national governments, on European level but also by the United Nations aimed at the improvement of individuals' competences to responsible 'consumption' were started and implemented by NGOs, a well-known example being the ecologic footprint. While it suggests that individuals can autonomously modify their resource use, actually the size of the ecologic footprint depends to a high degree on the region and society you live in. It has to be mentioned, however, that some of these project also refer to 'real' consumption of resources, but fail to properly distinguish between the two aspects.

To conclude shortly, we can see that the market, as the field of exchange, has become the place where discipline is enacted on individuals that allows also controlling their behaviour in other areas of society, e.g. the labour market. Individuals are forced to work through their appellation as 'consumers' and individuals are held responsible for the solution of societal problems. The logic of the market was established as hegemonic order of knowledge and, to achieve the acceptance of the governed, a respective set of discourses, institutions and instruments – as outlined above – is deployed to foster the subjectivation of individuals as 'consumers' and thus reproducing this order of knowledge in their every day practices.

This is what Foucault means, if he says that 'individualisation and totalisation', take place at the same time, the one is not to be achieved without the other (Gordon 1991: 3 f.). Neoliberal rationality did not spread all over the world because it forced all individuals to the same thoughts or behaviour, but exactly because its many different specifications and patterns reproduced by allegedly free individuals. The maintenance and extension of a hegemonic order of knowledge depends on the freedom of individuals to develop his/her unique identity according to this rationality. Thus 'Individuals are to be governed through their freedom' (Burchell 1996: 41). Through this mechanism the model of the market gets universal for all societal sectors, and so does the model of the customer. Since all social relations are organised as market relations between vendor and customers, individuals are addressed as customers in almost all situations and feel themselves as customers. The role of the customer increasingly covers the totality of individual identity and social practice, while the logic of the market tends to be applied to the totality of all social relations. As a consequence, the market turns out to be the place where social reputation can be gained, and from which social status can be derived. 'Consumption' – again mostly reduced to the choice in the supermarket or between shopping or not shopping – is a core category for people to shape their identity, to a high degree accepting the role as 'consumers' (in the sense of customers) imposed on them and including it in their technologies of the self. Whether they follow the call to buy as much as possible and hence define themselves through the newest car or trendy fashion, or they shape their identity according to the recommendations of conscious 'consumption' and thus reduce their demands but refer to organic and fair products, they subject themselves to the appeals imposed on them. Also collective identities grow around consumer behaviour, leading to controversial discussions even within social movements. And even those groups that refuse the identity of a 'consumer', have to refer to this concept, albeit negatively.

The concept of responsible 'consumption' draws on the self-perception of individuals as 'consumers', making them the target of moral appeals and disciplinary instruments and assigning responsibility to them. The burden of overcoming the different crises was thus to a high degree passed on to the individuals adding a strong moral aspect to the role of the 'consumer'. While the influence of individuals was reduced to 'purchasing acts', more responsibility was handed down to them and at the same time taken from politics and enterprises. It is exactly the emphasis on the maintenance of purchasing power that assigns responsibility to people for the use of the money they get. The 'responsible consumer' can be blamed for increasing costs of the health system as well as for growing CO_2 emissions. If we understand – following Foucault – neoliberal governmentality as a rationality of 'governing individuals through the market', this does not seem surprising and can be seen as continuous development.

The predicament of the 'responsible consumer'

This mode of subjectivation has one core implication: the 'enterprising self' is responsible for its own life, it has to improve its human capital to be able to fend for itself over the whole lifespan. The responsible 'consumer', however, is not only responsible for him/herself but also for social justice and for environmental problems. If we return to the above-mentioned conditions for imposing discipline on free individuals, namely that they are 'made responsible through their individual choices for themselves and those to whom they owe allegiance' (Rose 1996: 57), we can see that the range of 'those to whom they owe allegiance' has been enlarged. But, and this is a contradiction, they should not care for those in direct social interaction or in political action, but, on the contrary, social justice, human rights or prevention of climate change are supposed to be achieved by choosing the right products in daily purchasing acts.

There is no doubt that, drawing on the concept of responsible 'consumption', individuals gain new opportunities to get involved in governmental programs to improve the situation of people in developing countries, to foster conscious use of resources and to participate in projects on renewable energy and the reduction of CO_2 emissions. But they do so only if they accept the proposed solutions for the problems that – due to the hegemony of the market model – are only market based solutions. Whether it is about human rights or reduction of poverty, about the change to renewable energies or organic food, for all these problems the market is supposed to provide the best solutions. Thus the struggles of the environmental movements and the development movements could be integrated into the governmental programs like the struggle for workplace autonomy was before. And certainly some improvements for indigenous people or a certain degree of reduction of resources use or some support for organic farmers can be the outcome of such programs.

On the other hand, the attempt to solve social and environmental problems – which are at least partly a consequence of the free market system with its highly individualising effects – with more of the same, with even more individualisation and a further reduction of social interaction, implies several contradictions and paradoxes. Individuals, for example, in the supermarket have to decide whether they want to buy regional food, thus reducing CO_2 emission, organic food, even if it comes from a more distant region, but preventing soil and water pollution by pesticides, or fair trade products, supporting development projects but with long ways of transport. So they never can totally satisfy their ethical demands. Unemployed people, who have to accept jobs in remote cities, so, even if in their private life they don't use a car, may be forced to do it, to be able to earn their living. Finally, for many things we need we do neither know how they are produced nor do we have alternatives to get them. Thus all efforts seem to be unsatisfactory and individuals tend to blame themselves and try even harder.

Thus we recognize also on an ethical level a shift from an ethic of work to an ethic of consumption. Striking evidence that even moral values increasingly refer to the behaviour on the market, sometimes almost showing religions traits, is the appearance of 'ecotherapy'. An article in the New York Times says that questions of responsible consumption increasingly become sources for partner conflicts or even the break down of partnerships. A psychologist is quoted:

> Linda Buzzell, a family and marriage therapist for 30 years who lives in Santa Barbara and is a co-editor of 'Ecotherapy: Healing With Nature in Mind,' cautions that the repercussions of environmental differences can be especially severe for couples. 'The danger arises when one partner undergoes an environmental 'waking up' process before the other, leaving a new value gap between them'(Kaufman 2010).

The characteristic of governmentality, that the gain of freedom and a growth of possibilities to act in one sector – in this case the sector of the market – comes along with contradictions, unreasonable demands and a loss of opportunities and repression in other sectors, can be found also in this case.

As questions of human rights, ecological sustainability or energy change often conflict with market rationality, they can only insufficiently be solved by market instruments and people engaged in those projects have to deal with conflicting goals and discussions and negotiations are deadlocked. The overcoming of the economic crises requires restrictions in social spending that have to be accepted by those, supporting the recovery programs of the governments. The strive for competitiveness stands against the improvement of labour rights. The necessity of economic growth impedes the reduction of resources use, the change to renewable energy is supposed to cause the loss of jobs in the energy-sector. Through these contradictions the different goals and movements are pit against each other, conflicts arise not only between governments and citizens but also between different social groups and between NGOs and social movements participating in government programs and those refusing to do so. All solutions beyond the market, especially solutions to be achieved on the level of political action, get out of view. We face a de-politisation of these issues and discourses, social practices and struggles referring to political action and system change are suppressed and delegitimised.

But while struggles about labour rights and social rights have been marginalised by constituting individuals as 'consumers' instead as workers with entitlements to social rights and these issues are subjected to the logic of the market and thus restricted with the argument of overcoming the crises, with the rise of the 'consumer' subject also the importance of consumer protection legislation grew.

Trapped in 'consumer' protection?

If people are supposed to act and to take responsibility as 'consumers', it is evident that – especially against international corporations acting on a global scale – they have to be supported by laws. And if exchange activities are supposed to be the main source of economic prosperity it is reasonable to apply proper rules to them. But these regulations again focus on the process of exchange and thus actually are 'customer protection laws', as buying things is not necessarily linked with consumption, but first of all is an act of exchange.

Refering to EU legislation as an example for outlining governmental strategies and techniques is not about blaming the European Union. Rather referring to 'consumer' protection allows to problematise different aspects: Firstly, how, due to the rise of the importance of the 'consumer', 'consumer' protection law could become universally applied and thus, from its original intention to protect citizens in their position as customers, could turn into a means of control and restriction of citizen rights. Secondly, it illustrates the consequences and contradictions deriving from not differentiating between consumer and customer, and finally, it shows that governmental rationality and techniques are not restricted to the national level, but can also be deployed by supranational organisations, thus either multiplying the opportunities for discipline and control or those of appropriation and resistance.

All of us frequently take the role of customers, in the supermarket or in the bank, when we order things from the internet, when we buy a flight ticket or if we call a technician to repair the washing machine. In all these situations a 'customer protection law' gives us a stand against the vendor of these goods or services. It makes us sure that the things we buy, meet certain standards and we have the right to compensation if they do not. It guarantees that the terms of trade follow legal regulation and it strengthens our position on the court if we bring a charge against companies that do not keep up with those terms. We are protected against aggressive and misleading advertising through the right to withdraw from contracts.

But individuals' activities cannot be reduced to this role. All of us are also producers of those goods and services, we need for the reproduction of our living conditions, outside the market in social interaction with other individuals. There are groups of people organising their energy supply themselves, like in some energy autonomous communities or municipalities or in the Danish windmill-cooperatives. Or the farmers' market where producers (not only vendor) and consumers (not only customers) are involved in personal interaction, where they know each other and consumers come to buy food produced in a way they know and appreciate. We find parents organising childcare themselves according to their educational concepts. In all these activities individuals are not customers but co-producers and do not need to be protected by some 'customer protection law', because they have the possibility to participate in decision-making.

But since the logic of the market becomes hegemonic, also these societal activities tend to be integrated into this logic and it is almost impossible to satisfy one's needs outside of market relations. Thus an increasing number of activities are subject to 'consumer' protection law. If the same rules are applied to small organic farmers as to big food industries they cannot continue to produce their homemade food and people who would prefer this kind of food and like to support this kind of agriculture are forced to buy in the supermarket. Parents who organise childcare collectively have to meet the standards of official child care facilities, neighbourly help as well as voluntary work in associations is threatened by claims for damages, and all together might be charged with tax fraud.

If hikers use trails maintained by members of voluntary alpine associations, they are not customers buying a good, as well as these associations are not selling a kind of 'adventure holiday' but are providing a common good open to be used by everybody who wants. If these associations are held responsible for accidents happening there and thus have to expect claims of compensation they will not longer be ready to maintain alpine hiking trails in their leisure time. Treating hikers as 'consumers' of hiking trails with the right of compensation, finally shows the effect that these trails will either not be maintained any more, or that people have to pay to use them as it is already practiced in some places and thus once more extending the scope of market logic.

But in many of the contexts described above, individuals act as consumers in the sense of using resources – either natural or man-made – in so far as they consume food or electricity. In this role, as they are directly involved in processes of decision and production, they really could act as 'responsible' consumers, provided that these activities were supported by an adequate legal framework. But this cannot be achieved by a law made to protect customers.

A real consumer protection law, instead, had to protect individuals against the integration of their activities in market relations, against the pressure of big companies and against governmental policies that support that, like in Denmark, windmills built and run by local cooperatives were taken over by for profit companies (cf. Kruse 2009: 224). It should also protect them against laws that apply industrial standards to family enterprises or reduce the quality of child care facilities to building regulations. It had to guarantee the right to organise food and energy consumption autonomously or at least to participate in decisions made about how and what is produced. Only if individuals are involved in decision making, they can take the responsibility for what they do, for their behaviour as consumers.

But the current legislation on so called 'consumer protection' not only fails to meet this requirement, but even prevents such activities by treating individuals as customers in all their activities and thus transforming all their relations into market relations. It creates the 'total' consumer within the 'total' market, locating all other activities in a sphere outside the law or at least in a grey area. We can see that laws, made to protect individuals in specific situations, can be used as instruments of restriction and control if applied universally in fields they are not adequate for.

Overprotection always implies the danger of incapacitating individuals, to reduce their agency and control and thus strengthens hegemonic power. The reach of protection laws, the area they should cover, the space they should leave for individual arrangements, therefore cannot be fixed but have to be subject of social negotiations. In the case of 'customer protection' its scope had to differ according to the distance and the anonymity of the market relations and it had to leave open a space for individuals to actively engage in the production of things they need in local contexts and in decision making about how these products are produced and used.

To prevent misuse of law, individuals are vested with basic citizens rights, they can refer to against such attempts of governments and that make these borders between protection and control a field of struggle. Through the totalisation of the logic of the market, in the case of 'consumer' protection it was possible to disguise or at least to extend these borders.

That the jurisdiction of 'consumer' protection laws could enlarge to nearly all activities is a consequence of constituting individuals as customers and subjecting nearly all their activities to this role. Because governmental techniques have brought individuals to perceive themselves as customers the reduction of the realm of self-organisation and individual freedom in the name of 'consumer' protection had been accepted almost without resistance and is even appreciated by individuals who feel as customers and identify themselves with this role. So we can see that laws can be used as governmental strategies to gain trust, acceptance and legitimacy, even though reducing basic citizens' rights. Thus the enlargement of individuals rights as customers disguised the reduction of control and agency it includes.

It was already mentioned that the European Union puts a strong emphasis on 'consumer' protection and that this is one of the most appreciated aspects of the EU, which is easily to understand given the above outlined conditions. On the other hand, the reference to EU law on 'consumer' protection frequently is used by national governments to legitimate their own programs. In the context of 'multilevel governance' on each level the program may be adopted to the interests of the respective governing body, either national or regional governments, while they can blame the others for unintended side effects due of the lack of transparency in these multilevel processes. For the individuals confronted with this law it is not clear, whether its implications were intended by the EU, whether it was used by the national government to enact laws otherwise rejected by the population, or the regional government applying the law, used it for their purposes (cf. Benz 2004: 143). Thus people do not know whom to blame for negative effects, they do not know how to intervene and thus get the impression that one cannot do anything about it because critique or complaints seem to come to nothing. This possibly is one more reason why resistance against the weakening of basic rights remains on a marginal level.

But the main insight we can draw from this analysis is more general and not restricted to EU level and it brings us back to the beginning, when it was stated, that states are a 'function of changes in practices of government' (Gordon 1991: 4). The same holds for international state-like institutions. They are part of the arrangement for governing individuals. They, on the one hand, have to guarantee political stability, security and rule of law. But on the other hand – and partly exactly to meet these tasks – they are also institutions to preserve and reproduce the existing orders of knowledge and power and can turn into instruments of control an repression if a balance of social powers can not be achieved.

We have to be aware that

> Liberty is a practice ... The liberty of men is never assured by the institutions and laws that are intended to guarantee them. This is why almost all of these laws and institutions are quite capable of being turned around. Not because they are ambiguous, but simply because 'liberty' is what must be exercised. ... I think it can never be inherent in the structures of things to guarantee the exercise of freedom (Foucault 1986, quoted from Gordon 1991: 47).

But that, of course, does not mean that those laws and institutions should be abandoned. Rather we can assume that they are a precondition and have to be a target of social practices. It is only from this knowledge that we can develop perspectives for political activities that aim on changing power relations and overcoming the contradictions inherent to the generalisation of one single order of knowledge.

Questioning totalities – opening space for change

The emphasis on individual 'consumer' power and responsibility and – as a consequence – the focus on maintaining purchasing power and keeping individuals morally obliged to fulfil their duties as responsible 'consumers', allows interventions in the spheres of citizens rights, labour rights and social rights while keeping them outside the space of bargaining and struggles and also outside of the space of public perception. Instead of fighting for human or social rights, the 'consumer-subject' tries to achieve their implementation through acts of purchasing, Then everything, also human rights, social rights or ecological sustainability is subordinated to market rationality, can only be pursued under this rationality thus increasing the totality of its scope. Because the logic of the market stands against these goals, social movements are confronted with contradictions and impasses.

The mode of subjectivation as responsible consumer seems to promise profit and sustainability at the same time, and suggests that we all have to work together to overcome the different crises. Therefore class differences have to be postponed. It is important to be aware that we have not reached the end of class conflicts but only a new mode of their specification, with new techniques of power and new instruments for control, activation or repression. As shown above, the responsibility for more problems is handed down to the subordinate classes, while capital accumulation remains in the hands of the few who benefit from it. Nevertheless, the traditional logic of left and right may become questionable, as lines of conflict open across and within these social groups. While pretending to close the gap between capital and working class the discourse of responsible consumption opens lines of conflicts within the working class, further weakening its power.

Resistance from the perspective of governmentality, is not a resistance against the current order of knowledge proposing another, better one, to be implemented instead, because each world view that claims to be the 'right' one deploys hegemonic effects and powers of domination. Rather it means resistance against the totality of this rationality, against the totality of the market and the totality of the 'consumer subject'. Resistance then means to refuse the imposed mode of subjectivation and to develop different identities and counter-hegemonial practices.

Social movements as well as trade unions, should refuse the role of the 'responsible consumer' and their emphasis on maintaining purchasing power, but turn to the issues of control and agency. The latter cannot be reduced to the activity of 'shopping', but has to regain spaces for autonomy beyond market relations and state control for a need oriented reproduction of living conditions. In order to achieve this we have to understand how the neoliberal notions of 'freedom', 'emancipation' or 'participation' are constructed by governmental rationality and the respective programs and to use the gap between the target and the impossibility of achievement for processes of appropriation. In times of crisis, this gap tends to broaden, certainties break away and power constellations are challenged.

> Unleashed barbarism and humane civilisation were formed as elements, as seeds, as origins in the processing contradictions of capitalism. In times of crisis these elements could immediately be put together into entirely new totalities – into totalitatian fascisms, but maybe also into societies based on solidarity (Brie 2009: 17).

It is especially the field of energy that is of outstanding importance for the capitalist mode of reproduction, and thus for the respective power relations and therefore always has been a field of struggles. The turn from fossil to renewable energy provides the opportunity to upset power relations if only we recognise that the issue of energy is neither a question of technology nor individual responsibility, but we have to

> understand the use, production, and distribution of energy as moments of capitalist social relations of production. As such, energy and technology are both important sites of struggle, and are shaped by these struggles. (Abramsky/de Angelis 2008/9: 1).

The issues of climate change and peak oil are very contradictory between environmentalists and workers, between the poor, who cannot afford 'responsibility', and those better off, between workers in the old, 'dirty' industries and the innovative, 'green' industries. In addition, all individuals are concerned in more than one aspect, they are workers and consumers, workers and environmentalists, at the same time. So conflicts arise not only between individuals but also within themselves. Many different struggles emerged worldwide, grounded in these aspects and it is of crucial importance that these

> *struggles can find ways of collectively organizing and struggling that do not pit one struggle against another, but instead gives rise to a social force that is simultaneously able to set limits on capital and also create alternatives (ibid.: 5).*

If environmentalists continue the moral appeals for responsible 'consumption' they support the assumption that social and environmental problems can be solved by purchasing acts and reproduce these gaps and conflicts, instead of putting the problem back to where it belongs, namely into the fields of politics and production. Trade unions follow a similar fallacy when defending jobs in energy-intensive production or when claiming 'thousands of new green' jobs. It must made clear that social, environmental and democratic problems have the same source in the capitalist system of reproduction and hence have to be solved together and trade offs between them are not acceptable. Instead of enforcing the logic of anonymous markets the necessity of collective action and democratic control must be stressed.

From that point we can develop a concept of individual liberty and self-realisation that cannot be gained via free markets but is only to be realised within mutual interdependence and social interactions. It depends on modes of production and regulation that enhance both, sustainable use of natural resources and supportive social relations, the quality of these relations and the chances of individual development in the best case supporting each other. A paradigm drawing on this assumption is the Social Quality Approach brought forward by the European Foundation on Social Quality. Social quality

> *is defined as the extent to which people are able to participate in social, economic and cultural life and development of their communities under conditions which enhance their well-being and individual potential.*

From this perspective

> *[e]mpowerment is concerned with the means and processes and relations necessary for people to be capable of actively participating in social relations and actively influencing the immediate and more distant social and physical environment.[70]*

> *(see Herrmann in this volume: 216; see as well Herrmann, forthcoming)*

This kind of empowerment can certainly not be achieved through market relations but through collective action and democratic processes.

---

[70] http://www.socialquality.org/site/index.html

References

Abramsky, Kolya/Angelis, Massimo de (2009): Energy Crisis (Among Others) Is In The Air. In: The Commoner. Issue 13, Winter 2008-9 http://www.commoner.org.uk/N13/00-Introduction.pdf

Angelis, Massimo de (2007): The Beginning of History. Value Struggles and Global Capital. London: Pluto Press,

Angelis, Massimo de (2008a): Crisis: Neoliberal Impasse and Political Recomposition; ' http://www.commoner.org.uk/wp-content/uploads/2008/07/deangelis_crises1.pdf - 05/05/2010

Angelis, Massimo de (2008b): Next Lap in the Rat Race? From Sub-Prime Crisis to the 'Impasse' of Global Capital. http://www.commoner.org.uk/wp-content/ uploads/2008/06/deangelis_sub-prime.pdf - 05/05/2010

Araghi, Farshad (2010): The End of 'Cheap Ecology' and the Crisis of 'Long Keynesianism'. In: Economic and Political Weekly, January 23, 2010, Vol XLV no 4. http://beta.epw.in/static_media/PDF_folder/archives_pdf/latest_issues/ P012310_The_End_of_Farshad_Araghi.pdf - 05/05/2010

Benz, Arthur (Ed.) (2004): Multilevel Governance – Governance in Mehrebenen-systemen. In: Benz, Arthur: Governance – Regieren in komplexen Regel-systemen. Wiesbaden:VS Verlag für Sozialwissenschaften: 125 – 146

Biebricher, Thomas (2008): Staatlichkeit, Gouvernementalität und Neoliberalismus. In: Gesellschaftstheorie nach Marx und Foucault. Prokla no. 151, 2/2008, Münster: Westfälisches Dampfboot: 307 – 322

Brand, Ulrich (2007): The Internationalisation of the State as the Reconstitution of Hegemony. IPW Working Paper No. 1/2007. Vienna: Institut für Politikwissen-schaft Universität Wien

Brand, Ulrich/Sekler, Nicola (ed.): Postneoliberalism – A beginning debate. In: Development dialogue no. 51, January 2009. Uppsala: Dag Hammarskjöld Centre

Brand, Ulrich/Sekler, Nicola (2009a): Postneoliberalism: catch-all word or valuable analytical and political concept? – Aims of a beginning debate. In: Postneoliberalism – A beginning debate. In: Development dialogue no. 51, January 2009. Uppsala: Dag Hammarskjöld Centre: 5 - 13

Brie, Michael (2009): Ways out of the crisis of neoliberalism. In: Brand, Ulrich / Sekler, Nicola (ed.): Postneoliberalism – A beginning debate. In: Development dialogue no. 51, January 2009. Uppsala: Dag Hammarskjöld Centre: 15 – 31

Bröckling, Ulrich (2007): Das unternehmerische Selbst. Soziologie einer Sub-jektivierungsform. Frankfurt am Main: suhrkamp

Burchell, Graham (1996): Liberal government and techniques of the self. In: Barry Andrew/Osborne, Thomas/Rose, Nikolas (Ed.): Foucault and Political Reason. Liberalism, neo-liberalism and rationalities of government. Chicago: The University of Chicago Press: 19 – 36

Cleaver, Harry (1979): Reading Capital Politically. Austin: University of Texas Press

European Commission (2006): Communication from the Commission to the European Parliament, the Council and the European Economic and Social Committee: Implementing the partnership for growth and jobs: Making Europe a pole of excellence on Corporate Social Responsibility. COM(2006) 136 final Brussels, 22.3.2006
http://eur-lex.europa.eu/LexUriServ/site/en/com/2006/com2006_0136en01.pdf - 05/05/2010

European Commission (2009): Commission Working Dokument: Consultation on the Future of 'EU 2020' Strategy. COM(2009)647 Brussels, 24.11.2009 final http://ec.europa.eu/dgs/secretariat_general/eu2020/docs/com_2009_647_en.pdf - 05/05/2010

European Council (2000): Lisbon European Council 23 and 24 March 2000, Presidency conclusions. http://www.europarl.europa.eu/summits/lis1_en.htm - 05/05/2010

Foucault, Michel (1986): On the Genealogy of Ethics: An Overview of Work in Progress, interview with Robert Dreyfus and Paul Rabinow. In: Rabinow, Paul (ed): The Foucault Reader. Harmondsworth: Penguin Social Sciences

Foucault, Michel (1991): Governmentality. In: Burchell, Graham / Gordon, Colin / Miller, Peter (Ed.): The Foucault Effect. Studies in Governmentality. Hertfordshire: Harvester Wheatsheaf: 87 – 104

Frank, Stefan (2009): Die Weltvernichtungsmaschine. Vom Kreditboom zur Wirtschaftskrise. Saarbrücken: Conte Verlag

Gordon, Colin (1991): Governmental rationality: an introduction. In: Burchell, Graham/Gordon, Colin/Miller, Peter (Ed.): The Foucault Effect. Studies in Governmentality; Hertfordshire: Harvester Wheatsheaf: 1 – 51

Gorz, André (2004): Wissen, Wert und Kapital. Zur Kritik der Wissensökonomie; Zürich: Rotpunktverlag

Herrmann, Peter (forthcoming): Empowerment – processing the processed; in: van der Maesen, Laurent/Walker, Alan (eds.), forthcoming: Sustainable Welfare Societies and overall Sustainability; London et altera: Macmillan

Herrmann, Peter (forthcoming): Searching for Global Social Policy – Economy, Economics and Governance

Hirsch, Joachim (2002): Herrschaft, Hegemonie und politische Alternativen; Hamburg: VSA Verlag

Horx, Mathias (1985): Das Ende der Alternativen. Ein Rechenschaftsbericht. München: Hanser Verlag

Kaufman, Leslie (2010): 'Preserving The Planet, Taxing Relationships' In: The New York Times. Insert in Der Standard, Vienna, 03/01/2010

Kruse, Jane (2009): The End Of One Danish Windmill Co-Operative. In: The Commoner. Issue 13, Winter 2008-9: 223 – 224
http://www.commoner.org.uk/N13/15-Kruse.pdf - 05/09/2010

Lemke, Thomas (1997): Kritik der politischen Vernunft; Hamburg: Argument,

Neumann, Arndt (2008): Kleine geile Firmen; Hamburg: Verlag Lutz Schulenburg

Rose, Nikolas (1996): Governing 'advanced' liberal democracies. In: Barry Andrew/Osborne, Thomas/Rose, Nikolas (Ed.): Foucault and Political Reason. Liberalism, neo-liberalism and rationalities of government. Chicago: The University of Chicago Press: 37 – 64

Sum, Ngai-Ling (2009): Struggles against Wal-Martisation and neoliberal competitiveness in (southern) China – Towards postneoloberalism as an alternative? In: Brand, Ulrich/Sekler, Nicola (ed.): Postneoliberalism – A beginning debate. In: Development dialogue no. 51, January 2009; Uppsala: Dag Hammarskjöld Centre: 157 – 170

Empowerment – processing the processed

Peter Herrmann

Introduction – Localising Empowerment

To look at empowerment in the context of the social quality approach has to face two challenges,

- the one being the necessity to locate the orthogonality and embeddedness of empowerment in the context of discussing the other factors, namely socio-economic security, social inclusion and social cohesion;
- the other being concerned with elaborating the specificity of the factor and its distinctiveness in relation to other reference-theories of empowerment.

To put it simple, the first question is: How is empowerment linked to and actually defined by the other factors? The questions in the second complex are: Has empowerment a distinct meaning in the context of the social quality theory – distinct when compared with the understanding in other contexts? How is it differentiated in relation for instance to empowerment in the context of social work, learning theories and others? Of course, these questions are interrelated and in actual fact, in a way we have to answer both questions simultaneously.

The original definition of empowerment in the theory of social quality, as it had been iteratively developed (see Beck/van der Maesen/Walker, 2001) highlights the following five points:

- the fundamental reference to equity;
- the reference to capabilities and capacities and thus – logically – the interaction of action and structure
- the reference to the actor-orientation of the social-quality concept and thus the central role empowerment has to play;
- the 'practical' relevance of the concept, and its 'instrumental character' in terms of policy making;
- the reference to 'choice', again linking action and structure.

Seen in this light, empowerment had been defined in the following way:

> *Empowerment to realize human competencies or capabilities (versus subordination) primarily concerns the micro-level enabling of people, as 'citizens', to develop their full potential. Thus this component of social quality refers to developing the competence of citizens in order to participate in processes determining daily life.*

(Beck/van der Maesen/Walker, 1997: 290).

However, to get a clear understanding we have to look first at the question of power and the two analytically distinct dimensions. Helpful is briefly investigating the linguistic dimension. Taking the French *pouvoir,* we see clearer then in the English language the dimensions of being able to do something, to make on the one hand and on the other hand the dimension of power that is concerned with control. In Italian language we find synonyms as *potere, potenza* and as well *forza* and *autorità.* And in German we see the strict link of *Macht,* the root being *machen,* i.e. making. This suggests seeing power as category very much concerned with actually bridging two main dimensions which are in social thought usually seen as independent and/or dichotomous, namely the social and the economic. This characteristic dichotomisation is not just a matter of two areas but reaches the core of social thinking, namely the confrontation between idealist and materialist social theory.

But this is, of course, very much a reflection of real social developments, namely the falling apart of these different dimensions. Niklas Luhmann once characterised this by writing "Alles könnte anders sein – und fast nichts kann ich ändern." (Luhmann, 1969: 44) [All could be different but I nearly cannot change anything.]. However, the question arises why and in which way everything actually could be different? And why can we not change anything?

Crucial moments in this context – as matter of real development and also as matter that is important when it comes to the epistemological dimension of contemporary analysis – are the two secular shifts we can detect as decisively characterising historical developments: the one is the increasing juridification and more specifically contractualisation – this is not least a matter of increasingly undermining genuine social patterns and replace them by somewhat artificial glues (see Herrmann, 2009 a). We see from here the particularly strong link between empowerment and cohesion. The other secular trend is that around commodification, semi-commodification and decommodification. Though have to acknowledge the limitation of such statement, we may say that the commodification-decommodification axes links heuristically empowerment to both, the dimension of socio-economic security and to inclusion.

From here, the most important questions about empowerment and the search for relevant indicators have to concentrate on the following issues. (i) the determination of citizenship and with this the determination of internal divisions and external borders; (ii) the determination of power inequalities and their debate in the context of 'gaining societal wealth' for their (pseudo-)justification; (iii) the discussion of power distribution between win-win and zero-sum games. – Before looking at these issues, some general remarks are required.

Empowerment – some mainstream issues

If we look for empowerment and how it is reflected in contemporary debates, we can see in particular two strands. The one is very much dealing with issues on the individual level, concerned with matters of the empowering individuals in settings of their immediate sociability. As such, relevant considerations are very much linked to the subject of social psychology and as much as they can claim following an emancipative ethos, they are following very much an affirmative notion: being geared towards individuals developing 'ownership' over the immediate environment. The fundamental limitation is given by such approaches being concerned with individuals' development: it is the individual that is encouraged to develop such ownership, proposing that such identification contributes to the enhancement of affirmative (non-) action: systemic attachment rather than systemic development and change are at the centre of this orientation.

On the other hand, empowerment is promoted as strategy of governance, replacing and/or complementing democracy. Again, the fundamental notion is affirmative, actually not meant to deal with the issue of societal power. Moreover, it is not even dealing with the distribution of power within a given system as it rigidly accepts the framework setting without considering the complex interrelationship of relational and processual issues of empowerment. To understand empowerment in a more appropriate way it is useful to start from a tensional field in which power – and subsequently empowerment – can be understood. This field spans on the one hand between individual and societal and is on the other hand characterised by appropriation and control. It is characteristic that the latter dimension is – as appropriation – primarily concerned with the relationship between humans and nature and – as control – primarily seen as matter of social relationship. However, it has to be emphasised that this is true by way of interpreting contemporary relationships rather than being employed with the generic dimension of power. Generically, we are dealing with a socio-environmental relationship: social processes are linked into and depending on the natural environment; and vice versa, the natural environment does barely exist as such: it is predisposed by the way in which individuals and societies are actually dealing with it and in which way this is a process that is shaped by the socio-environmental presuppositions.

As heuristic tool the following matrix may be helpful:

	individual - (power of individuals)	societal - (power of society)
appropriation		
ruling and control of others		

Figure 9: Power, Appropriation and Ruling[71]

In this light it is clear that as much as the social quality concept aims in general on overcoming the methodological individualism which underlies – explicitly or implicitly – most of social science, it is in particular the centrality of *empowerment as an objective factor* that makes it possible to grasp the dialectical relationship between *(a)* actor and structure and thus *(b)* between the individual and soci(et)al.

As already briefly mentioned, empowerment is commonly positioned at the borderline of the different dimensions of the individual and the social, actually meaning that it claims to fulfil a bridge-function, making it possible to combine in a single act the two dimensions which had been spelled out by *James S. Coleman* as

> *character of macro-to-micro and micro-to-macro transitions*
>
> *(Coleman, 1990: 11 f.)*

---

[71] See in this context as well the reflections on the different traditions of conceptualising the state in theories of social contract as elaborated in Herrmann 2007

The challenge of defining empowerment is seen as overcoming the apparent disparity of

- the *Durkheimian* understanding of the social, pointing on an independent entity in its own rights and

- the original definition of the social quality approach according to which

    the social is not existing as such but it is the expression of constantly changing aspects of processes by which individuals realize themselves (verwirklichen) as interacting beings.

    (Beck et altera, 2001: 310)

In actual fact, what seems to be suggested as contradiction between the approaches is more a contradiction in earlier formulations of the social quality approach itself as at the same location it is said that

our endeavour is to develop a scientific framework and a political programme which assume the social as an authentic entity.

(ibid.)

In other words, this approach itself presumes a certain independence of the social, whereas it states at the same time that the social 'is not existing as such'. Here the attention is turning to another emphasis of the definition, seeing it as

both the ever-present condition (material cause) and the continually reproduced outcome of human agency. And praxis is both work, that is conscious production, and (normally unconscious) reproduction of the conditions of production, that is society.

(Bhaskar, 1979: 43 f.; cited in Beck at altera, 2001: 312)

Seen in this light, empowerment is central to the entire concept of Social Quality. Deciphering the definition of the social, we can highlight as a forgotten matter of interest that an explicit link between the living-together of people and the definition of citizenship is established.

Following the proposal to point out a trinominal structure, *(a)* the subject matter of empowerment is the provision of the means of and for communication as foundation of the social as interactive process. Whereas other factors concentrate on available material resources *(socio-economic security),* the integration into different relationships *(inclusion)* and trustworthiness of relationships *(cohesion),* the concern of *empowerment* is the availability and reliability of the availability of access, necessary to establish the capability of participation.[72] *(b)* The specific nature, i.e. the resources needed being knowledge and rights, necessary to put the potential into reality. *(c)* Taking these considerations seriously when looking at empowerment, we can say that this is a variable that is

- to some extent the point of departure, the factor on which the realisation of the others is build upon and
- at the same time the 'result' of the other factors.

In other words, *empowerment is very much a conditional and – when related to the other factors – a resulting factor.* We have to take this already into account when we are looking for a definition of empowerment. The definition proposed is – so far as follows:

> *Social Empowerment is concerned with the means and processes and relations necessary for people to be capable of actively participating in social relations and actively influencing the immediate and more distant social and physical environment.*

Or shorter we can say that

> *Social Empowerment is the degree to which the personal capabilities are and the ability of people to act is enhanced by social relations.*

Empowerment is then the core of the entire project of social quality (see Herrmann, 2005). From here, the Social Quality Approach is very much understandable as dialectical theory of action. It is not solely and even primarily concerned with transfer of knowledge, enabling the individual to cope with given structural situations. Rather, empowerment is concerned with enabling the person individually and socially to

- adapt to a given situation,
- to cope with changes of situations and
- to actively influence social developments, i.e. to evoke and maintain changes.

---

[72] This refers largely to the definitions of the other components, recapitulated by van der Maesen, 2003: 23

The notion of enlightenment

This stands against commonly used traits of dichotomising the nature in social sciences in which empowerment is usually located on the micro-, the meso- or the macro level alternatively. This does not draw immediate attention to the relational character of the social. Such relational perspective is not simply a matter of relations between people but as well and more importantly a matter of relations between individual and the soci(et)al. – Although this cannot be elaborated, it has to be mentioned that such a conceptualisation largely helps to overcome the dichotomy between structure and agency. As such, the social concerns

> the outcomes of reciprocal relationships (dialectic) between processes of self-realisation of individual people as social beings and processes leading to the formation of collective identities. Its subject matter concerns the outcomes of this reciprocity. ...
>
> The definition of social quality is based on this reciprocity. Social quality is the extent to which people are able to participate in the social and economic life of their communities under conditions which enhance their well-being and individual potential.
>
> (van der Maesen, April 2004)

A very general, i.e. philosophical orientation on empowerment, employing an individualising bottom-up approach, comes from the notion of enlightenment which derives the social from the notion of rationalisation and of translating increasing cognition by the individual into the basis of the social fabric and finally society. In the perspective of the *Kantian* imperative

> act so that the maxim of thy will can always at the same time hold good as a principle of universal legislation
>
> (Kant, 1788)

the social is nothing else than an 'invisible contract', drawn between individuals not on grounds of necessary control of individual behaviour but on grounds of a higher natural law of reason and the ability as well as duty of the individual to accept responsibility.

As such this can be already seen as an acknowledgement of power, although it fundamentally divides the individual and the social – power is then equalled with responsibility – responding in accordance with the ability to rationally perceive the world and to act accordingly. The social is not seen as a genuine 'goal and framework' in and by which individuals realise themselves. Moreover, the social is not considered as being an entity sui generis, constituted by social actors. Rather, the social is understood as construct, a conglomerate emerging from isolated individual acts, based on knowledge and constituted by the individual's efforts to coordinate their actions and activities.

Such a perspective is taken up even by the *Frankfurt School,* the *Institute for Social Research.* There, *Max Horkheimer* in his *Eclipse of Reason* importantly points on the loss of objective reason as guiding code (see Horkheimer 1947: 4-6), however, he then fails to clearly derive the criteria for 'empowering subjective-social rationality' from the social action itself. On the one hand, he refines such rationality by the allusion to religious or quasi-religious value systems; on the other hand, it is a matter that is suggested as being inherent to the objects and processes. Without exploring this further, the relevance for mentioning this approach lies in the fact that we can concede a continuation of these thoughts in terms of empowerment as communicative act. It is here, where *Juergen Habermas* suggests drawing on trust as voluntarily established basis for empowered – and further empowering – societal structures, itself based on practical but in particular intellectual insight. Actual soci(et)al practice as practice of change, however, is replaced by contemplation and consensus, based upon ethical principles. It is the 'universalistic humanism' which *Max Horkheimer* already mentioned, writing:

> The basic ideals and concepts of rationalist metaphysics were rooted in the concept of the universally human, of mankind, and their formalization implies that they have been severed from their human content.

> (ibid.: 62)

The *Theory of Communicative Action,* then, uses this as disguise. Referring to *Max Weber,* we read that

> [t]he social is not absorbed as such by organized action systems; rather, it is split up into spheres of action constituted as the lifeworld and spheres neutralized against the lifeworld. The former are communicatively structured, the latter formally organized. They do not stand in any **hierarchical** relationship between levels of interaction and organization; rather, they stand **opposite** one another as socially and systematically integrated spheres of action. In formally organized domains, the mechanisms of mutual understanding language, which is essential for social integration, is partially rescinded and relieved by steering media. (Habermas, 1989: 309; emphasis in original)

218

This means, however, that in actual fact questions of power are dislodged, and defined as a matter of systems and sub-systems rather than as relationship between real social beings.

As much as *Habermas* draws attention upon the necessity of the intellectual appropriation and the knowing individual – the person, being able to understand and act in accordance with the environment on the basis of a 'mutual understanding and acceptance', as much he falls short of the actual unity of the world in which the individual shapes his/her life. Of course, under given social conditions of contemporary societies we find without any doubt the contradiction between different parts of society. However, *Habermas* draws a strict distinction between system world and life world, and goes in particular beyond *Loockwood's* concept. On the one hand, he applies a voluntarist concept – interpreting the system world as result of 'irresponsible action' by the ruling forces. On the other hand and contradicting, the system world is an apparently eternal, time- and even more actorless framework, perpetuing inevitable alienation between actor and a *dues ex machina,* developing just in the sense of the *Weberian* iron cage of bureaucracy. Social quality, if *Habermas* would consider such a concept at all as 'anti-colonialist', could only be a 'set of eternal values, set against the colonialiser'. However, neither the objective dialectic of the different domains nor the dialectical relationship between subjective and objective factors and domains would be understandable as in immediate part of the entire idea of Social Quality. Of course, this is a deviation of the original concept of the critical school. However, it goes even further in the sense that by taking 'communicative act(ion)' as basis of any progressive development, the actual 'social action by real people under real social conditions' is faded out. 'Social quality' in this perspective would degenerate into an idealist concept. Although this can be justified by the Kantian elements of the social quality approach itself, it fundamentally contradicts its action perspective which is fundamental for giving empowerment such a central place. Rather than empowering people as individuals and society as a conglomerate of rationally behaving people by enhancing their discursive power and trusting the 'power of ratio', empowerment in terms of social quality breaks up analytically. In other words, locating empowerment as one of the objective factors, linking it to the biographical and soci(et)al dialectically development overcomes the wrong dichotomy of 'systems, institutions, organisations' on the one hand and 'communities, configurations, groups' on the other hand, or in *Habermas'* terms system world and life world. – The debate of how close this can be linked into an *Eliasian* perspective of civilisation has to be spared although such a side-remark may stimulate for further thoughts.

However, this vision of 'empowerment by knowledge' is very vague. As much as *Kantian* thinking is of course idealistic, it would allow well for the further development of in particular

- orienting on the 'absolute idea' as particularly suggested by *Hegel*
- mechanical materialism as primarily developed by *Feuerbach* or
- a dialectical-materialist perspective as it is well known from *Marx*.

Empowerment – Overcoming Economist Perspectives

Leaving these debates aside, empowerment had been only recently re-invented and defined as explicit issue of social science. In particular, it has to be mentioned that the new interest emerged from a perceived need for action-oriented approaches of integration, well recognising that the relative openness of modern societies on a structural level, was nevertheless clearly limited by providing an inactivated (i.e. passivising) structure. One major reason for this explication can be seen in an increasing gap between private and public. On the one hand, the public gained more and more momentum – we can see it in the growing meaning of social (policy) actions, the interpenetration of daily life by public measures and the strictly defined responsibility of 'the public', meaning predominantly the state and its 'attached' bodies, combined with a decreasing control of these entities. At the same time, however, we find an increasing dependency of individuals by these bodies and as well a kind of 'privatisation', definitely a 'closure'. For example one expression of this general shift can be seen in the fact that more and more people are covered by social measures of one or the other kind.[73] However, such a 'public system' is at the same time increasingly 'private' as the general interest is getting less and less important, its definition follows private decisions rather than being an issue of real public discourse or let alone public action (see Herrmann, 2006).

Going back to such disparity between individual and social regulation and action, in particular two notions of empowerment are getting prevalent – the one being concerned with a technical approach of increasing the accessibility of given – and uncontested – structures; the

---

[73] As for example the increasing coverage of the people by social insurance systems independent of their employment status.

other being concerned with developing a vision of increasing the power of the individual in control over his/her own life, overcoming the limitations of traditional economist thinking.

(1)

The first perspective, strongly an individualist strategy, has two dimensions. The one is concerned with the opening of structures. Although it is not geared to fundamental change, the concept is concerned with altering the structure of society. Powerlessness is then seen as result of a mismatch between individual and structure, requiring a simplification of the structures. We find such theorising in particular in reflections on management and of political sociology, looking at questions of government's responsiveness and the respective 'crisis of governance' and 'crisis of governability'. All these approaches assume basically an irreconcilable relation between social and individual. The social is designed as largely independent of the actors, determined *(a)* by an (undetermined) elite and/or *(b)* as undetermined entity, a kind of *deus ex machina*. Empowerment in such a context is understood as defining access points that allow successively finding a common language of 'actors' and 'structures'. Although alienation is – even if not necessarily explicitly – accepted as unavoidable, empowerment is interpreted as bottom-up strategy of opening the system to allow for 'participation'.

In theoretical terms, this approach is based in political science on the one hand, and more broadly it can be traced back to systems theory, as brought forward by *Niklas Luhmann*. Though *Luhmann* claimed to start from 'open systems', he established the presumption of mechanisms which in actual fact closed the different entities by referring *(a)* to functionality of the systems and *(b)* – especially in later years – the reference to autopoitic self-reproduction.[74] In terms of empowerment – though not explicitly elaborated by *Luhmann* – it meant that we find potentially two forms.

The one can be seen as 'internal empowerment', being concerned with establishing and developing mechanism of internal control of own resources. In other words, here we can talk of 'empowered management', increasing the effectiveness and efficiency of using respective 'general media' as they are used by the (sub-)system in question.

---

[74] It is a worthwhile debate in its own right to look at how far actually such a closure of system theories reflects in actual fact reality or is simply an expression of certain ideological limitations of systems theory.

The other can be seen as mechanism of enhancing communication skills between (sub-)systems. The 'general media' are bound by the 'formula of contingency' as limitations of what a single system can actually deal with. As such these media cannot be 'translated' and consequently exchange is limited.[75] However, this does not make the necessity of 'co-ordination' redundant. One way of coordination is putting mechanisms of 'structural coupling' into place. In a way, these can be seen as effort of translation – for instance 'rights' can be seen as a typical example where the legal code is actually used as an answer on civil, political and social challenges (see Marshall, 1950). Such a perspective would allow a way of passive empowerment. The actual power basis is not even looked at; however, the changes which are controlled, are the procedures by which the actual execution of power takes place (in *Luhmann's* terminology the 'legitimation by procedure').

Another mechanism is more active, i.e. it is defined by the actors or the respective subsystem itself. This starts from the presumption that the different systems are well able to produce an effective 'noise' which requires at least the targeted system to answer in some way. This kind of action can well be interpreted as empowerment as it is conceptualised by theories of government. Politically, as we will see, it finds its expression in strategies of 'better government', orientation on governance and 'strategic management' by creating 'one-point-access', improved and simplified information etc.

At the end, in this light empowerment is reduced on the partial redistribution of power, enhancing the abilities of the individual to access power points. Turned around, this means however, that power as such is not availed off by the individuals. *(a)* It is individuals who (may) increase their own power rather than changing the actual power structure. This can be interpreted as an increase in 'quality of life', but is alien to increasing 'social quality'. *(b)* Power is basically seen in terms of a zero-sum game – collective power, though in modern theories of governance mentioned, is not at the core of such theories. Moreover, here the understanding as it is grounded in (though individualistic) the process of modernisation as matter of enlightenment and cognition of the world is left behind in favour of an entirely mechanical individualist approach.

What can be valuably borrowed from such an approach, however, is the requirement of clearly defining the reference points of the analysis. In

---

[75] As Luhmann mentioned it is not possible to exchange for instance lawfulness by capital gains and vice versa.

regard of the debate on empowerment it is necessary *(a)* to clearly define over what power is actually exercised and *(b)* to make out on which level it is actually exercised – this latter point may be concerned with the reference to the same aggregate level and as well with the power which reaches across the different levels. We have to distinguish in particular between

- sub-systemic exchange, i.e. the execution of power on the same aggregate level (individual power),
- systemic exchange, i.e. the execution of power in the immediate environment (social power), and
- exchange with the environment, i.e. the execution of power in the wider environment (societal power).

(2)

The other approach – and one which is very inspiring for understanding empowerment from a social quality perspective – focuses on capacities and capabilities. In particular *Amartya Sen* can be seen as representative – and even initiator – of such an interpretation. The characteristic moment is that such a view takes capacities and capabilities together, thus emphasising the connection between *(a)* objective conditions of availing of power and *(b)* the ability to make use of these 'opportunities'. Not least, this is based on a critique of parts of traditional mainstream economic theory. *Sen* argues against simplifying economist theories of motivation which suggest

> *to see rationality as internal consistency of choice, and the other ... to identify rationality with maximization of self-interest.*

> *(Sen, 1987: 12)*

Instead, for him rational decisions are only one element of decision making. In consequence, there are as well other moments that finally decide over the power of individuals. The one aspect is simply the economic power in the sense of objectively given resources 'as such'; however, another aspect is the 'value' of these resources in terms of what a person actually can achieve with them.

By developing such a perspective, *Sen* articulates in particular the reinterpretation of poverty as matter of accessing means by which the individual can gain control over the own living circumstances. Philosophically, such a perspective is based on Stoicism and its emphasis of the independence of the individual, the 'engagement by gaining distance and independence' (Nussbaum, 1998: 58). Sociologically, such an approach is closely (though not directly and explicitly) linked to interpretative sociology as it looks for structures and resources insofar – and only insofar – as they represent a certain 'meaning'. In other words, the form is only relevant as far as it determines – and allows for – a specific and enhanced content. Here, empowerment is very much linked to its etymological root – the *pouvoir*, the ability which can be understood as

> the expansion of the 'capabilities' of persons to lead the kind of lives they value – and have reason to value.
>
> *(Sen, 1999: 18)*

Consequently, *Sen* writes:

> The concept of 'functionings', which has distinctly Aristotelian roots, reflects the various things a person may value doing or being. The valued functionings may vary from elementary ones, such as being adequately nourished and being free from avoidable disease, to very complex activities or personal states, such as being able to take part in the life of the community and having self-respect.
>
> *(ibid.: 75)*

This is followed by the remark:

> There can be substantial debates on the particular functionings that should be included in the list of important achievements and the corresponding capabilities. This valuational issue is inescapable in an evaluative exercise of this kind, and one of the main merits of the approach is the need to address these judgemental questions in an explicit way, rather than hiding them in some implicit framework.
>
> *(ibid.)*

Nevertheless it has to be seen that this debate is mainly based on an economic approach of 'balancing resources', aiming on equilibrium and orienting on 'coping with situations of shortage'. On the one hand, *Sen* rejects a purely economic approach and argues in particular against welfarism on the basis of Pareto-optimal distributions, which he argues are only concerned with efficiency criteria.

He states that

> *welfarism is the view that the only things of intrinsic value for ethical calculation and evaluation of states of affairs are individual utilities.*

(Sen, 1987: 40)

On the other hand, it can be very much argued against him that – by referring to agency – he only adds another moment to individual motivations underlying their decision making. although he mentions the 'creation of social opportunities' (see Sen, 1999: 40), the said limitation gets clear as he does not attempt to overcome the individualist perspective of the much referred Stoicism and the reference to

> *four distinct categories of relevant information regarding a person, involving 'well-being achievement', 'well-being freedom', 'agency achievement', and 'agency freedom'.*

(Sen, 1987: 61)

Furthermore, with this there is an undeniable danger to slipping down into a solely subjectively defined 'meaning'. Here a similar critique would apply as it had been brought forward in the debate of *Pierre Bourdieu's* class analysis and the notion of – at least partially – interchangeable 'concept de capital' (see Bourdieu 2000)and its culmination in the 'esprit de calcul' (see ibid.,: 17). Although power – and with this empowerment – is not infinite and not even quantifiable it is by no means a matter of contingencies. This is true in terms of the range of power and as well in terms of the foundation of power.

An important point in overcoming the difficulties can be seen in establishing a strong link between empowerment and citizenship. This is not only concerned with pointing on rights based aspects of the conceptualisation of empowerment strategies. Of course, strong points can be made in this regard – drawing attention to the historical development as pointed out primarily by *T.M. Marshall (see below),* but as well at least in terms of the established welfare states, in particular in form of legally codified systems.[76] Despite this, however, there is a

---

[76] In this context it is interesting that we find in German social science alongside with the term welfare state (Wohlfahrtsstaat) the term of the social state (Sozialstaat), the first referring more to the general pattern of the welfare-related governance, the different actors and the outcome of any kind of well-being, security and 'social embeddedness' (see in this context Gøsta Esping-Andersen), the second reflecting the judicial codification of social policy in its relation to

second strand of the debate which focuses on the meaning of citizenship. As much as this is a matter of existing – and withheld – rights we have to go a step beyond. The question of citizenship and rights is very much a matter of 'openness', of existing opportunities to participate (= take part in a given system), but as well of exploring and developing an in general open space. In other words, empowerment has to be concerned not solely and mainly with the realisation of the given social space but as well with the realisation of the self by which then the social space itself develops.

It is somewhat striking that recent debates on empowerment have their origins on the one hand in community work and community development, the latter including settings which deal by and large with ethnic minorities and/or migration issues. One of the most pronounced representatives is probably Paulo Freire, working on a 'Pedagogy of the Oppressed' (Freire, 1972). Though largely concerned with pedagogy and in particular with developing learning strategies in Latin America, the focus which is of interest in the present context is the emphasis of transformative action as a concept which claims to link dialectically the two sides of the consciousness, i.e. the subjective and the objective side. It is important that in this perspective 'teaching' and the 'appropriation of knowledge' does not equal the reproduction of knowledge. Rather, Freire interprets learning as an act, beginning with 'The Act of Study' (Freire, 1985: 1-4). He explains on another occasion:

> In reality, consciousness is not just a copy of the real, nor is the real only a capricious construction of consciousness. It is only by way of an understanding of the dialectical unity, in which we find solidarity between subjectivity and objectivity that we can get away from the subjectivist error as well as the mechanical error. And then we must take into account the role of consciousness or of the conscious being in the transformation of reality.
>
> (Freire, 1973: 153 f.)

Actually it means as well to understand power as a 'passive' factor in the sense of something 'one has or does not have' and at the same time as a process one can use, leaving for the present open the question for what it is actually of use, in who's interest it is executed.

The last formulation makes already clear that power – and with this empowerment – is a matter that relates not only to subjective and objective aspects but – subsequently – as well to individual and

---

the 'politics of [soci(et)al] order' (Ordnungspolitik).

collective aspects. Although it is an individual who avails of power, it is always the establishment of identification of the individual with a collective identity by way of self-actualisation.

> *The 'us and them' of the pluralist form of community were to be interpenetrated into a collective 'us' through a linking of 'public and private interest' formed in open and public dialogue.*

(Heskin, 1991: 63 f.)

Thus the reasoning behind selecting the indicators is getting very clear: This is clearly shown in the outline of the indicators which is provided above. Importantly, the indicators can and have to be forcefully welded into the debate on the two tensions: between communities and institutions on the one hand and between biographical and societal development on the other hand.

This interpretation opens the view on structures and the question if they are characterised by reciprocity (equalling empoweredness) or lack of reciprocity (equalling a lack of empoweredness). In the words used above, it is the reflection of the dialectical relationship between *(a)* actor and structure and thus between *(b)* the individual and soci(et)al.

Heskin reminds us of the relevance of *Gramscian* ideas and the fact that the Italian politician and scientist pointed on the necessity of an alternative hegemony, encapsulating the process of what dialectics called *Aufhebung,* the process of simultaneous sublation and supersession.

A major challenge remains to be followed up. Although power is in this understanding in the mentioned approaches – apart form the *Gramscian* view – basically open for the development of an 'easing' between different interests and allowing for the development of power in the 'common and general interest', there is at the same time the contradicting notion according to which power of communities seems to be somewhat prior to power of individuals, whereas then again the power of the communities seems to be always in danger of being subordinated by the power of society. In other words, these approaches – being fundamentally individualist – seem to presume as irrevocable fact – as general social law – that societal structures emerge in a way that makes them led by interests independent of actors. In other words, the alienation between structure and agency appears in this light as indispensable.

Consequently, we find a kind of 'normative gap', namely that community work and development approaches draw on the one hand attention on objective mechanisms of inequality; on the other hand, however, they seem to be ready to leave a high degree of openness to the predisposed normative definition of what empowerment, then, is about although they represent themselves in an objectivist manner. This gets in particular clear by confronting the following statement by *Fetterman* with the just mentioned contradiction which is established by many of those approaches between individual, community and society.

> *Empowerment has roots in community psychology, action anthropology, and action research. Community psychology focuses on people, organizations, and communities working to establish control over their affairs. ... work in action anthropology focuses on how anthropologists can facilitate the goals and objectives of self-determining groups ... .*
>
> *(Fettermann, 2001: 10)*

The links from here to the first two of the three steps of empowerment evaluation, namely

- *'establishing a mission or vision'*
- *'identifying and prioritizing the most significant program activities'*

(ibid.: 5)[77]

remains problematic as they are not part of a clearly set overall goal or evaluation respectively. Consequently the relationship between individual and soc(et)al and as well between objective and subjective dimension remain fuzzy, not allowing their translation into the analysis of a concrete social formation.

Empowerment – its relevance in European politics

Strangely, empowerment went through a weird career as part of European (social) policy making. Basically we find the following three notions in the debates.

First, we can see a general, not in concrete politics nor policies reflected philosophical approach. The importance of *Kant* and the tradition of enlightenment had been mentioned before and without exaggeration this can be seen – as positive basic feature as well as limited by the individualist and idealist perspective – 'European common sense',

---

[77] the third step, Fetterman mentions is 'charting a course for the future.' (ibid.: p. 6)

defining the European Social Model (see for a debate Herrmann, 1998 a; 2006; Leibfried/Pierson, 1995). Thus, the notion for instance of the Summit in Paris in the 1970s, emphasising that economic growth cannot be an end in itself but has to serve the well-being of the people can be interpreted in this sense.

Second, this general notion had later been translated into what may be called 'social work' perspective, being recognised as an important moment of programme policies particularly in the social area (see for instance Herrmann, 1995; 1997; 1998 b; 2009 b). The core was largely concerned with a strategy of solely enhancing individual's capacities and capabilities of adaptation. This is, by the way, important to note with view on cohesion and inclusion alike. In these terms of 'empowerment by and in programme policies' it can be said that failure of inclusion and lack of cohesion hat been seen as a matter of individual capacities lagging behind untouchable (and not responsible) conditions in the social fabric, a strategy of blaming the victims.

Third, this had been translated back again into a wider social and societal strategy, however one, which had been entirely concerned with matters of economic integration. Interestingly it can be noted that on the one hand the explicit reference to empowerment as it had been spelled out in social policy programmes had been more or less eliminated and replaced by the orientation of activation. This opened the way to an explicit link to welfare and social policies as it is outlined as part of the triangle which had been put forward by the *European Commission* in the Social Policy Agenda of 2000 (cf. Baars et altera, 2000).

The Framework

Domains and dimensions – developing an analytical tool

The term 'domain' captures the aspect of 'property' as well as the one of 'master(ing)'. The subject matter of empowerment had been defined at the end of section one 'as a matter of control over living conditions and life'. It is of particular importance to keep this twofold orientation in mind, i.e. the orientation on living conditions – thus reflecting the 'structural side' – and life – by this reflecting as well the side of the 'actor'. 'Action', then, can be taken as the factual bridge of these two dimensions. Theoretically, this reflects very much the age-old sociological debate of functionalism and structuralism (their absolute meaning and relation to each other) and the more recent questions, raised by *Giddens, Archer* and others. What can be recorded so far is that 'living conditions' and 'live', i.e. 'structure' and 'acting' can be taken as dimensions (on a first level), describing a tensional matrix, against which 'empowerment' is measurable as simultaneity of the self-realisation of the individual in and through the social.

Determining the dimensions for the development of indicators further, we have to go back to the subject matters of the different domains, which can be briefly summarised by the following:

Resources for social relations	Capabilities for participating in social relations
Integration into social relations	Strength of social relations

Figure 10: Dimensions of Social Relations

This is in a way the reflection and even dialectic reproduction of the four objective domains inside of the domain of empowerment, namely

Socio-economic security	Empowerment
Inclusion	Cohesion

Figure 11: Inside of Empowerment

However, this approach is by no means identical with the notion of a simple reproduction, i.e. the search for indicators in the other domains and their use as dimensions of empowerment. Instead, understanding the domains for our purpose as dimensions, they provide the basis to develop indicators that are sensible towards the question of *'what matters?'*. As empowerment – even more than all other domains – is fundamentally

- processual
- relational and
- historical

it has to be considered in this twofold context and tension of the simultaneity of biographical and societal development. The difficult task will be to avoid the limitation of using indicators as means of 'descriptive measurements'. Instead, the crucial point is to explore the individual's capacity of appropriation in terms of the enhancement of his or her own control over

- the living conditions
- the life
- and – perhaps most importantly – the 'comfortable', 'appropriate' and 'suitable' matching of both.

These terms – 'comfortable', 'appropriate' and 'suitable' – point into the direction of the subjective dimension which has at least to be kept in mind. For this, it is useful to explore the link *(a)* to socially agreeable or even agreed values[78] and *(b)* to the subjective conditional factors, namely the collectivisation of norms, participation, sensitivity towards values and social recognition. – At this stage these subjective conditional factors are simply taken from the given set of considerations, admittedly a tentative concept which has to be further elaborated. Though these subjective factors have to be considered already here, they will be at the same time developed from the elaboration of the objective factors – as conditional factors, they are the material and objective basis from which the subjective factors dialectically emerge.

Locating Indicators

From here it is easily possible to develop a framework in which we can locate indicators for empowerment.

First, it is important to note that, although we concentrate at this stage only at the conditional factors we have to guide the search by keeping at the same time the other two sets of factors, namely the constitutional and normative factors in mind.

Second, it had been said in the beginning that an important aspect of compiling the list of indicators has to consider the orthogonality and embeddedness of indicators, ie. we have to look at the question of how they actually link into the overall system of conditional factors.

And third, it is important to emphasise that we are concerned with a systematic connection between the different factors that – at least in the long durée – the social as the outcome of the interaction between people (constituted as actors) and their constructed and natural environment.

As said elsewhere in this volume, indicators are not measuring instruments in the strict sense. Instead they are means of investigating the borders of a field in which relations are established and processes are

---

[78] though socially agreeable does not necessarily mean that they are uncontested

developing. As such we propose to characterise in the following as step before coming to the domains the actual meaning of empowerment in respect of empowerment within the quadrangular tension, namely the tension between biographical and societal development and also between communities and institutions. With this in mind we have as well an instrument at our disposal that allows a clear classification of the domains as instruments that are able to understand relationships and processes in context – namely in reflection of their reference to communities and institutions on the one hand and to biographical and societal developments on the other hand. This brings us to the following outline of domains and sub-domains.

Empowering active personalities

Freedom as a substantial, though barely explicitly mentioned, part of social quality, has to be understood in our context – that of the social quality approach in general and that of empowerment in particular – as potentially problematic as it is caught in the tension between individualist (hedonist) and voluntarist attitudes on the one hand and a complete give away of individual control and decision making power, allowing the accumulation of 'enabling resources and enhanced possibilities' on the other hand. It is a major challenge to get this on the theoretical level right as we are actually not simply dealing with information and its processing. Knowledge is about developing insights in social contexts and, going even a step further, broad educational processes, understood as matter of socialisation – in German language this refers to *Bildung* and *Bildungsprozesse*. Though literally possibly translated as formation, such term does not really carry the entire meaning which has to be closely linked to concepts of humanism in a broader understanding. Surely going beyond contemporary notions of the 'information society'. It is difficult to fully reflect this is in the search for indicators. The choice is therefore aiming on allowing an understanding that considers the importance of knowledge as matter of socialisation: enhancing individual knowledge as means that allows participation and gaining social freedom. As subdomains we find consequently application of knowledge, availability of information and user-friendliness of information.

A word of warning may be appropriate: in this light we have to be careful, avoiding the trap of utilitarian approaches towards knowledge that aim on an understanding that is limited to knowledge solely as means to enhance labour market integration.

Though personal relationships name another domain and are linked to empowering social actors (see below), they are hugely relevant as well under the present heading dealing with empowering active personalities, emphasising the aspect mentioned that is already highlighted in the definition of the social, namely the orientation on people constituted as actors. In this sense personal relationships close the circle of the four areas and five domains.

The indicators that are of relevance are in particular concerned with the enhancement of knowledge as condition for controlling the conditions in respect of their potential development. If we then look at the indicators, namely the extent to which social mobility is knowledge-based (formal qualifications), per cent of population literate and numerate, availability of free media, access to the internet, provision of information in multiple languages on social services, and availability of free advocacy, advice and guidance centres we can clearly see the actual point of reference: we are speaking of real knowledge that is concerned with the understanding of situation and processes rather than technical knowledge as it would be reflected in instrumental reasoning. This has huge implications as well for the quality of educational processes that are under scrutiny. With this we can see a close link that is established by empowerment as central factor in welding individual and social dimensions. The indicators are chosen by their relevance of allowing personalities to develop themselves as conscious social actors.

Empowering institutional systems

If we look at the domain of openness and supportiveness of institutions, we can maintain the orientation of linking the domains with the discussion of the tensional fields. In the present case it is obviously an important aim of the domains to develop an understanding of the meaning of the institutional system for people's everyday life. Whereas we had been dealing in the first instance with the actors and their self-referential capacities, we are now looking at the second dimension contained in the definition, namely the 'framing structure, which translates immediately into the context of human relationships'. In concrete terms we are then dealing with the openness of political systems and the openness of the economic system as sub-domains. One important aspect of this is that the political and the economic sphere are getting understandable in their mutual interwoveness: the political is economic as much as the economic is political, both being a matter of the social.

The indicators that had been chosen – existence of processes of consultation and direct democracy, number of instances of public involvement in major economic decision making, percent of organisations/institutions with work councils – are explicitly aiming on developing an understanding of the dynamic aspects of institutions. Such dynamism is, however, in a social quality orientation only relevant if it goes beyond any notion of learning organisations, i.e. the assessment of the dynamic of institutions themselves. Rather, the really important aspect is the assessment of organisations as stepping-stones which can be used by active personalities. In this understanding they are very much concerned with building an opening for citizens in order to make their activities soci(et)ally relevant.

Empowering active citizens

All this makes only sense if it is moved towards and within the public space which is considered as a further domain, thus enforcing an understanding of empowerment as matter of active citizens. The term active citizen puts into a nutshell that biographical and societal development are welded together. Public space allows and enforces then the emergence of support for collective action and cultural enrichment as subdomains.

Looking at the indicators – percent of the national and local public budget that is reserved for voluntary, not-for-profit citizenship initiatives, marches and demonstrations banned in the past 12 months as proportion of total marched and demonstrations, proportion of public budgets allocated to cultural activities, number of self-organised cultural groups and events, proportion of people experiencing different forms of personal enrichment on a regular basis – are decisively chosen in a way to highlight the process-character of empowerment. All these indicators aim on reflecting social action as (i) people, going together with others and (ii) acting in the public space in a way that aims on this space itself, rather than changing positions and endowments of individuals.

Empowering social actors

Personal relationships as last domain are – as said earlier – providing a bridge. Provision of services supporting physical and social independence; Personal support services and Support for social interaction are the relevant subdomains and it should get clear that this dimension of is not concerned with isolated individuals. Rather, the focus is on processes of social production and reproduction: the way in which people engage with their environment in a process of social (re-) production.

The indicators chosen – percentage of national and local budgets devoted to disabled people, level of pre-and-post-school child care, extent of inclusiveness of housing and environmental design – are obviously of special relevance as they clearly show that the indicators aim at assessing (and changing) the intertwinement of soci(et)al conditions and individual actors. In particular the indicators in this area show also that we are not dealing with direct measurement but with indicators, i.e. indirect measurements that help to grasp a situation: process and structure by pointing out what the different dimensions of the conditions are. This allows us to understand as well the potential as it is given in any situation.

Labour market issues, referring to a fifth domain, are crosscutting. Employment and labour market issues already play a decisive role in the area of socio-economic security – and there are surely as well qualitative moments included in their discussion. However, when it comes to discussing labour market issues in the context of empowerment the qualitative moment is centre stage and we are dealing in particular with issues around the control of points of entry, exit and change, the domains being control of the contract, prospects of mobility and reconciliation-issues. All these issues are currently prominently on the political agenda: on the one hand as matters of attempting a policy of flexicurity – at least claiming to bring together flexibility as matter of control by employees on the one hand and on the other hand as a matter of globally increasing precarisation (see Tabak, 1996; Hepp, Rolf (ed.), 2009; Herrmann, Peter/van der Maesen, Laurent, 2008).

A brief reference has been made to freedom as central, though not elaborated feature of the social quality approach. The elaboration cannot be dealt with on this occasion. However, one hint may be useful to stimulate further consideration. It is Ernst Bloch's exploration

of four different kinds of possibilities, allowing us with this an informed approach to understanding them in their objectivity. He points on (i) the formally possible – what is possible according to its logical structure; (ii) the objectively possible – possible being based on assumptions on the ground of epistemologically based knowledge; (iii) the objectively possible – possible as it follows from the options inherently given by the object; (iv) and the objectively real possible –

possible by following the latency and tendency which is inherent in its elementary form.

(Herrmann, 2010; with reference to Bloch, 1959: 258-288)

Having derived from the foregoing this list of indicators we can discuss further the actual meaning of empowerment not as matter of ascribing a certain status. Instead, empowerment is to equal parts concerned with matters of actors, relationships and processes. This means also that empowerment can only be understood as matter of embedded structuration of complex processes. Quoting David Miller, Nicholas Barr states

> *'The whole enterprise of constructing a theory of justice on the basis of choice hypothetically made by individuals abstracted from society is mistaken, because these abstract ciphers lack the prerequisites for developing conceptions of justice'. Or, if they do manage to make choices it must be in terms of culturally acquired attitudes.*

(Barr, 2004: 51; citing Miller, 1976: 341)

This may explain that looking at theories aiming on means of increasing the power of the individual over his/her life confronts us with theories of learning and psychologically oriented strategies of enhancement of self-esteem – power being equalled with individual abilities. But it shows also that looking at the individual cannot be reduced on looking at utilitarian strategies of maximising utility values but is even as such part of a more complex process.

A critical review empowerment as a matter of control over living conditions and life

Clearly spelt out, empowerment in the debate of the institutionalised Europe is very much a concept which in actual fact does not refer to power but instead to capabilities in a liberalist sense. As much as capabilities are the main point of reference, indeed, the crucial question is how to decide between the political, social and scientific conceptualisation of empowerment between societal power and individual capabilities. It is only by referring to the social dimension that this question can be answered. Then, it has to be answered if empowerment is understood as a matter of shaping the situation of an isolated individual – an individual being on his or her own – or if it focuses on the individual as fundamentally social entity and the dialectic of individual and soci(et)al development.

236

Considering empowerment as process, the latter means that the first and most important question is to determine the actual aim of empowerment. In other words, the question is who benefits from empowerment. And again in other terms we have to ask *for what* a person shall be empowered. At the first glance this is – and actually it should be – the person who is being empowered. However, in actual fact it can be seen especially in recent times that empowerment had been understood as an instrument to 'enhance the performance of people in terms of the system'. We find management strategies of which the aim had not been the development of the people concerned but the enhancement of their responsibility in favour of production. Another strand of utilising empowerment for the sake of the system is the widespread use of the concept in the context of welfare (state) reform.

I suggest to define the ***aim of social empowerment*** in the perspective of Social Qualityas **enhancing the participation of people to enable them to balance personal development and coordination with the immediate social and physical environment** and the more distant social and physical environment. In other words, the Social Quality approach understands empowerment as a means to enable people to control the personal, communal and societal environment to foster their own development. Such control comprises of gaining influence over the environment as well as accessing the environment to enrich the socio-personal life.[79]

Thus, empowerment has the three dimensions of

- access,
- participation and
- control.

It is clear that the separation between the different dimension of power – technical ability and control over others – as it had been mentioned in the beginning, comes into play.

For the later search for indicators this means that we have to look for input indicators (namely factors that enhance the abilities of the individual/group) and equally important output indicators (namely factors that are available to the individual/group to actively take part in social and societal life). It means as well to be aware of the fact that

---

[79] It would be necessary to discuss the different approaches of methodological individualism, a task that cannot be approached here.

empowerment always has the two angles of passive and active. However, the particular difficulty is to make clear that the 'passive' moments are actually only then 'real' if and when they are actually put into practice. This is meant when it is emphasised that we are dealing with real processes where the rights as such are only then meaningful if they are translated into actual action – in particular in looking for indicators this is an important point which has to be kept in mind. In other words, we are already dealing with compassion and social responsiveness as matters of activating collective identities.

This has huge implications as well in regard of the localisation of empowerment in the process of social development. Besides the requirement of determining an aim in the sense of who is profiting in which way from empowerment, another aspect of discussing the aim of empowerment is concerned with locating empowerment between the poles of social integration on the one side and social change on the other side – again a matter which is by way of status and development concerned with the passive and active side of empowerment. Though closely linked to the before mentioned aspect it is important to note that whereas before we dealt with the actor perspective – combining input aspects into 'the system' and output aspects regards the individual/group – we are now dealing with the perspective of the impact, concentrating solely on the output. Looking for an answer to the question if social integration or social change is reached we actually have to be clear about the character of social integration. This can have two dimensions,

- the one being concerned with the integrity of the system – and as such it can absolutely be an 'emancipative' instrument, changing the social conditions and the social system respectively,

- the other being concerned with the integration into the system, a kind of subordination of the individual/group.

It is important to clarify which side, namely the individual/group or the social setting is taken as dependent and which as independent variable.

This is closely connected with the question if empowerment is based on the idea of distributing power in society as a zero-sum constellation. Establishing such a perspective means to consider the link between the individual and society. Interpreting power as zero-sum constellation means that power is a subordinating process. The individual/group is seen not in relation to the environment along the lines of access and participation; rather, in the conceptualisation of power as zero-sum constellation the relationship is set between individuals/groups. However, the Social Quality perspective requires to think of power and empowerment as establishing and designing a relationship between people, but the actual aim is – as mentioned – access and participation in the sense of changing the environment. In other words, the output is personal power in its combination to social power. In practice, this has two dimensions,

- the one being 'competition', i.e. the redistribution of power
- the other being self-realisation of the individual/group, utilising the social for own purposes and 'enriching the social' by reaching a higher degree of sociability.

The question of re-distribution of power, though being strongly linked to empowerment, can be better dealt with in the framework of in particular the factor of socio-economic rights and cohesion. In other words, it is here where actually the complementarities between empowerment on the one hand and in particular socio-economic security and social cohesion on the other hand have to be discussed. On the other hand, self-realisation is suggested to be an original question of empowerment.[80] Then, what the individual gains actually equals what is gained on the soci(et)al level. In other words, we are concerned with a process of socialisation as mutual enhancement.

However, it has to be noted that despite the fact of mutual benefit there will be some groups loosing their own power. What actually happens in the ideal case is that subordinating forms of power cannot persist under generally empowered and empowering conditions.

Finally, it is important to put the debate on empowerment into a wider perspective of rights. This can contribute to avoiding an individualist approach to empowerment, based on the idea of 'enhancing individual performance', thus requiring educational support for the individual rather than securing soci(et)al conditions which are accessible and allow participation of individuals and groups. A rights based approach can link to *T.M. Marshall's* historical perspective on civil, political and social rights. It has to be emphasised, however, that the different rights are in actual fact only different dimensions of the same right, i.e. the right of what we might call 'active social inclusion', i.e. social inclusion on terms

---

[80] In the further discussion of the connection between the four or even eight factors it will be getting clear that there can be major constraints of one factor stemming from the performance of (an)other factor(s).

and conditions of the individual rather than inclusion as subordination. As it is suggested to talk of 'active social inclusion', the granting of the set of different rights can be seen as a major factor of empowerment.

Going back from here, we have to re-establish the link to the relationship between biographical and societal development. This had been understood as a conditioning, mutually beneficial and enriching relationship. Following this line, we can say that the three dimensions of empowerment, namely access, participation and control are centred on the common link to autonomy. Individuation thus is not only complementing (let alone opposing) socialisation and vice versa. On the contrary, individuation is a form and expression of socialisation and socialisation realises itself as individuation. Seen in this light, the frequently found interpretation of individuation is a form of increased socialisation – we can establish a strong link to the *Kantian* understanding of the enlightened societal development as putting freedom as realisation of necessity into place.[81] This should not be confused with other forms of individuation which are simply a matter of anomie, where actually individuation translates into forms of isolation (see in this context Herrmann, 2006).

Taking up *Marshall's* consideration of rights we have to emphasise again that the three rights, which in his historical analysis appear to be distinct from each other are in actual fact historically emerging into the one right of what is in the meantime understood as civic citizenship. As such, it can be considered to look at social quality as a matter of merging the rights – civil, political and social – into the one right of civic participation. This again can be seen as merging of biographical and societal development as being concerned with the means and processes and relations necessary for people to be capable of actively participating in social relations and actively influencing the immediate and more distant social and physical environment. Having the definition of empowerment given above in mind, this dimension can be seen as central for societal development. Moreover, this debate is clearly marking a necessary shift in the welfare state. It is not simply concerned with the realisation of opportunities which are given in principal and which we want to be given for everybody. Instead, a welfare state of high social quality has to be concerned with the self-realisation of the individual in the social context and as such the mutual development of the individual

---

[81] Though the idealist turn within the Kantian paradigm is of course a major obstacle.

and the social. Loyalty is then achieved by evoking a critical distance. This means not least that

- 'social security' is not simply the provision of replacements for otherwise commodified provisions
- 'education' cannot be solely concerned with teaching technical skills and retrievable knowledge,
- 'participation' is not only the opening of existing structures.

Instead, empowerment requires truly open structures, starting from the needs of the people concerned and the management of reciprocity of structure and agency.

Of course, this has to be understood not least as qualification of the orientation on capabilities and capacities necessary – *A. Sen's* work had been addressed before.

To summarise, we can take up the requirement of the trinominal structure. The *subject matter* is the autonomy as capability and right to act. Then, the *resources* are knowledge and rights. This establishes a *relationship to the other factors* utilising and actually realising *(verwirklichen)* socio-economic security, social inclusion and social cohesion as a reference for the action of the individual. At the same time, empowerment serves as Procrustean bed for striving for the other factors.

Conclusions and Challenges

Up to now we had been concerned with the measurement of the actual degree of empowerment. Although this is the core interest from a social quality perspective and in particular the current project, it makes some sense to go a step further, looking for indicators of empowering structures and mechanisms. In other words, a Social Quality perspective is geared to finding

- indicators of the character of empowerment *('aim'),*
- indicators of the state of empowerment *('structure'),*
- indicators of the process of empowerment *('process').*

Thus, in addition of measuring empowerment by the indicators suggested above it is here promoted to look as well for indicators on a different and additional level.[82] These are concerned with the activities and structures

---

[82] It has to be decided to which extent this can finally be implemented – in any case

supported by various soci(et)al actors – considering that, as has been developed, empowerment is a social process and a relationship rather than an individual 'capability'.

The following are to be mentioned as main – general – actors:

- non-governmental/non-profit organisations (including self-help groups)
- community development groups/social movements[83]
- non-governmental/non-profit institutions[84] (as e.g. trade unions, employers organisations, political parties, the church …)
- state bodies[85]
- statutory support organisations as for example advisory bodies
- employers[86]
- institutions with a controlling and advising function (as 'ombudspersons', complaints bureaus and the like, as well psychological consultancies, child guidance clinics etc.)
- individual services as psychological consultancies.

Despite this it may be useful to consider other actors when it comes to the debate of empowerment in connection with a specific project. Then, for example, beneficiaries or very specific organisations and/or decision makers may play a decisive role and should be investigated separately.

---

the respective considerations always should be made at least in the discussion of the indicators and the assessment of the dimension of empowerment of Social Quality.

[83] There will be a huge overlap with the previous group; however, it is reasonable to distinguish between the two categories as the latter is not to the same 'organised' as the first.

[84] This category is introduced, taking account of the general exclusion of organisations mentioned here from the NGO/NPO/Third sector (as for example in the explicit discussion of this aspect in the framework of the Johns-Hopkins-Project; e.g. Salamon/Anheier, 1996)

[85] Probably it is useful to subdivide according the classical division of power, i.e. to look separately at legislative, judicative and executive bodies.

[86] The difficulty to deal with is that it can be useful to look at 'employers' in general, referring to the 'entrepreneurial culture' for example in a country, region or a specific time period and/or to look at individual employers.

Annex – domains, subdomains and indicators

Domains	Sub-domains	Indicators
Knowledge base	Application of knowledge	Extent to which social mobility is knowledge-based (formal qualifications).
	Availability of information	Per cent of population literate and numerate.
		Availability of free media.
		Access to the Internet.
	User friendliness of information	Provision of information in multiple languages on social services.
		Availability of free advocacy, advice and guidance centres.
Labour market	Control over employment contract	Percent of labour force that is member of a trades union (differentiated to public and private employees).
		Percent of labour force covered by a collective agreement (differentiated by public and private employees).
	Prospects of job mobility	Percent of employed labour force receiving work-based training.
		Percent of labour force availing of publicly provided training (not only skills based).
		Percent of labour force participating in any 'back to work scheme'
	Reconciliation of work and family life (work/ life balance)	Percent of organisations operating work life balance policies.
		Percent of employed labour force actually making use of work/life balance measures (see indicator above).

Openness and supportiveness of institutions	Openness and supportiveness of political system	Existence of processes of consultation and direct democracy (e.g., referenda).
	Openness of economic system	Number of instances of public involvement in major economic decision making (e.g., public hearings about company relocation, inward investment and plant closure).
	Openness of organisations	Percent of organisations/institutions with work councils.
Public space	Support for collective action	Percent of the national and local public budget that is reserved for voluntary, not-for-profit citizenship initiatives.
		Marches and demonstrations banned in the past 12 months as proportion of total marched and demonstrations (held and banned).
	Cultural enrichment	Proportion of local and national budget allocated to all cultural activities.
		Number of self-organised cultural groups and events.
		Proportion of people experiencing different forms of personal enrichment on a regular basis.
Personal relationships	Provision of services supporting physical and social independence	Percentage of national and local budgets devoted to disabled people (physically and mentally).
	Personal support services	Level of pre-and-post-school child care.
	Support for social interaction	Extent of inclusiveness of housing and environmental design (e.g., meeting places, lighting, layout).

References

Baar, Niocholas (2004[4]) Economics of the Welfare State; Oxford: Oxford University Press

Baars, J. et altera (2000) Social Quality. A Sustainable Project for Europe. Briefing Paper for the Round Table of the European Commission, Amsterdam, The European Foundation on Social Quality, 1.11.2000 – the text is on the website www.socialquality.nl – 4.5.2004, 6.51 pm; linked from Annual Reports, Annual Report 2000

Beck, Wolfgang/van der Maesen, Laurent/Walker, Alan (1997) Social Quality: From Issue to Concept; in: Beck, Wolfgang/van der Maesen, Laurent/Walker, Alan [eds.], 1997: The Social Quality of Europe; The Hague et altera, Kluwer Law International, 263-296

Beck, Wolfgang/van der Maesen, Laurent/Walker, Alan (2001) Theorizing Social Quality: The Concepts Validity; in: Beck, Wolfgang/van der Maesen, J.G. Laurent/Thomése, Fleur/Walker, Alan (Eds.) (2001) Social Quality: A Vision for Europe, The Hague/London/Boston, Kluwer Law International, 307-360

Bhaskar, R. (1997) The possibility of Naturalism: A Philosophical Critique of the Contemporary Human Sciences, Brighton, The Harvester Press

Bloch, Ernst (1959) Prinzip Hoffnung; Frankfurt/M: Suhrkamp [written in 1938-1947; reviewed 1953 and 1959]: 258-288

Bourdieu, Pierre (2000) Les structures sociales de l'Économie, Paris, Éditions du Seuil

Coleman, James S. (1990) Foundations of Social Theory, Cambridge et altera, The Belknap Press of Harvard University Press

Fetterman, David M. (2001) Foundations of empowerment Evaluation, London et altera, Sage

Freire, Paolo (1972) Pedagogy of the Oppressed, Sheed&Ward; Penguin

Freire, Paolo (1973) A conversation with Paulo Freire. The Institute of Cultural Action; in: Freire, 1985: 151-164

Freire, Paolo (1985) The Act of Study; in: The Politics of Education. Culture, Power and Liberation, Massachusetts, Bergin&Garvey Publ.

Habermas, Juergen (1989) The Theory of Communicative Action. Vol. 2: Lifeworld and System: A Critique of Functionalist Reason, Oxford, Blackwell

Hepp, Rolf (ed.), 2009 The Fragility of Socio-structural Components/Die Fragilisierung soziostruktureller Komponenten; Bremen: Europaeischer Hochschulverlag

Herrmann, Peter (1997) Sozialpolitik in der Europäischen Union, Rheinfelden/Berlin, Schäuble

Herrmann, Peter (1998 a) European Integration between Institution Building and Social Process. Contributions to a Theory of Modernisation and NGOs in the Context of the Development of the EU, New York, Nova Science

Herrmann, Peter (1998 b) Partizipationskulturen in der Europäischen Union. Nichtregierungsorganisationen in EU-Mitgliedstaaten, Rheinfelden/Berlin, Schäuble Verlag

Herrmann, Peter (2005) Empowerment – the Core of Social Quality; in: The European Journal of Social Quality; volume 5; New York/Oxford, Berghahn Journals: 292-302

Herrmann, Peter (2006) Person-oriented services and social service providers in comparative and European perspective. Current debates on changes by liberalisation in a perspective of a theory of modernisation, New York, Nova Science

Herrmann, Peter (2006) Politics and Policies of the Social in the European Union, New York, Nova Science

Herrmann, Peter (2007) Social Professional Activities and the State; New York: Nova

Herrmann, Peter (2009 a) Gemeinschaft der Gesellschaft – die Suche nach einem Definitionsrahmen für Prekarität; in: Hepp, Rolf (ed.): The Fragilisation of Socio-structural Components/Die Fragilisierung soziostruktureller Komponenten; Bremen: Europaeischer Hochschulverlag: 76-107

Herrmann, Peter (2009 b) Die Europaeische Union als Programmgesellschaft. Das europaeische Gesellschaftsmodell, die Sozialpolitk und der Dritte Sektor; Bremen, Europaeischer Hochschulverlag

Herrmann, Peter (2010) Human Rights, Health and Social Quality – Realisations and Realities; in: Laurinkari, Juhani (Ed.) Health, Wellness and Social Policy. Essays in honour of Guy Bäckman; Bremen

Herrmann, Peter [ed.] (1995) Europäische Integration und Politik der Armutsprogramme – Auf dem Weg zu einem integrierten Sozialpolitikansatz?, Rheinfelden/Berlin: Schäuble

Herrmann, Peter/van der Maesen, Laurent (2008) Precarity – Approaching New Patterns of Societal (Dis-)Integration; Working Papers of the European Foundation on Social Quality; Munich: Munich Personal RePEc Archive; MPRA Paper 10245, January 2008;
http://mpra.ub.uni-muenchen.de/10245/;
http://mpra.ub.uni-muenchen.de/10245/1/MPRA_paper_10245.pdf

Heskin, Allan David (1991) The Struggle for Community, Boulder et altera: Westview Press

Horkheimer, Max (1947) Eclipse of Reason, New York, Continuum

Kant, Immanuel (1788) The Critique of Practical Reason, Translated by Thomas Kingsmill Abbott;
http://eserver.org/philosophy/kant/critique-of-practical-reaso.txt

Leibfried, Stephan/Pierson, Paul [eds.] (1995) European Social Policy. Between Fragmentation and Integration, Washington, The Brookings Institution

Luhmann, Niklas (1969) Komplexität und Demokratie; in: Luhmann, Niklas: Politische Planung. Aufsätze zur Soziologie von Politik und Verwaltung; Opladen 1971: 35 ff.

Marshall, T.M., (1950) 'Citizenship and Social Class' in Citizenship and Social Class; T.H. Marshall/Tom Bottomore; London et altera: Pluto Press 1992

Nussbaum, Martha C. (1998) Cultivating Humanity. A Classical Defense of Reform in Liberal Education, Cambridge/London, Harvard University Press

Salamon, Lester M./Anheier, Helmut K. (1996) The emerging nonprofit sector. An Overview, Manchester/New York, Manchester University Press

Sen, Amartya (1987) On Ethics and Economics, Oxford: Basil Blackwell

Sen, Armartya (1999) Development as Freedom; Oxford/New York, Oxford University Press

Tabak, Faruk (1996) The World Labour Force; in Hopkins, Terence K./Wallerstein, Immanuel: The Age of Transition. Trajectory of the World-System 1945-2025; London/New Jersey: Zed Books/Leichhardt: Pluto Press Australia: 87-116

van der Maesen, Laurent (2003) Elaborating the Theory of Social Quality and its four Components (Discussion Paper)

van der Maesen, Laurent, April (2004) Internal Working Document

www.ingramcontent.com/pod-product-compliance
Lightning Source LLC
Chambersburg PA
CBHW032128020426
42334CB00016B/1080